The Vietnam Experience

A Nation Divided

by Clark Dougan, Samuel Lipsman,
and the editors of Boston Publishing Company

Boston Publishing Company/Boston, MA

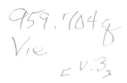

Boston Publishing Company

President and Publisher: Robert J. George
Vice President: Richard S. Perkins, Jr.
Editor-in-Chief: Robert Manning
Managing Editor: Paul Dreyfus

Senior Writers:
Clark Dougan, Edward Doyle, David Fulghum, Samuel Lipsman, Terrence Maitland, Stephen Weiss
Senior Picture Editor: Julene Fischer

Researchers:
Kerstin Gorham (Chief), Sandra M. Jacobs, Christy Virginia Keeny, Denis Kennedy, Carole Rulnick, Ted Steinberg, Nicole van Ackere

Picture Editors:
Wendy Johnson, Lanng Tamura
Assistant Picture Editor: Kathleen A. Reidy
Picture Researchers:
Nancy Katz Colman, Robert Ebbs, Tracey Rogers, Nana Elisabeth Stern, Shirley L. Green (Washington, D.C.), Kate Lewin (Paris)
Picture Department Assistants:
Suzanne M. Spencer, Kathryn J. Steeves

Historical Consultants:
Thomas Griffith, Ernest May, Charles E. Neu

Picture Consultant: Ngo Vinh Long

Production Editor: Patricia Leal Welch
Editorial Production:
Sarah E. Burns, Karen E. English, Pamela George, Elizabeth C. Peters, Theresa M. Slomkowski, Amy P. Wilson

Design: Designworks: Sally Bindari

Marketing Director: Jeanne C. Gibson
Business Staff: Amy Pelletier

About the editor and authors

Editor-in-Chief *Robert Manning*, a longtime journalist, has previously been editor-in-chief of the *Atlantic Monthly* magazine and its press. He served as assistant secretary of state for public affairs under Presidents John F. Kennedy and Lyndon B. Johnson. He has also been a fellow at the Institute of Politics at the John F. Kennedy School of Government at Harvard University.

Authors: *Clark Dougan*, a former Watson and Danforth fellow, has taught history at Kenyon College. He received his M.A. and M.Phil. at Yale University. *Samuel Lipsman*, a former Fulbright Scholar, received his M.A. and M. Phil. in history at Yale. Mr. Dougan and Mr. Lipsman have coauthored other volumes in *The Vietnam Experience*.

Historical Consultants: *Thomas Griffith* is a former senior editor of *Time*, editor of *Life* magazine, and author of two books on life in America. *Ernest May* is Charles Warren Professor of History at Harvard University. *Charles E. Neu*, a professor of history at Brown University, specializes in American foreign policy.

Picture Consultant: *Ngo Vinh Long* is a social historian specializing in China and Vietnam. Born in Vietnam, he returned there most recently in 1980. His books include *Before the Revolution: The Vietnamese Peasants Under the French* and *Report From a Vietnamese Village*.

Cover photo: Before a violent clash between peace demonstrators and National Guardsmen at the Pentagon on October 23, 1967, a protester plants pink carnations in the guardsmen's rifle barrels. By then, the nation was beginning to come apart over the Vietnam War.

Library of Congress Catalog Card Number: 84-72040

ISBN: 0-939526-11-5

10 9 8 7 6
5 4 3 2 1

Contents

At six o'clock EST on the evening of November 3, 1964, the first election returns flashed onto the screens of millions of television sets across the country. With only one-fifth of 1 percent of the vote counted, incumbent President Lyndon B. Johnson was leading his opponent, Senator Barry Goldwater of Arizona, by 77,572 to 74,139, or 51.3 percent to 48.7 percent. By seven o'clock, with 2 percent of the national vote in, the president's plurality had increased to 273,000, or 59.6 percent. By 10:00 P.M. his lead had swelled to nearly 4 million votes and his share of the total to over 60 percent. Throughout New England, the Midwest, and the Far West, in industrial states like Ohio and Illinois and in rural states like Wyoming and Idaho, even in such Republican strongholds as Kansas and Indiana, Johnson was winning handily.

Watching the results with his family and friends at the Driskill Hotel in Austin, Texas, the

president was not surprised. Nor were most Americans. Johnson had run an effective campaign. A year before he had succeeded to the presidency at a moment of tragedy and crisis, promising to complete the work that his predecessor, John F. Kennedy, had only begun. And in many ways he had made good on that promise. Retaining many Kennedy advisers, he had carried on the tradition of strong executive leadership that so many identified with the Kennedy presidency. He had overseen Congressional passage of the Kennedy tax cut and twisted some arms to insure enactment of the Kennedy civil rights bill. From the very beginning of that first year in office, however, he had known that he would have to secure his own mandate if he were to proceed any further. To build his Great Society on the foundations of Kennedy's New Frontier, he would have to forge his own "consensus"—that was the word he used—among the American people.

Yet as Lyndon Johnson knew perhaps better than anyone else, the main outlines of that consensus had already been drawn. They had slowly taken shape not in the previous three years of the Kennedy administration, but in the twenty years after the end of World War II. A political disciple of Franklin D. Roosevelt, Johnson had been there at the beginning, and during more than twenty-five years as congressman, senator, and vice president of the United States, he had watched the consensus grow. It was a frame of mind based on a variety of assumptions and ideas about the nature of American society, the meaning of democracy, and the function of the federal government. Its central propositions were these: first, that limitless economic growth held the key to social harmony and progress; second, that international communism represented the principal threat to the American way of life; and third, that it was the responsibility of the government to insure sustained economic progress at home and to contain communism abroad.

It was to these widely held beliefs that Johnson had appealed throughout the 1964 election campaign. Running on a platform of "Peace and Prosperity," he vowed not only to increase the American economic pie, but to distribute the individual slices more equitably than ever before. He also promised to meet the danger of Communist aggression, while affirming his intention not to escalate the war in Vietnam. At the same time, he isolated his Republican opponent on the right by hammering away at every utterance Barry Goldwater had made and every vote he had cast that fell outside the purview of the consensus. Senator Goldwater was depicted as the "war candidate," a man not content with merely "containing" communism in South Vietnam but determined to widen the war into the North. Having voted against the civil rights bill and having advocated the dismantling of the social security system, the senator was also identified as an enemy of all government measures designed to promote social progress in America.

In the end, Johnson got the mandate he wanted. When all the ballots were counted, he had received 43,126,218 out of 70,621,479 votes cast—the greatest margin (nearly 17 million votes) and percentage (61 percent) of victory that any president had ever drawn from the American people. Senator Goldwater had carried only six states—his home state of Arizona and five states of the Deep South.

Having established himself as president by right, and not by default, Lyndon Johnson could now look to the future with fresh confidence. As president of "all the people," he would move beyond "the rich society and the powerful society" that America was "upward to the Great Society" that America could be—a society in which poverty, hunger, and racial injustice no longer existed and in which "equal opportunity" for all was not just a promise, but a reality.

In 1964, however, the "Great Society" was still a dream. The growing American military involvement was a fact. By the time of Johnson's election there were more than 22,000 American military advisers in Vietnam, as well as thousands of tons of American war materiel. The U.S. Air Force had flown more than 12,000 sorties. And more than 200 Americans had been killed in hostile action. As a proportion of the nation's total resources, the cost of the war had been small. But it was growing, and as it grew, so did the concern of the American people. The president nevertheless remained confident that he could bring the war in Vietnam to a successful conclusion while continuing to wage war on poverty in America. Just how he would accomplish those goals, not even he knew for sure. Yet this much was clear: As he made his decisions for the future, his options would be circumscribed by the assumptions of the past.

America at the zenith

"America stands at this moment at the summit of the world," Prime Minister Winston Churchill declared to the British House of Commons in early August 1945, one week after the United States had dropped a second atomic bomb on the Japanese city of Nagasaki. Several weeks later President Truman echoed his ally's assessment. In a nationally broadcast radio address on V-J Day, September 1, 1945, he told the American people that they possessed "the greatest strength and the greatest power that man has ever reached." No one could accuse either man of exaggerating the simple truth.

The America that emerged from World War II was undeniably the most powerful country in the world; indeed, in the history of the world. In addition to its monopoly on the most devastating weapon yet devised, the atomic bomb, the United States in its moment of victory in 1945 had more men and women under arms (11,913,639) than any other nation and, more important, the unrivaled capacity to equip them with whatever aircraft, ships, guns, and munitions they required. Because the United States, alone among the major warring powers, had been spared the ravages of war on its own soil, full wartime mobilization had not only pulled the American economy out of the last throes of the depression, but also created an industrial behemoth that would dominate the world economy in the years to come. Already endowed with an abundance of land, food, raw materials, and trained manpower, the United States had come out of World War II with its industrial plant intact and more money to spend on new production facilities, new processes, and new research than any of its competitors.

Despite these advantages, the future prosperity of the U.S. economy hardly seemed certain in 1945. Haunted by memories of the Great Depression, many Americans feared that the process of reconversion from a war to a peace economy would mean a return to the hard times and bitter social conflict of the 1930s. As government war contracts dried up and the public clamor to "Bring Our Boys Home—Now!" reached a strident pitch, leading economists grimly predicted that the sudden influx of millions of job-seeking veterans would create unemployment on a grand scale. At the same time, the growing demand for an end to rationing as well as a relaxation of wartime wage and price controls threatened to precipitate runaway inflation.

Nor was the state of the economy the sole source of apprehension. Although sheer military strength provided the nation with an unprecedented measure of security, Americans remained divided over the ends to which that power should be used in the future. On the right a vociferous minority argued that a lasting peace could be secured only by ridding the world of the menace of Soviet communism and therefore urged the president to pursue a policy of direct confrontation with Stalin's state. To their left stood those who believed that further cooperation between the United States and its wartime ally was both possible and desirable and favored a foreign policy aimed at aiding the nationalist aspirations of Europe's former colonial dependencies. Between these two positions, a wide variety of conflicting, and often confused, points of view could be found. Appealing to a strain of isolationist thinking dating back to the first years of the Republic, some Americans contended that the country had already fulfilled its international responsibilities and should concentrate its attention on its own domestic affairs. Others shared the desire to return to normal life as quickly as possible but also recognized that the U.S. would have to play an important role in the shattered postwar world.

The return to prosperity

The man most responsible for charting America's course in the postwar world, President Harry S Truman, both understood and accepted the burdens of leadership. "I feel as though the moon and all the stars and all the planets have fallen on me," he had told a group of reporters in April 1945 after learning of Franklin Roosevelt's death. "Please, boys, give me your prayers. I need them." Cocky yet humble, inexperienced yet decisive, he had made mistakes during his first months in office (at one point casually signing an order that abruptly cut off lend-lease aid to Great Britain and the Soviet Union) but succeeded in guiding the nation through the last months of the war. Now, as peace returned, he turned his attention to the new challenges that confronted him at home and abroad, beginning with the economy.

Buffeted by the competing claims of the country's most powerful economic blocs—businessmen calling for a return to free enterprise, labor unions seeking an end to wage controls and protection against unemployment, and farmers demanding a continuation of governmental price supports—the president began by dispelling any doubts that he intended to continue within the tradition of his predecessor's New Deal. In a message to Congress delivered just four days after V-J Day, and in six additional addresses over the next three months, he outlined the principal elements of what would later be called the "Fair Deal," including full-employment legislation, farm-price supports, public housing, and an extension of New Deal legislation on conservation, social security, and minimum wages. At the same time, he attempted to calm the fears of businessmen by gradually lifting price controls and by taking stern measures against striking unions.

None of these actions proved sufficient to forestall an economic crisis in 1946. But, in 1947, the sputtering economy began to pick up speed, and by the end of the year a boom was under way. Government figures released in early 1948 showed that the United States, with only 6 percent of the earth's people, was producing one-half of the world's manufactures: 80 percent of its new automobiles, 62 percent of its oil, 57 percent of its steel, and 43 percent of its electricity. Unemployment was declining, prices were stabilizing, and the gross national product, which had already doubled during the war years, was beginning its ascent along an upward curve to heights previously unimaginable.

The new prosperity gradually seeped into every pore of the economy. Aided by easy money at low-interest rates, and by a generous federal mortgage policy, millions of Americans were able for the first time to buy their own homes, often in trim new suburban subdivisions. Construction boomed, and sales of such "consumer durable" goods as cars, refrigerators, and washing machines skyrocketed. Government officials exulted. "The American people are

Postwar Prosperity

PRICES SOAR, BUYERS SORE
STEERS JUMP OVER THE MOON

So read a New York *Daily News* headline in the summer of 1946, when a relaxation of wartime price controls, a nationwide rash of labor strikes, and pent-up consumer demand combined to create chronic shortages of many basic commodities, including beef. Widespread fears of a return to the economic hardship and social turmoil of the 1930s nonetheless proved unfounded. By 1948 the process of "reconversion" from a war to a peace economy was all but complete, and a new boom was underway. For the first time in nearly twenty years, most Americans could look forward to a future of continuing prosperity.

Life in the U.S. quickly returned to business as usual after World War II. Left. Main Street, Mission, Texas, on the eve of the annual citrus festival in January 1948. Above. Customers crowd a local drugstore in Louisville, Kentucky, September 1947.

in the pleasant predicament of having to learn to live 50 percent better than they have ever lived before," Fred Vinson, the U.S. Director of War Mobilization and Reconversion, had declared in 1945. By the end of the decade many considered that a conservative estimate.

Although the resurgence of the American economy contributed handily to Truman's startling triumph over Thomas Dewey in 1948, the prosperity of the late 1940s was in fact less the result of astute government policy than of a fundamentally sound economic structure. As "Rosie the Riveter" abandoned the factory for the maternity ward and returning veterans gradually found jobs, production of consumer goods steadily increased until it caught up with demand, thereby stabilizing prices and widening profit margins. While some government measures, like the GI Bill and the Employment Act of 1946, eased the impact of "reconversion" and helped to sustain the recovery once it began, their most important effect was far more subtle. Through its willingness to take action to restore economic order, the Truman administration reinforced the popular belief—a belief nurtured during the days of the New Deal—that prosperity required governmental intervention in the economy.

Cold war

If the role of the Truman administration in resuscitating the economy was less than it seemed at the time, the same cannot be said of its influence in the realm of international affairs. Long before most Americans had given any thought to such matters, members of what came to be described as the nation's "foreign policy establishment"—a group that included high-ranking government and military officials, international lawyers and businessmen, and prominent academicians and journalists—had taken steps to insure that the United States would not withdraw from the world after World War II as it had after World War I. Under FDR, they had been instrumental in launching the United Nations, in hammering out a series of international economic agreements, and in settling some of the outstanding differences among the Big Three allied powers prior to the end of the war. With the accession of Truman to the presidency in April 1945, they continued their efforts to commit the United States to an unambiguously "internationalist" foreign policy.

Led by Secretary of War Henry Stimson and future Secretary of State Dean Acheson, and supported by such notable converts from isolationism as Senator Arthur Vandenberg, the Michigan Republican, these men realized that American strategic interests in Europe and the Near East had long been served by the rapidly dissolving British Empire. With the weakening of Great Britain as a global power, they believed, it was imperative that the United States fill the vacuum if the danger of a third world war was to be averted.

In the opinion of many policymakers, the chief source of that danger was the Soviet Union. Not only were the United States and the U.S.S.R. ideologically antagonistic, they contended, but in many ways and in many places the geopolitical interests of the two nations were bound to collide. Having been invaded twice from the west in the twentieth century, having lost an estimated 20 million people during World War II, Soviet Russia was determined to establish a secure buffer zone in Eastern Europe after the war. The U.S. was equally determined to halt the extension of Communist rule before it engulfed Western Europe. It was in the interest of the Soviet Union to secure access to the Mediterranean Sea by controlling the Straits of Dardanelles and to gain a foothold in the Near East. It was in the interest of the United States to keep the Russians out of those areas.

Not everyone agreed with this line of reasoning. Echoing a view once held by President Roosevelt, Secretary of War Stimson went before the cabinet in September 1945 and argued for a continuation of the wartime policy of cooperation with the Soviets. "The only way you can make a man trustworthy is to trust him," Stimson said, and he even went so far as to suggest that the U.S. allay Russian suspicions by sharing the technology of the atomic bomb.

Ultimately the Stimson approach lost out, in part because of the course of international events after the war and in part because when the hard-liners pressed their views on the new president they found a ready listener.

From the beginning Harry Truman was far more wary of Stalin's intentions than his predecessor had been, and, in some ways, he had far more reason to be. Soviet moves to consolidate power in Eastern and central Europe during the spring and summer of 1945, including the attempt to impose a pro-Soviet regime in Poland, seemed clear indications that the Soviet Union had embarked on an aggressively expansionist policy in violation of the agreements reached the preceding February at Yalta. Stalin's contention that he was acting in accordance with a "spheres of influence" pact made with Winston Churchill in October 1944 did not prove persuasive. The time has come, President Truman declared, to stop "babying" the Russians and take a "firm line." By February 1946, when Stalin delivered a speech suggesting that war between the great capitalist and Communist powers was inevitable, even the skeptics among Mr. Truman's advisers could only agree.

That same month, February 1946, a telegram to Washington from George Kennan, who for eighteen months had been serving as deputy to Ambassador Averell Harriman in Moscow, underscored the prevailing interpretation of Soviet strategy. Although the professed fear of "capitalist encirclement" can be attributed to a "traditional and instinctive Russian sense of insecurity," Kennan began, the manifestation of that insecurity posed a direct threat to the United States.

The Establishment

Democratically minded Americans rebel against the notion that a nonelected elite in any way determines American policy. Yet if ever there were such an "establishment," as journalist Richard Rovere later called it, it was the group of men who formulated and carried out U.S. foreign policy after World War II. It was a group that included individuals who belonged to both political parties and differed over how to get things done but who shared a collective perception of the role of the United States in world affairs.

The personal ties between men whose paths continually crossed—in schools, clubs, and board rooms—threaded this network of influence. Most came from upper-middle-class Protestant families who instilled in their offspring a tradition of public service and a sense that the doors of power were open to them. As youths they generally attended private eastern schools and went on to Harvard, Yale, or Princeton. The majority took up professions in law, finance, or academia. And many of them joined the Council on Foreign Relations.

A private New York discussion club for businessmen and lawyers that in 1921 was transformed into an institute for international affairs, the Council on Foreign Relations was composed of committed internationalists who had been roused to action by America's reversion to isolationism after World War I. They continued their lobbying efforts throughout the twenties and thirties, and when war broke out in Europe in 1939 these men and their successors strove to commit the U.S. to the conflict. After the war council members gained influence as advisers to, and then as members of, the State and War departments. Ivy League lawyers such as Henry Stimson (alternately secretary of war and state under three presidents), Robert Lovett (an undersecretary of state under Truman), and John Foster Dulles (Eisenhower's future secretary of state), all belonged to the council and drew heavily on council membership when looking for help. Stimson's assistant secretary of war in charge of personnel, financier and future council chairman John J. McCloy, recalled that "[w]henever we needed a man we thumbed through the roll of council members and put through a call to New York."

The national security bodies that emerged after the Second World War—the Department of Defense, the CIA, and the National Security Council—opened new avenues of power and influence to members of the foreign policy establishment. Robert Lovett went on to become secretary of defense, and Allen Dulles, the brother of John Foster, became director of the CIA. Allen Dulles was among those who had been recruited from Ivy League schools to serve in the Office of Strategic Services, precursor to the CIA, where many gained a permanent taste for power. "We were kids, captains and majors, telling the whole world what to do," recalled Carl Kaysen, a member of the Council on Foreign Relations who eventually became assistant national security adviser in the Kennedy White House.

There was a touch of the religious crusade in their vision of the United States as the upholder of liberty and justice in the world, but at heart these were pragmatic, nonideological men. For the most part Anglophiles who saw the U.S. as part of a North Atlantic community, they realized that the protection of American security and prosperity had long been a joint venture with Britain, with U.S. military power concentrated in the Pacific and the British in control of the Atlantic and Mediterranean. In their eyes the demise of the British Empire meant that the mantle of world leadership had now passed to America.

Among those who most forcefully articulated this point of view was Dean Gooderham Acheson, a secretary of state under Harry Truman. The son of an Episcopal bishop, Acheson grew up in Connecticut in a world that reflected the values, manners, and outlook of English landed gentry. He did all the right "establishment" things: attended Groton, Yale, and Harvard Law School, became a prominent Washington attorney, and joined the government. As a State Department advocate on Capitol Hill, Acheson was known for his barbed tongue, elitist ways, and disdain for Congress. Acheson did develop a close, though patronizing, relationship with Truman. He once told an aide that "that little fellow across the street has more to him than you think." Some suspect, however, that Acheson's loyalty derived in part from the president's acquiescence to his foreign policy advice.

In formulating that advice Acheson, like most of his establishment colleagues, was strongly influenced by the encounter of the Western liberal democracies with the Nazi Reich in World War II. The effort to appease Hitler that led to the Munich agreements they viewed as a failure of moral courage on the part of their allies, and from it they drew the lesson that giving in to aggression only encourages more. The Munich analogy became the framework for assessing the postwar moves of the Soviet Union in Eastern Europe and the Near East. Hitler's "salami tactics" became the postwar "domino theory": the belief that the collapse of one country to a Communist aggressor would initiate a chain reaction in which a succession of adjacent countries would also fall. Out of this assessment came the American doctrine of containment.

The U.S. foreign policy establishment, in the opinion of Walter Lippmann, overemphasized the lesson of Munich. The doctrine of containment, originally designed to apply to Europe, came to be applied to Asia as well, and "international communism" replaced the Soviet Union as the perceived threat. In the name of containing communism and defending its national security, the United States would multiply its commitments abroad and eventually send one-half million troops to fight in an obscure corner of southeast Asia called Vietnam.

Acheson and Weapon

11

We have here a political force fanatically committed to the belief that with the U.S. there can be no permanent modus vivendi, that it is desirable and necessary that the internal harmony of our society be disrupted, our traditional way of life destroyed, the international authority of our state be broken, if Soviet power is to be secure . . . .

A year later Kennan elaborated on his views in an article published under the signature "X," in *Foreign Affairs.* Outlining a policy he defined as "containment," he called for "the adroit and vigilant application of counterforce at a series of shifting geographical and political points" to thwart Soviet expansionism. What he had in mind at the time, Kennan later wrote, was "not the containment by military means of a military threat, but the political containment of a political threat." Nevertheless, as the term "containment" caught on as a description of the United States' postwar foreign policy, the distinction was soon forgotten. So, too, was the fact that Kennan's analysis had been based not on an interpretation of Communist ideology, but on a consideration of Russia's traditional geopolitical interests.

Although the Truman administration had already shown its willingness to stop "pussyfooting" with the Soviets, it was not until 1947 that the newly formulated doctrine of "containment" was put to the test. Following one of the harshest winters on record, the European economy in the spring of that year teetered on the brink of collapse. Poverty, hunger, and disease gripped the entire continent, strengthening the appeal of the indigenous Communist parties of Western Europe and, as a result, expanding the influence of the Soviet Union. "The patient is sinking," warned Secretary of State George Marshall, "while the doctors deliberate."

At the same time, the deteriorating economic situation had forced Great Britain to renege on its commitment to Greece, where British-backed forces were engaged in a civil war against Communist guerrillas supported by Yugoslavia and other newly established Eastern European Communist states. Having already exhausted a U.S. loan of $3.75 billion to reduce its staggering balance-of-payments deficit, the British government informed Washington on February 21, 1947, that it would have to withdraw its support for the Greek government within five weeks. Unless the United States were prepared to move into the breach, a Communist victory in Greece seemed likely.

The U.S. response to the mounting European crisis was twofold: economic in the form of the Marshall Plan and military in the language of the Truman Doctrine. Conceived by and named after the new secretary of state, the Marshall Plan set forth a bold program for restoring Europe's devastated economy through a massive infusion of American economic aid. Although the Soviet Union and its satellites refused to participate in the plan, Western European leaders immediately embraced the idea, and in the long run it proved extraordinarily successful. As 12.5

billion dollars poured into the Continent over the next four years, industrial output rose sharply, unemployment fell, and the political threat from the left faded. By 1951 countries cooperating in the plan had raised their overall production 40 percent over 1938 and, more important, created the framework for further expansion and integration of the European economy.

As an antidote to the imminent danger of a Communist takeover in Greece, the Truman Doctrine was equally effective. Yet, in a sense, its success was purchased at a much higher price. For in order to win Congressional approval for his proposed grant of $400 million in military aid to Greece and Turkey, the president had decided that he had to "scare hell" out of the country and awaken the American people to the threat posed by Soviet expansionism. Speaking before Congress in early March, Truman had declared his belief that "it must be the policy of the United States to support free peoples who are resisting attempted subjugation by armed minorities or outside pressures." And he had left little doubt about who was responsible for arming those minorities and applying the "outside pressures."

Alarmed by the sweeping language of the Truman Doctrine, critics right and left attacked the concept of containment. In Congress, traditional isolationists led by Ohio Senator Robert A. Taft openly questioned the nation's financial and moral capacity to sustain an interventionist foreign policy. Others charged that a hardening of policy toward the Soviet Union would inevitably lead to war. Still others, like journalist Walter Lippmann, challenged the logic of a doctrine that seemed so open-ended as to defy any limitation of legitimate U.S. interests.

Doubts about the wisdom of the administration's foreign policy faded, however, after the Communists staged a coup in Czechoslovakia in February 1948 and the Soviets blockaded West Berlin several months later. As the nation took the first steps along the road that would lead it "from Korea to Berlin to Cuba to Vietnam," to quote Senator William Fulbright, the long-range implications of the doctrine of containment were brushed aside. Originally designed to meet a specific threat at a specific moment in time—a time when American military supremacy was insured by exclusive possession of the atomic bomb—the decision to "contain" the spread of Soviet influence in Europe and the Near East soon mushroomed into an ideological crusade against "World Communism." And Truman, having successfully "scared hell" out of the American people in order to gain their support for his policies, nonetheless found himself vilified by conservatives for being too "soft" toward the very threat he had identified.

What occasioned the transformation of the policy of containment from a geopolitical strategy to a global ideological struggle, however, was not so much the actions of the Soviet Union as a far more monumental event—the Chinese Revolution. That revolution had been long in the

The Berlin Airlift, June 1948 through September 1949. In response to the Soviet blockade of West Berlin, British and American planes delivered over 2 million tons of food, petroleum, and other supplies in more than 250,000 flights.

making, fueled by forces that made the eventual triumph of Mao Tse-tung's Communist army all but inevitable. Ruled by an incompetent and corrupt Nationalist government, further victimized by capricious feudal landlords, and beset by famine and pestilence of immeasurable proportions, millions of Chinese peasants had joined the Communist cause during the Second World War. When the war in the Pacific came to an end and civil war broke out, Mao's troops already controlled one-fifth of China's territory and more than 100 million people, and the ranks of his legions were growing steadily.

By that point some American officials stationed in China believed that any further efforts to prop up Chiang Kai-shek's Nationalist government were doomed to failure. But the Truman administration remained unconvinced and continued to funnel military and financial assistance to Chiang. In late 1945, the president also dispatched 50,000 American troops to China to support the Nationalist campaign in Manchuria. The campaign failed, however, as did efforts to negotiate a settlement between the Nationalists and Communists in 1946.

Outraged by Chiang's intransigent opposition to any compromise with the Communists, General Marshall, who had led the U.S. negotiating team, returned to Washington urging disengagement. The alternative, he told the president, was "a continuing commitment from which it would be practically impossible to withdraw." Although many Asian experts in the State Department agreed with Marshall's assessment, American aid continued over the next few years while support for the Nationalist regime inexorably eroded.

The fall of China

By February 1949 the Nationalists had lost nearly half their troops, mostly by defection, and 80 percent of their U.S.-supplied military equipment had fallen into Communist hands. Two months later, when Mao's army crossed the Yangtze River and began to sweep across southern China, President Truman made the decision to terminate U.S. support. Chiang and his supporters fled to the offshore island of Formosa, where they set up a rival

Nationalist government and began plotting the eventual reconquest of the Chinese mainland. "The unfortunate but inescapable fact," wrote Secretary of State Dean Acheson in an official white paper issued the following August, "is that the ominous result of the civil war in China was beyond the control of the government of the United States." Rather, he concluded, the victory of the Communists must be attributed to "internal Chinese forces" that might only have been offset by "full-scale intervention," and even then success could not have been assured.

From the point of view of the American foreign policy establishment, the decision to withdraw from China thus represented the only rational course of action in the face of intractable events. Yet to other Americans, and notably a group of influential conservatives who composed the so-called "China Lobby," the "loss" of China to Mao Tse-tung and the Communists was nothing less than an act of treason on the part of the Truman administration. Accusing the president of "selling out" China and the free enterprise system, they gained support from many Americans who could not understand why the greatest power on earth had been unable to defeat an army of Communist insurgents. Not recognizing the role that nationalism had played in the revolution, they interpreted the "fall of China" as evidence of a monolithic Communist movement bent on conquering the world. In so doing, they helped to perpetuate the belief that the United States was engaged in an ideological holy war and that it was the government's duty to resist the spread of communism no matter what the cost.

The conservative attack on the Truman administration's China policy had other far-reaching consequences. Not only did it broaden the purview of "containment" to include all of Asia as well as Europe, but it also pushed the postwar foreign policy consensus to the right. By feeding popular fears that the United States had become perilously weak, it made it a political liability for any president to be perceived as being "soft" on communism or to be accused of having "lost" a nation to Communist revolutionaries. By ignoring the responsibility of the Nationalist Chinese government for its own demise, it induced the American government to pursue a policy of nonrecognition toward the world's most populous nation. And by nurturing suspicions that the "loss" of China had been the work of "conspirators" inside the U.S. State Department, it set the stage for one of the darker chapters in the history of the Republic.

Shortly before the Communists take control of China in 1949, a U.S. ship, emblematic of America's new role in the postwar world, moves through Shanghai Harbor. Inset. Earlier in the war, in December 1945, General George C. Marshall meets with Generalissimo and Madame Chiang Kai-shek in Nanking hoping to negotiate a peace settlement between the Communists and the Nationalists.

McCarthyism

"The reason we find ourselves in a position of impotency," declared Senator Joseph McCarthy of Wisconsin, speaking before the Women's Republican Club of Wheeling, West Virginia, on February 9, 1950, "is not because our only powerful potential enemy has sent men to invade our shores but, rather, because of the traitorous actions of those who have been treated so well by this country.

"I have here in my hand," he went on, "a list of two hundred and five [individuals] . . . known to the Secretary of State as being members of the Communist Party and who nevertheless are still working and shaping the policy of the State Department." No one knows if McCarthy actually said 205. The sole recording of the speech was immediately erased, the senator himself was never able to locate his notes, and in the days following the Wheeling address the alleged list shrank in McCarthy's telling to 57, swelled to 81, then back up to "over two hundred card-carrying Communists." Nor were any of the names on his list ever identified. When pressed by reporters or his Senate colleagues for more specific information about the individuals involved, the Republican senator either evaded the question entirely or simply promised that the guilty would be exposed in time.

Much more significant than the actual number of names on McCarthy's notorious list, however, were the charges that the list purported to substantiate. As news of the senator's allegations splashed across the front pages of the nation's newspapers, the public was led to believe that McCarthy had uncovered a vast network of conspiracy inside the bowels of the American government. Announcing that he had penetrated "Truman's iron curtain of secrecy," he condemned the administration for pursuing a "weak, immoral, and cowardly" foreign policy of "appeasement, retreat, and surrender" before communism and for having "perpetrated a fraud on the American people." But that was just the beginning. Emboldened by the publicity that his accusations generated, he escalated and multiplied his attacks as time went on to the point where virtually no one was beyond suspicion as a "security risk." The Democratic party, he asserted in the weeks after Wheeling, was in the hands of "men and women who wear the political label stitched with the idiocy of a Truman, [and] rotted by the deceit of an Acheson." A year later he would denounce General Marshall, a man regarded by many of his fellow countrymen as "the greatest living American," as part of "a conspiracy so immense and an infamy so black as to dwarf any previous venture in the history of man." And by 1953, as chairman of the Senate Permanent Subcommittee on Investigations, he would be conducting sweeping witch-hunts through the State Department, the army, and other institutions of government looking for evidence of Communist "subversion."

So outlandish were most of the senator's charges, so

flimsy was his putative "evidence," it later was difficult to understand how McCarthy and McCarthyism became such powerful forces in American politics during the early 1950s. But they did. In the course of his brief, lurid Congressional career Joseph McCarthy not only destroyed the reputations of numerous government officials, many of whom were in effect banished for life from public service, but he also managed to intimidate two presidents and much of the American public.

At least in part, McCarthy's mercurial ascendancy could be attributed to the policies and actions of the very administration he so viciously denounced, for it was President Truman who had first raised the issue of "subversion" within the government and instituted a federal loyalty program in 1947, just six days after he had pronounced the Truman Doctrine. The real source of McCarthy's success, however, was his ability to articulate, and manipulate, the fears and frustrations of many Americans.

The pro-Soviet coup in Czechoslovakia and the Berlin blockade in 1948, the fall of China in 1949, the startling news that the Soviet Union had detonated an atomic bomb in August 1949, all contributed to a growing sense of vulnerability and, to use McCarthy's own term, "impotency," among large segments of the American population as the decade ended.

A series of unforeseen developments in January 1950 only heightened these apprehensions. On January 12 Secretary of State Acheson, in a speech to the National Press Club in Washington, seemed to define the American "defensive perimeter" in such a way as to exclude Korea. Although Acheson subsequently explained that Korea was protected by a separate treaty, his remarks provoked calls from Republican members of the Senate for a vote of censure on the administration and for Acheson's resignation. On January 21 Alger Hiss, the brother of one of Acheson's law partners and a former senior State Department offi-

cial under Roosevelt, was convicted of perjury in New York for having denied under oath that he had passed State Department papers to Whittaker Chambers, an admitted Communist spy. Less than a week later Washington learned that Klaus Fuchs, a German-born physicist who had worked on the highly sensitive Manhattan Project, had been arrested by Scotland Yard for passing secrets about the atomic bomb to the Soviets.

Yet if the mood of the country in early 1950 assured Senator McCarthy a receptive audience, it was the outbreak of war in Korea that gained him a certain credibility. When Communist North Korean troops launched a surprise invasion across the thirty-eighth parallel on June 25, 1950, charges that the Truman administration was grossly mishandling U.S. foreign policy suddenly seemed more persuasive. Pointing a finger at Acheson's description of the American "defensive perimeter" five months before, Senate Majority Leader Robert Taft declared that the administration's Far Eastern policy, and particularly its "Chinese policy," had "encouraged" the North Koreans to attack. "If the United States was not prepared to use its troops and give military assistance to Nationalist China against Chinese Communists," he asked, "why should it use its troops to defend Nationalist Korea against Korean Communists?"

The president's quick decision to send American soldiers to Korea, backed by a United Nations Security Council resolution condemning the invasion and sanctioning the U.S. response, rallied the nation behind him and quieted his critics for a time. But when Chinese Communist troops began to pour across the Yalu River in November 1950, preempting an anticipated victory by UN forces and then sending them into retreat, conservative assaults on the administration's policies resumed in earnest. An open clash between Truman and General Douglas MacArthur over the conduct of the war, culminating in the president's decision to recall MacArthur in early April 1951, caused an outburst of indignation from those who shared the general's belief that "there is no substitute for victory" and therefore that the United States should strike at the "source of aggression" in China. In the months that followed, as the war dragged on, as the cost in American lives and dollars rose, and as the frustrations of fighting a "limited war" mounted, the Truman administration found itself increasingly on the defensive.

In the meantime, the McCarthyite search for the "enemy within" continued, with profound consequences for American foreign policy. The oft-repeated charge that "Communist sympathizers" within the Truman administration were responsible for the nation's "impotency" in international affairs implied that anyone who dissented from the rigidly anti-Communist right-wing line was "un-American," or a "traitor," and thus effectively silenced all criticism from the left. As recently as 1948, left-wing opposition to the anti-Soviet thrust of the containment doctrine had found a spokesman in Henry Wallace, the former vice president who ran as the presidential candidate of the Progressive party. By 1951, however, such voices of dissent were barely audible, as even the more moderate members of the foreign policy establishment—the architects of the original geopolitical policy of containment—were compelled to support the broadly defined goals of the anti-Communist ideologues. That year, for example, Dean Acheson and General Marshall both testified during Senate hearings on Far Eastern policy that they would never so much as "consider" the recognition of Communist China or support its admission to the UN.

Acheson and Marshall were not alone. Throughout the Department of State McCarthy's heresy hunts bred suspicion, insecurity, and above all caution. Witnesses to the purge of the country's leading Asia experts—men whose chief transgression was to have dutifully reported the failings of the Nationalist Chinese government—the officers of

the U.S. foreign service learned their lessons well. It would be advantageous for the career-minded to filter their assessment of any international situation through the lens of anti-Communist orthodoxy and to ignore whatever did not accord with it.

Eisenhower: consensus affirmed

The inauguration of Dwight D. Eisenhower as thirty-fourth president of the United States on January 20, 1953, brought with it great expectations. Having pledged during his election campaign to "clean up" the "mess in Washington," having also promised to "go to Korea" and bring the war to an end, the former war leader had raised hopes that many of the ills afflicting the nation would soon be cured. Among conservative Republicans, the end of twenty years of Democratic rule brought the prospect of a

reversal of New Dealism at home, a more vigorously anti-Communist policy abroad, and a halt to the steady aggrandizement of presidential power that had begun during FDR's first term. At the same time, moderate Republicans and Democrats alike hoped that General Eisenhower's stature would allow him to stand up to McCarthy and rid the nation of the noxious menace that the senator represented.

At the beginning it seemed as though the conservatives would have their way. Openly vowing to "restore" the constitutional balance between the president and Congress, and decrying such federal projects as the Tennessee Valley Authority as examples of "creeping socialism," Eisenhower projected the image of a president intent upon minimizing his personal role in the government. Relatively inexperienced in domestic affairs, he gathered around him men whose principal qualifications seemed to be their own financial success as well as their opposition to governmental meddling in the economy. The new secretary of the treasury, George M. Humphrey, was a strong-willed, deeply conservative Ohio businessman who believed that New Dealism was spending the country into bankruptcy and planning it into chaos. When the new secretary of defense, former General Motors president Charles E. Wilson, was asked how he might resolve any conflict between his business interests and his public duties, he replied: "I cannot conceive of any because for years I thought what was good for our country was good for General Motors, and *vice versa.*"

General of the army Douglas MacArthur, commander of U.S. forces in Korea, enters his Tokyo headquarters on April 11, 1951, shortly after learning that he has been relieved of his command by President Truman.

Equally heartening to conservatives was the appointment of John Foster Dulles as secretary of state; the grandson of one secretary of state (John Foster) and nephew of another (Robert Lansing), Dulles had impeccable credentials within the foreign policy establishment. Yet unlike the majority of his fellow diplomats, he had long advocated abandoning what he called "the negative, futile and immoral" policy of containment in favor of a more aggressive policy of "liberation." Containment, he argued during the 1952 election campaign, committed the United States to a policy of indefinite coexistence, whereas the proper goal was not to coexist with the Communist threat but to end it—to "roll back" the Communists and "liberate" their "captive peoples." The president echoed these views in his first State of the Union address when he promised to unleash Chiang Kai-shek and his Nationalist forces for the presumed reconquest of China and further repudiated "all commitments contained in secret understandings such as those of Yalta which aid Communist enslavement."

For all the talk of dismantling the New Deal at home and "rolling back" communism abroad, however, in practice the Eisenhower administration proved far more moderate. Despite his promise to put an end to economic "statism," the president made no serious attempt to repeal major New Deal legislation and repeatedly took steps to insure continued economic growth. In 1954, and again in 1958, Eisenhower violated traditional Republican orthodoxy by pursuing a modest course of deficit spending to pull the economy out of recession, and in 1956 he committed the federal government to paying 90 percent of the construction costs of the new interstate highway system.

Nor did Eisenhower make good on his promise to curb the growing power of the presidency. Instead he created an elaborate staff system to extend presidential control and jealously guarded the prerogatives of office that had accrued during the previous two Democratic administrations. When Senator McCarthy demanded access to Department of Defense files in May 1954, for example, Eisenhower claimed "an uncontrolled discretion" to refuse any information originating in the executive branch, and in the years that followed he invoked that right, under the name of "executive privilege," more often than any president in U.S. history up to that time. Congressional attempts to place limits on the president's authority in international affairs met with similarly stern resistance. In early 1954 Eisenhower successfully fought off a proposed constitutional amendment requiring Congressional approval of all international agreements, in addition to formal treaties, on the grounds that the measure was "isolationist." The threat did prompt the president, however, to seek "blank check" Congressional authorization during the crisis over Formosa in 1954–55 and during a crisis in the Middle East in 1957. The same tactic would be used by President Lyndon B. Johnson in the case of Vietnam in August 1964.

In its foreign policy, the Eisenhower administration soon abandoned the bellicose rhetoric of "roll back" and embraced the policy of containment. Far from rushing to the aid of "captive peoples," the president refused to encourage Chiang's plans for an invasion of mainland China, refrained from intervening directly during the anti-Soviet rebellions in East Germany in 1953 and Hungary in 1956, and refused to rescue the French at Dien Bien Phu in 1954. Instead, under the stewardship of Secretary of State Dulles, the administration broadened the scope of the containment doctrine and, in effect, institutionalized the Cold War through a series of mutual defense treaties and military aid agreements.

In Southeast Asia, where the U.S. had underwritten much of the cost of the ill-fated French war against the Communist Vietminh, the danger of further Communist expansion was met by the formation of the Southeast Asia Treaty Organization (SEATO) in September 1954. When the Soviets launched an ambitious aid program in 1955 that eventually brought military and economic assistance agreements with fourteen nations in Asia and the Middle East, the United States countered by engineering the Baghdad Pact, later known as CENTO (Central Treaty Organization), "to create," in Dulles's words, "a solid band of resistance against the Soviet Union." Two years later, in March 1957, Congress fortified the U.S. commitment to the Middle East by endorsing the so-called "Eisenhower Doctrine," which granted the president the authority to commit American forces to the region in the event of "overt aggression from any nation controlled by International Communism."

What was most striking about the Eisenhower administration's "pactomania," as some critics called it, was that it rested on a series of problematical assumptions about the nature of the Communist threat to U.S. interests abroad. Not only did the administration assume that "International Communism" was a monolithic movement controlled at a single source, but it also interpreted goals of that movement in almost exclusively military terms. Furthermore, while Secretary Dulles once stated that it was "counterproductive . . . to oppose nationalism," the United States tended to ignore the role of nationalism both in the foreign policies of the Soviet Union and Communist China and in the Communist movements of the Third World. As a result, American foreign policy during the Eisenhower years was marked by a contraction of economic aid programs and a steady extension of military commitments around the world.

The military

The extraordinary expansion of American military power in the postwar era began with the reorganization of the country's entire defense establishment in 1947. Under the provisions of the National Security Act passed that year, the previously autonomous Departments of the Army and

Navy, and the newly constituted air force were brought together to form what was called the National Military Establishment under the "general direction, authority, and control" of a civilian secretary of defense. The same act also set up a permanent Joint Chiefs of Staff, a National Security Council, and the Central Intelligence Agency, an outgrowth of the wartime Office of Strategic Services.

To meet the manpower requirements of the streamlined U.S. military machine, a year later President Truman pressed Congress for a new conscription law that would require compulsory universal military training. While most legislators favored the reinstitution of the Selective Service draft, which had formally ended in March 1947, many were wary of the idea of universal military training—some for economic reasons, others because of opposition within their constituencies. As a result, the final version of the new draft law remained decidedly "selective," applying only to males between the ages of eighteen and twenty-five and providing for a wide range of deferments and exemptions. By the end of the year the total number of American men and women under arms had risen from a postwar low of 1.4 million to 1.6 million.

Although some military officials maintained that the ranks of the armed forces should be augmented even further, both strategic and budgetary considerations argued against the need for a large conventional fighting force. Relying upon the presumably unmatched power of the atomic bomb, American military strategy in the early postwar years was based on the concept of "deterrence"—the belief that any potential aggressor, notably the Soviet Union, could be deterred by the unspoken threat of a retaliatory atomic air strike. Although the army sharply criticized the logic of deterrence, the air force, arguing that the next war would be fought with "machines, not men," lobbied hard and successfully to gain acceptance of a strategy based upon air power. As a result, while the Truman administration kept a tight lid on overall defense expenditures between 1947 and 1950, the air force's share of the military procurement budget increased enormously.

Once Washington learned that the Soviet Union had developed its own atomic capability, however, America had to reappraise its strategic position and priorities. The president immediately charged the National Security Council with that task, and in April 1950 it presented its report. Among the recommendations of NSC–68, as the document was titled, were an increase in military expenditures from 5 to, if necessary, 20 percent of the gross national product; the rapid build-up of conventional forces; the development of the H-bomb (a huge improvement in destructive power over the A-bomb) to meet the danger of a growing Soviet atomic arsenal; a strong network of alliances directed by the U.S.; and the mobilization of American society behind the administration's policies, including a "consensus" on the need for "sacrifice" and "unity." Two months later, the eruption of war in

Korea underscored the findings of NSC–68 and exposed—or so it seemed—the weakness of a military strategy based upon air-atomic power.

By almost any measure, the American military was not prepared for the Korean War. Not only had the bulk of U.S. occupation forces left South Korea in June 1949, but by the beginning of 1950 the overall troop strength of the armed forces had once again fallen to the predraft level of 1.4 million men. The army had only ten active divisions and 593,000 soldiers, roughly half the number they had had three years before. The navy was staffed by 381,000, down almost 70,000 from the previous year. And throughout the military there were grave shortages of arms, ammunition, and supplies.

Bolstering the ranks of conventional forces was therefore the most immediate task facing the Truman administration as it committed the nation to war. On July 10 the first draft calls went out, greeting 50,000 young men with news of their impending induction. Across the country local draft boards sprang into action, processing centers went into operation, and factories began to retool to meet the military's wartime needs. By early 1950 draft calls were running at 80,000 per month; by midyear 1.8 million men, including 609,000 reservists called up to active duty, had been added to the armed forces; and by the time the war ended in July 1953, all three services had more than doubled their personnel.

In the years that followed, those numbers steadily shrank—from 3.3 million in 1954 to 2.8 million in 1956 to 2.5 million in 1959—in part because the nation was at peace and in part because the Eisenhower administration once again redefined U.S. strategy in a way that minimized the need for conventional military forces. In the view of Secretary of State Dulles, the principal lesson of Korea was not that the United States should prepare itself to fight limited local wars, but that it should maintain a "deterrent power" so formidable that no nation would dare to transgress upon America's strategic interests. Placing the U.S. nuclear arsenal at the center of his new strategy, Dulles outlined the doctrine of "massive retaliation," as it came to be known, in a speech to the Council on Foreign Relations in January 1954. "The only way to deter aggression is for the free community to be willing and able . . . to retaliate, instantly, by means and at places of our own choosing," he stated. In other words, in the future, local aggression would be met, not by committing conventional forces to a limited war, but by a threat to launch a massive nuclear attack against the Soviet Union or Communist China.

The "New Look" military posture of the Eisenhower administration did not, however, represent a wholesale abandonment of the U.S. commitment to interventionism. Rather, the repudiation of limited-war capability meant an increasing reliance on clandestine CIA operations to protect American interests abroad. Under the Truman administration the CIA had been used primarily to infiltrate

Communist bloc countries in Eastern Europe and to counteract Soviet influence in Western Europe by aiding non-Communist parties, trade unions, and newspapers. Now, under the direction of Allen W. Dulles, the secretary of state's brother, the powers and purposes of the CIA were greatly expanded to include the active subversion of perceived foes as well as the support of friends. In Iran in 1953 and Guatemala in 1954, the CIA was instrumental in the overthrow of governments considered to be pro-Communist. In Egypt (1954) and Laos (1959), it helped to install supposedly pro-Western regimes. And in 1960 it plotted assassination attempts against pro-Communist leaders Fidel Castro of Cuba and Patrice Lumumba of the Congo.

From the outset a number of high-ranking army officers strongly objected to the Eisenhower administration's new military policies. Seeking some middle ground between the sledgehammer of massive retaliation and the slingshot of covert intervention, they advocated a conventional ground force adequate to meet the demands of less than all-out war. But the air force enthusiastically supported the "New Look," and in the end the advocates of air power held sway. Congress, too, endorsed the plan, after being persuaded by Secretary Dulles that it would provide "more basic security at less cost" or, as Secretary of Defense Wilson put it, "more bang for the buck."

Nevertheless, in concrete terms the new emphasis on cost-effectiveness meant military budgets that were on average three times larger than those before the Korean War. The lion's share of those outlays went to the air force, which saw its budget grow from $15.5 billion to $19 billion between 1954 and 1960. During the same period navy and Marine Corps expenditures held steady at $10 billion to $11 billion per year, while spending on the army fell from $14.5 billion to $9.4 billion. Waste, duplication, and inter-service rivalry inflated those budgets, as each military branch lobbied to procure whatever new weapons happened to be on the drawing board and to protect its own turf within the defense establishment. Moreover, even when the Department of Defense did try to cut back on unnecessary spending, it often found itself opposed by congressmen whose political fortunes rested on their ability to secure juicy military contracts for their constituencies. It was during the late 1950s, for example, that Henry Jackson of Washington State became known as the "Senator from Boeing," and Richard B. Russell and Carl Vinson joined together to stuff twenty military installations into Georgia. The undisputed king of the Pentagon pork barrel, however, was Lucius Mendel Rivers of South Carolina, the future chairman of the House Armed Services Committee, who managed to bring to his district an air force base, an army depot, a Marine Corps training center, a Coast Guard mine-warfare school, and a navy shipyard, supply center, and weapons station, as well as defense plants with hundreds of millions of dollars in contracts.

In his farewell address to the nation in January 1961,

President Eisenhower called attention to "this conjunction of an immense military establishment and a large arms industry" whose "total influence—economic, political, and even spiritual—is felt in every city, every State house, every office of the Federal Government." He warned, "We must guard against the acquisition of unwarranted influence by the military-industrial complex." Eisenhower's words of caution notwithstanding, the unprecedented peacetime military budgets of his administration had had at least one salutary effect. By nurturing some 40,000 "prime" defense contractors and hundreds of thousands of lesser ones across the country, the government had helped to sustain a level of economic growth and prosperity that most Americans, by the mid-1950s, had come not only to expect, but to take for granted.

Affluent America

The Affluent Society. The Consumer Culture. The Post-Industrial Order. Such were some of the terms used to describe American society during the bountiful years of the 1950s, a decade in which virtually every index of economic growth and material well-being climbed steadily upward to new record highs. The real GNP rose fully 50 percent, industrial investment ran at a pace three times greater than in the "golden twenties," output per man-hour increased more than 35 percent, and the average income of Americans went up more than 25 percent. During the 1950s, in short, more Americans found themselves better off than they had ever been before. And the great leap of the sixties still lay ahead.

If swollen defense expenditures, brought on by the Korean War and sustained by the cold war budgets of the Eisenhower administration, helped push the economy along the road to prosperity, rising consumer demand pulled it the rest of the way. Stimulated by the lure of installment credit, by mortgage policies that made it possible for the majority of Americans to buy their own homes, and by a rapidly growing advertising industry that encouraged every whim, the American people created an ever-expanding home market for the cornucopia of manufactured goods pouring out of the nation's industries. Particularly in suburbia, where more than four-fifths of all new homes were built during the 1950s, buying on time and surrounding oneself with the accouterments of the good life became something of a national passion.

In part because of the increased distance from home to work place, and from home to local shopping center, car sales rose 50 percent during the decade while the number of two-car families increased by an average of 750,000 per year. Sales of other necessary adjuncts of suburban living or, as the advertisers preferred to say, "modern conveniences"—automatic washers and dryers, electric dishwashers, power lawnmowers—also shot up. Yet perhaps most remarkable of all was the mass consumption of an

Defense build-up. Above. Specially equipped for long-range, high-altitude reconnaissance, new B-36s near completion on an assembly line at Consolidated Vultee Aircraft Corporation in Fort Worth, Texas, 1950. Left. Secretary of Defense Charles E. Wilson, surrounded by models of the most advanced American weaponry, poses for photographers at his first press conference in 1953.

entirely new technological marvel, the television set. From approximately 7,000 sets manufactured in 1946, production leaped to more than 7 million per year by 1953, and by 1960 an estimated 86 percent of all American homes had at least one TV.

Further expansion of the economy was guaranteed by the unparalleled growth of the American population. The so-called "baby boom" had begun in 1946, when a record total of 3,426,000 births—one every nine seconds—occurred in the United States. Although demographers initially regarded the surge as a temporary aberration, brought on by rapid postwar demobilization, the same trend continued for the next twenty years. From 1947 to 1951 an average of more than 3.7 million babies were born per year; in 1952 and 1953 the figure climbed to 3.9 million; and beginning in 1954 it surpassed 4 million—a pace of population growth that would continue until the midsixties.

Not only did the ongoing "baby boom" provide a constant source of parental demand for diaper services, baby food, and toys but, as *Time* magazine noted at the end of 1948, it meant that several million "more consumers" were arriving in the United States each year. Ten years later *Life* picked up the same theme when the cover of the June 16, 1958, issue carried the headline: "Kids, Built-in Recession Cure—How 4,000,000 a Year Make Millions in Business." So great was the perceived economic worth of infants, in fact, that one economist even suggested they be viewed not only as consumers but as "consumer durable goods expected to yield a stream of psychic satisfaction through time."

Nuclear anxiety: A back yard bomb shelter is constructed behind a home in Hermosa Beach, California, 1951.

The "baby boom" generation undeniably had an enormous impact on the economy of the 1950s. The youthful bulge in the U.S. population not only lured the attention of advertisers hawking toy guns and coonskin caps, hi-fis and hula hoops, but also placed a strain on the nation's educational resources. With some 4 million children reaching school age each year, public spending on primary and secondary education tripled during the decade, and even then many communities were unable to remedy the shortage of classrooms and teachers. In New Jersey, for example, where the school population increased 62 percent between 1950 and 1960, 47,000 students were crowded into half-sessions taught by underqualified teachers, while in Los Angeles the addition of one new

school a week and a thousand teachers per year proved insufficient to meet the expanding city's needs.

Yet for most Americans, living in the midst of unprecedented plenty, such matters hardly seemed cause for serious concern. Indeed, throughout the decade the fundamental strength of the American economy nourished the widespread belief that ever-increasing prosperity would eventually wash away the nation's social problems. It was a belief that rested upon a shared set of assumptions about the virtues of the American capitalist system and the essential goodness of American society. Codified in a series of official and semiofficial statements that appeared in the 1950s—from the panel reports of the Rockefeller Brothers Fund to the report of President Eisenhower's Commission on National Goals—those assumptions were often expressed in the form of a syllogism. Beginning with the proposition that a reinvigorated free enterprise system had brought about the new age of abundance, and observing further that uninterrupted economic growth had raised the standard of living of the vast majority of American citizens, it followed—or seemed to follow—that the continued success of American capitalism would eventually bring prosperity to all and virtually eliminate social and political conflict. "Production has eliminated the more acute tensions associated with inequality," wrote John Kenneth Galbraith in *The Affluent Society*, voicing an opinion shared by many of his colleagues in the social sciences. The American worker, said the editors of *Fortune* magazine, had become "a middle class member of a middle class society."

Set against the background of the 1930s and early 1940s, when many American economists were predicting the end of capitalism and many American workers were calling for it, such statements are striking. More significant, however, is the extent to which they reflected popular attitudes during the 1940s. To cite but one index of the transformation that occurred, in 1942 a poll taken by Elmo Roper for *Fortune* found that only 40 percent of respondents opposed socialism, 25 percent favored it, and as many as 35 percent were undecided. By 1949, a Gallup poll found that only 15 percent wanted "to move in the direction of socialism," while 62 percent wanted to move in the opposite direction. Five years later the pollsters did not even raise the question.

The booming economy, of course, was not the sole

source of the new mood of consensus that descended upon America in the 1950s. Equally decisive in shaping public opinion, and in silencing fundamental criticism of American society, was the fervently anti-Communist posture of the U.S. government. Cast in the role of both international and domestic bogeyman, magnified by the missionary rhetoric of the Cold War and the machinations of McCarthy, the specter of communism loomed over the nation as a perpetual threat to what was commonly called "the American way of life." Intensified by the ever-present possibility of war between the superpowers, fear of communism became the opposite face of the renewed sense of confidence that gripped the country during the 1950s. For if unprecedented prosperity held out the promise of ultimate perfectability, the unprecedented vulnerability posed by the threat of nuclear war shrouded the future in dark uncertainty.

This stark, almost Manichaean dualism of consciousness found expression in many ways. The very works that celebrated the accomplishments of American capitalism, for example, typically included warnings about the "challenge" or "menace" confronting the nation from without. One of the Rockefeller Brothers Fund reports thus speaks of "the mortal struggle in which we are engaged" and "the basic underlying Soviet danger," while the National Goals report warns that "the nation is in grave danger, threatened by the rulers of one-third of mankind." Organized labor also gave its official imprimatur to the belief that the American economic system offered the best means of achieving social progress and that communism was its Number-One Enemy. When the American Federation of Labor and the Congress of Industrial Organizations finally joined forces in 1955, one of the formal articles of merger read:

The merged federation shall constitutionally affirm its determination to protect the American trade union movement from any and all corrupt influence and from the undermining efforts of Communist agencies and all others who are opposed to the basic principles of our democracy.

Perhaps most important of all, the same attitudes, assumptions, and fears permeated the major institutions entrusted with the transmission of ideas and values to the American public: the news media and the universities.

The distorted mirror

Among the more frequently asked questions about the performance of the American news media in the 1950s is, why didn't more newspapers and newspapermen stand up to the menace of McCarthyism? Or, to put it more accurately, why didn't they expose Senator McCarthy for what he was and what he was doing sooner than they did? Many journalists knew that the senator often lied, that he had little, if any, evidence to support his charges, and that his actions were destroying the lives of many reputable people. Yet until 1953 few editorialists and even fewer columnists were willing to challenge directly the validity of McCarthy's charges.

One explanation is that most journalists simply did not think it was their job to confront Senator McCarthy. Rather, they believed that their professional responsibility was only to report "facts," to recount what happened and how it happened, and not to insinuate their own judgments into their stories. As the eminent Walter Lippmann explained: "McCarthy's charges of treason, espionage, corruption, perversion are news which cannot be suppressed or ignored. They come from a United States Senator and a politician. . . . When he makes such attacks against the State Department and the Defense Department it is news which has to be published." Looking back on its own coverage of a McCarthy investigation, the *New York Times* echoed Lippmann's views. "It is difficult, if not impossible," wrote the *Times*, "to ignore charges by Senator McCarthy just because they are usually proved false. The remedy lies with the reader."

In part this attitude derived from a desire to maintain professional journalistic standards that had been honored, frequently in the breach, for at least the preceding half-century, standards of "objectivity" that included a presumed duty to report accurately whatever any prominent public official had to say. But there were other factors at work as well. The growth of the wire services had at once accelerated the pace of news gathering and nationalized information as it moved from reporter to wire to print in dozens of newspapers across the country. The development of national radio networks had a similar impact. As competition to get the news out fast *and* first intensified, there was less time to look back and reflect upon what had already transpired or to compare, for instance, what Senator McCarthy said two weeks before with what he said today.

There were many exceptions to these general trends. Throughout the nation there were still hundreds of local newspapers and radio stations that were little more than partisan mouthpieces for individual publishers and owner-operators. And even those journals that had national audiences, or aspired to national audiences, typically followed a strong editorial line. Overall, however, what was notable about the mainstream news media in the 1950s—local as well as national, liberal, or conservative—is the extent to which they mirrored and reinforced the broad tenets of the postwar consensus: the notion that international communism represented the greatest threat to national well-being and the belief that the structure of American society was essentially sound.

In many ways this homogeneity of opinion was understandable. Then as now, members of the news media, no matter how much they sought to objectify their views, were strongly affected by the dominant ideas and values of their time. The propensity to accept official views, moreover, and particularly government views of foreign policy matters, was heightened by a desire to gain access to privileged information. Many politicians in turn played upon the needs of the press as a means of shaping public opinion—planting a story with a favored correspondent, creating a rumor, providing selective "background" information on a given subject.

On the other hand, publishers and journalists often attempted to press their own views on the government. Henry Luce's Time, Inc. was a case in point. A man who liked to keep a tight editorial grip on his publishing empire, which then included not only *Time* but also *Life* and *Fortune* magazines, Luce strongly believed in his absolute right to express his own opinions in his own journals, and he endeavored to assure that stories dealing with his special areas of concern contained no apostasy. A fervid anti-Communist who had been raised by missionary parents in China, he frequently refused to credit reports from correspondent Theodore White in the 1940s that criticized the Nationalist government and instead threw the considerable weight of his highly subscribed publications be-

hind the "China Lobby." Throughout the 1950s he continued to champion Chiang Kai-shek's Taiwan government, to uphold the quixotic dream of reconquest of the mainland, and to denounce any hint that the United States might formally recognize the existence of "Red China."

The Luce magazines, and to a lesser degree such national journals as *Newsweek* and *U.S. News and World Report*, exerted impact, but for sheer power to influence public opinion, no publication or set of publications could match the newest of the news media, television. It was not until the early 1960s that television became the primary news source for most Americans, but the exponential growth of the TV industry in the 1950s nonetheless had a profound effect on peoples' perception and understanding of the world around them. It could heighten awareness of important issues and events through first-rate public affairs programs like Edward R. Murrow's "See It Now"; but it could just as easily stultify consciousness by portraying reality as one long episode of "Ozzie and Harriet." During the early 1950s television offered both kinds of fare, balancing its serious news coverage with entertainment pro-

Prime Time

Throughout the 1950s serious public affairs programs vied with light-hearted comedies and other escapist fare for the TV networks' prime time slots. Upper right. Columbia University instructor Charles Van Doren, later implicated in quiz show scandals, wins the jackpot on NBC's "Twenty-One." *Inset left.* Lucy, Ricky, Ethel, and Fred leave New York for sunny California in one episode of "I Love Lucy," *the most popular show of the decade. Inset right.* Edward R. Murrow, *the most esteemed broadcast journalist of his time, reports for CBS News.*

grams designed to divert rather than inform. But as that decade wore on, and the enormous advertising potential of the medium began to yield windfall profits, that balance increasingly shifted away from hard news in favor of melodramas and variety shows.

The change was not simply a function of ratings. In 1955 "See It Now" lost its regular weekly time slot because its sponsor, Alcoa Aluminum, had disapproved of Murrow's interview with controversial atomic physicist J. Robert Oppenheimer, as well as a Murrow report on land scandals in Texas, where Alcoa was planning to increase its investments. Several years later the nation's preeminent broadcast journalist returned to prime time but this time as the host of "Person to Person," a "soft news" interview program relatively insulated from issues of controversy. Nineteen fifty-five was also the first big year for an entirely new genre of television programming—the quiz show. That was the year that CBS introduced "The $64,000 Question," a show so successful that it prompted the network's president, Frank Stanton, to conclude: "A program in which a large part of the audience is interested is by

that very fact . . . in the public interest." For the next half a decade the quiz shows ruled the television airwaves, while the amount of broadcast time devoted to news programs steadily diminished.

Then, in 1959, the FCC uncovered evidence that several of the quiz shows had been rigged. Although initially the FCC agreed to keep the scandal quiet, the public soon learned that contestants on CBS's "Dotto" and NBC's "Twenty-One" had been furnished beforehand with answers to the questions they were later asked. In the wake of the quiz show scandals, the chairman of the FCC called the heads of all three networks down to Washington and ordered them to produce at least one hour of public affairs programs each week that did not coincide with a similar hour on another network. That decision marked a turning point not only for TV journalism, but for the American public as well, because it induced the networks to expand their news divisions and coverage of live events. It thereby insured that four years later, when crisis came to Birmingham and Dallas, Saigon and Washington, the cameras would be there and the nation would be watching.

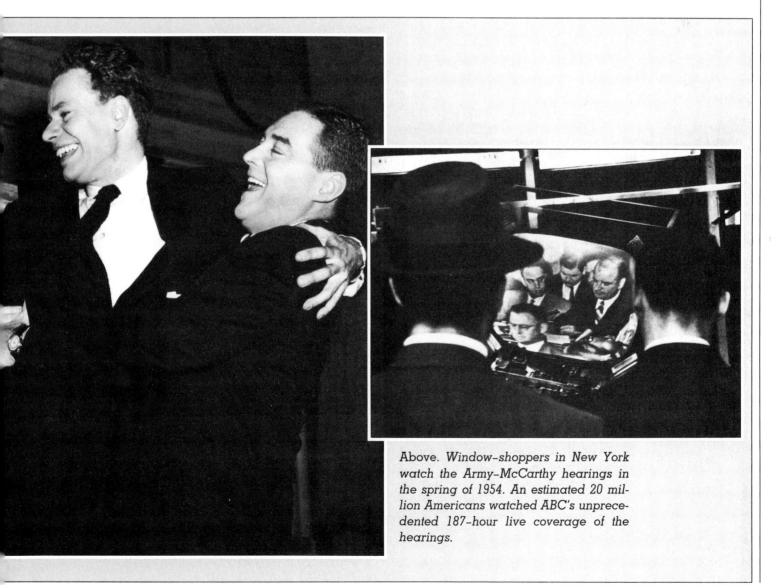

Above. Window-shoppers in New York watch the Army-McCarthy hearings in the spring of 1954. An estimated 20 million Americans watched ABC's unprecedented 187-hour live coverage of the hearings.

The rise of the "multiversity"

If the 1950s were "the age of bland in the media," as one journalist put it, in the nation's universities they were the golden age of complacency. Across the country enrollments were rising, endowments accumulating, new universities springing up, and old ones expanding. Monies from federal and state governments as well as from private foundations and industry were pouring in on a scale previously undreamed of. And the salaries and social status of university professors were steadily rising.

The great change began in the late 1940s, when the federal government extended its commitment to higher education in two significant ways. First, it stimulated enrollment by providing, under the terms of the GI Bill, financial support to World War II veterans who wanted to obtain a college education. At the same time, it increased direct aid to universities by offering long-term, low-interest loans for dormitory construction as well as lucrative research grants under auspices of the Department of Defense, the Atomic Energy Commission, and other governmental agencies.

In response to the unanticipated influx of veterans and the lure of federal funds, many state governments began to expand, improve, and coordinate their university systems. In California, where a dizzying rate of population growth put additional pressure on the state to plan for the future, a special commission appointed in 1947 recommended a series of sweeping reforms designed to provide an "equal opportunity for all to get a good education." Drawing up a blueprint for what later would be known as the "UCAL model," the commission called for the reorganization and rapid expansion of the state's three-tiered system of higher education under centralized direction.

Other states quickly followed California's much-publicized lead. The establishment of state boards to oversee planning, construction, and expenditures became increasingly common, and in some cases—Ohio and Illinois, for example—the boards were granted even greater authority than in California. In addition to bringing their existing institutions of higher learning into coordinated statewide systems, most states began building new colleges and junior colleges and, at the same time, augmented the graduate, professional, and research capacities of their universities. Even then, it was often difficult to keep pace with rising demand. During the decade total college and university enrollment shot up 70 percent (from 2.1 million in 1951 to 3.6 million in 1960); in California the figure was nearly 150 percent.

Aided by the flourishing economy, and by an ever-expanding array of federal, state, and private scholarship and loan programs, not only a greater number, but a greater percentage of Americans attended institutions of higher education every year. Although most students still came from upper-middle- and middle-class families, the number of second- and third-generation immigrants and members of the working class going to college was also on the rise. Once the privilege of the wealthy few, a college education came to be regarded by the end of the 1950s as a virtual necessity for anyone hoping to climb the American social ladder.

As the size and structure of the American university changed, so too did the reigning definition of its role in society. The traditional ideal of the university as a "community of masters and students" joined together in a "spirit of free inquiry" gradually yielded to the new idea of the "multiversity" as a source of socially "useful" knowledge. As envisioned by University of California President Clark Kerr, whose 1963 essay on "The Uses of the University" introduced the term "multiversity," the mission of higher education was not to cultivate scholarship for its own sake, but rather to serve the practical needs of society at large. The new university, according to President Kerr, functioned like a "factory" whose "invisible product, new knowledge . . . is the most important factor in economic and social growth."

Encouraging this redefinition of purpose was the ever-increasing flow of federal money into the nation's leading universities, much of it earmarked to support scientific research in the interest of "national security." This was the original rationale behind the establishment of the National Science Foundation in 1950, which spent more than $100 million during the following ten years to promote education and research in the sciences, as well as the National Defense Education Act of 1958, which provided loans, grants, "work-study" assistance, and graduate fellowships to hundreds of thousands of students. The same reasoning was used to justify a multitude of research projects sponsored by the Department of Defense, ranging from advanced missile development to an air force study (through the Rand Corporation) on the toilet training of the French. By 1960 the federal government was doling out an estimated $1 billion per year on university-affiliated research and an additional $500 million on scholarships and teaching programs—a total that amounted to 15 percent of all university budgets for that year and 75 percent of university expenditures on research.

Although many administrators believed that government-sponsored research comprised "an area of public service . . . in line with education proper," as a dean of the University of Washington stated in 1959, others openly worried that it might compromise academic freedom. Even Clark Kerr conceded that "the federal colossus had the power to influence . . . the most ruggedly individual of universities." By withholding or granting funds, government agencies could add to or subtract from the prestige of a major university and make or break the reputation of an individual professor.

More than increased government subsidies to higher education contributed to the quietude of American campuses in the 1950s. The real causes ran deeper. Like the media, the universities felt the sting of McCarthyism and, like the media, they reacted with timidity and a heightened sense of caution. Witch-hunts within the walls of the university were relatively rare, though there were some long-festering cases, but the tendency to shy away from social criticism and political dissent became commonplace. In English it was the age of the "New Criticism," which approached literature as if it had been written in a timeless vacuum. In the study of American history it was a time in which "consensus" interpretations prevailed. And in political science and sociology it was a decade in which critical theorizing stagnated and empiricism of the narrowest sort triumphed. It was, in short, an era in which many basic assumptions went unchallenged, pressing questions went unasked, and persistent problems were ignored. In this sense the new "multiversities" clearly reflected the mood of the nation, even if they were not fully serving its "needs."

The portrait of America in the 1950s as a society steeped in complacency can, of course, be overdrawn. Like any generalization about any society at any time, it necessarily blots out the ideas, aspirations, and experiences of many people who dissented from the majority point of view. Even before attorney Joseph Welch sealed the demise of Senator McCarthy during the televised army hearings in 1954 with the simple phrase, "Have you no sense of decency, sir?" there were some who spoke out forcefully against the scourge of "red-baiting" and "loyalty oaths." Others questioned the benefits of a form of prosperity that still left millions in poverty and the logic of a foreign policy that multiplied the nation's commitments abroad without any assurance that those commitments could be met. Still others criticized what they regarded as the progressive "homogenization" of American society, the ascendancy of the "organization man," and the decline of nonconformity.

University of California President Clark Kerr (foreground), *the originator of the term "multiversity," poses with the chancellors of the nine UC campuses in May 1964.*

Voices of dissent

The strongest surge of dissent during the age of consensus came from black Americans as a group. Long denied a proportionate share of the nation's wealth, relegated to the bottom rung of the social ladder, and still deprived in many areas of the right to vote, blacks in the 1950s began to demand an end to institutionalized racism in the United States and elevation to the status of first-class citizenship.

In mounting their challenge to the ruling white majority, however, the early civil rights movement did not directly attack the ideology of the postwar consensus. Although at times accused of being Communists, they consistently supported the foreign policy priorities of the U.S. government and advocated not a radical restructuring of American society, but "equal opportunity" within the existing structure. If sustained economic growth were to bring genuine social progress, as current theory held, then blacks would have to compete on equal terms with whites for the fruits of that growth. Discrimination against blacks in education, housing, and the job market would have to be eliminated. If America were to live up to its professed democratic ideals, then blacks would have to be guaranteed the same political and civil rights as whites—the right to vote, the right to hold public office, the right to "due process of law."

The principal target of the civil rights movement in its early years was the intricate and pervasive system of legal and quasi-legal racial segregation. After successfully lobbying to integrate the armed forces in 1948, but failing to gain Congressional approval of a fair employment practices law, black civil rights champions increasingly concentrated their efforts on desegregating the nation's public schools. In the early 1950s there were still seventeen states, plus the District of Columbia, that maintained dual systems of public education—one for white children, another for blacks. It was an arrangement sanctioned not only by state and local laws, but also by the U.S. Supreme Court, which had held, in the famous *Plessy v. Ferguson* decision of 1896, that separate public facilities for Negroes were constitutionally permissible so long as those facilities were "equal" in kind. Yet in practical terms the "separate-but-equal" doctrine had led to a situation in which states with segregated schools were spending approximately three dollars on each white student for every two spent on blacks, and in some southern states the differential was much greater.

Beginning at the local level and working its way up through the courts, the National Association for the Advancement of Colored People (NAACP) led the legal assault that eventually culminated in the reversal of the

Plessy doctrine. On May 17, 1954, in the case of *Brown v. Board of Education of Topeka*, the Supreme Court unanimously ruled that compulsory school segregation violated the "equal protection of the laws" clause of the Fourteenth Amendment. "We conclude," wrote Earl Warren, the new chief justice, "that in the field of public education, the doctrine of 'separate but equal' has no place. Separate educational facilities are inherently unequal." A year later the Court asked state school authorities to submit plans for desegregation, gave local federal courts responsibility for insuring "good faith compliance," and ordered that action move forward "with all deliberate speed."

In practice "all deliberate speed" proved to be an exceedingly slow pace. Particularly in the states of the Deep South—South Carolina, Georgia, Alabama, and Mississippi—resistance to the court ruling was strong and sustained. In 1955 militant segregationists began forming White Citizens Councils throughout the South, and in 1956 101 members of Congress, all from former Confederate states, signed a "Southern Manifesto" calling for "massive resistance" to desegregation. In Virginia attempts were made to get around the problem by diverting state funds to newly established, and exclusively white, private school systems and then closing down the public schools. In other places, like Clinton, Tennessee, efforts to integrate the schools met with violence.

The crisis over school integration reached a climax in the fall of 1957, when Governor Orval Faubus of Arkansas defied a court-approved plan to admit nine black students to Central High School in Little Rock and mobilized the state's National Guard on the pretext of maintaining public order. Although Faubus's actions represented a direct challenge to federal authority, President Eisenhower's initial reaction was tentative and restrained. Reiterating his familiar contention that "you cannot change people's hearts merely by laws," he invited Faubus to meet with him and eventually persuaded the governor to withdraw his troops. But when a mob of angry whites tried to bar the black boys and girls from entering the high school several days later, it became clear that the president would have to take sterner measures. For the first time since Reconstruction, federal troops were sent into the South to protect the rights of blacks. Order was quickly restored, and on September 25, 1957, the black children entered the school.

That same year brought further federal support for the cause of racial justice in the form of the first civil rights act passed by Congress since 1875, a statute that authorized the Department of Justice to bring suits on behalf of blacks denied the right to vote. Three years later, in 1960, a second act provided for the appointment of federal referees to safeguard voting rights. The impact of this new legislation, however, was far more symbolic than real. Enforcement of the provisions of both acts was at best spotty, and by the time Eisenhower left office the vast majority of southern blacks still could not exercise their franchise. In Mis-

sissippi, for example, where blacks made up more than 40 percent of the population, only 4 percent were registered to vote in 1960.

In the meantime the leaders of the civil rights movement broadened the front of their attacks on segregation and adopted some new tactics. While continuing to wage battle in the courts, they also took to the streets, launching a campaign of "nonviolent direct action." It began in December 1955, in Montgomery, Alabama, when a forty-three-year-old black seamstress, Mrs. Rosa Parks, was arrested for refusing to yield her bus seat to a white man. Under the inspiration of a young minister, Dr. Martin Luther King, Jr., the leaders of Montgomery's black community protested against the arrest by organizing a boycott of the city's bus system. When local white authorities retaliated by indicting King and a hundred other blacks on a charge of conspiracy to violate the city's segregation laws, King counseled his followers to avoid provocation and to confront "physical force with an even stronger force, namely, soul force." Strongly influenced by Thoreau and Gandhi, King believed that only the tactics of "passive resistance" could overcome the deep-seated fears and hatred that underlay the philosophy of white supremacy.

It took a year, but ultimately the Montgomery boycott, carried through a series of suits in federal courts, succeeded in desegregating the city's bus system. Yet for blacks and whites alike, the significance of the Montgomery experience went far beyond this single local triumph over racial prejudice. The emergence of the charismatic and eloquent Reverend King marked the arrival of a new kind of civil rights leadership. King was young, black, and a southerner. The effectiveness of the techniques of nonviolent protest added a new dimension to the moral force of the civil rights crusade. For blacks it provided an example to be emulated in bus stations, in public parks, and at lunch counters across the South; to whites it dramatized the courage and determination of those who struggled against racial oppression. While real progress toward the goal of full equality lagged in the late 1950s, the moral case against racial discrimination gradually won new adherents among moderate whites in the South as well as in the North. Forced to confront a problem that had long been ignored, a growing number of Americans were becoming convinced that if America and Americans were to live up to their avowed ideals, blacks would have to be accorded the same rights as whites.

Voices of alienation

Although the incipient black revolution was unquestionably the most profound social issue facing the nation in the late 1950s, it was not the only one. In the view of some social observers, stirrings of discontent among the nation's youth also gave cause for concern. A marked rise in the juvenile delinquency rate and the proliferation of urban

Whites objecting to court-ordered desegregation assault a black on-looker in Little Rock, Arkansas, as black students attempt to enter Central High School on September 23, 1957.

Rock 'n' Roll Rebellion

Girl: "What're you rebelling against?"
Marlon Brando: "Whatta you got?"
   —from The Wild One, *1953*

"I'm gonna rip it up, gonna rock it up..."
   —Little Richard, 1956

James Dean (center) plays the restless teen-ager in Rebel Without a Cause.

By the midfifties, many American parents were convinced that their children had gone crazy. Sneering at authority and responsibility, young people seemed to the older generation to represent a breakdown in the morals, standards, and order of postwar America. From the wearing of leather jackets to the violation of weekend curfews, many teen-agers considered themselves rebels, although they were not exactly sure of what they were rebelling against. Instead, cinematic antiheroes like Marlon Brando and James Dean set the tone for an attitude of general alienation and disinterest among youth. One teen-ager remembered that after he saw *Rebel Without a Cause*, "I was changed. James Dean had turned me around. ... The whole dopey decade was like one big mashed potato sandwich. Except for James Dean."

Nowhere was the restlessness and rebellion of youth more evident than in its music. "Rock 'n' roll is here to stay," Danny and the Juniors sang, and it seemed that all semblance of order was gone for good. When Bill Haley and the Comets exhorted kids to "Rock Around the Clock" in 1954, he was using a metaphor for sexual intercourse long employed by rhythm and blues singers. When Little Richard, in full make-up and glittery costume, screamed "Good golly Miss Molly/You sure like to ball," the decadence of the music seemed obvious to all. "Rock 'n' roll inflames and excites youth," warned a Boston priest, "like jungle tom-toms readying warriors for battle." In April 1956 the *New York Daily News* castigated rock 'n' roll as an "inciter of juvenile delinquency." Boycotts and burnings of records became common, especially in the Deep South.

The embodiment of all that was alarming about rock 'n' roll was a young man from Tupelo, Mississippi, named Elvis Presley. To youth, he was the symbol of the emergent style of rebellion. "The identification teenagers made between Marlon Brando's bitter lone-wolf biker and the Elvis Presley of two years later was not only automatic, it was correct," one music critic wrote later. Appearing on "The Ed Sullivan Show" in September 1956, Presley was shown only from the waist up, because the producers believed that the television audience would be scandalized by his trademark gyrating hips. Critic John Crosby of the *New York Herald-Tribune* called Presley "an unspeakably untalented performer" and asked, "Where do you go from Elvis Presley, short of obscenity?" In spite of—or perhaps because of—such disapproval, the trademark Elvis sneer and the apparent defiance of convention, both musical and social, made Presley the role model for millions of young men and a sex symbol for a comparable number of women.

It was a time of raucous fun for youth and increasing irritation for parents. Rock 'n' roll shows drew thousands of screaming fans, sometimes resulting in riots. Civic authorities refused to grant licenses for shows, citing fears of disturbance of the peace. Reports of teen-agers rioting after rock 'n' roll movies like *The Blackboard Jungle* came from all across the country. A used car dealer in Cincinnati promised to break fifty Elvis Presley records for each car he sold; five people took him up on his offer in one day.

By 1960, however, the hard-driving, mean style of rock 'n' roll was gone. Elvis Presley was drafted into the army in March 1958 and never did recover the swagger and style that had entranced his earlier audience. Little Richard dropped out of sight to devote more time to his career as an evangelical minister. In February 1960 a House committee unearthed evidence of radio disc jockeys having taken payments from record companies to play certain records on the air. To many people the "payola" scandal reinforced the long-standing belief that rock 'n' roll was the instrument by which shifty record producers and artists sought to control and degrade America's youth. The music was so bad, some thought, that kids would never listen to it unless they were tricked by greedy DJs.

The early sixties saw a return to the smoother, less threatening pop that had filled Top Forty charts for years. With the continued popularity of Dick Clark's "American Bandstand" program, which had first appeared on TV in 1957, artists such as Fabian, Pat Boone, and other "teen idols" sang songs that were pleasant, albeit sappy. Many kids shed their leather jackets for bathing suits, and the California vogue of "surfer" songs and beach movies set in. Singers no longer snarled with the restlessness of "Rip It Up." Instead, the romantic ballad was the mainstay of early sixties pop. The hard edge and rebellion had for the time being gone out of pop music. It would be several years before the music would get angry once again.

Elvis Presley in action. To parents he was scandalous and obscene, to teen-agers he was exciting and sexy.

street gangs, the popularity of teen-age "antiheroes" and the emergence of nonconformist "beatniks," even the spread of "rock 'n' roll" music, all seemed to indicate a growing dissatisfaction among young Americans with the prevailing cultural ethos. Whereas earlier in the decade there had been frequent complaints about the unimaginative conformity of what some labeled "The Silent Generation," by the end of the 1950s many adults were more troubled by the apparent alienation of the young than by their apathy.

To a certain extent the perceived "problem" of youth was simply a function of numbers, since by the late 1950s the first great wave of the "baby boom" generation was entering its teen-age years. But there was also some substance to the emerging "youth culture" of the 1950s. Whether depicted in films like *Rebel Without a Cause*, captured in the pulsating rhythms of rock 'n' roll, or articulated in poems like Allen Ginsberg's "Howl," the sense of rebellion against prevailing cultural standards and mores was too pointed and too widespread to be dismissed lightly. Ironically, perhaps, the target of revolt was often the very technology, materialism, and abundance that made the youth of the 1950s the first "post-affluent" generation in history. When Ginsberg railed against the "robot apartments! invincible suburbs!" and "monstrous bombs!" of "Moloch" America, he found an audience among those who felt stifled by the mundane routines of everyday life. When Bill Haley and the Comets promised to "Rock Around the Clock" and when James Dean revved up his engine to head off in the night, each of them appealed to the restlessness of a generation taught to believe in limitless possibilities yet faced with unavoidable restrictions.

While some commentators attributed these signs of discontent to simple adolescent zest, others found them symptomatic of a much deeper malaise. One California criminologist, for example, maintained that the increased hostility of youth reflected both the rise in world tensions and the glorification of violence by the mass media—an interpretation that gained support from those who believed that a generation schooled in nuclear "air-raid drills" had developed an acute case of "H-bomb jitters." Other sociologists laid blame on the "decay of moral and spiritual values" brought on by the excesses of materialism. And still others agreed with journalist Harrison Salisbury that the origins of the problems of the "Shook-Up Generation," as he termed it, were "lack of love and care and attention" in the home.

There were, of course, important distinctions to be made among the forms of youthful alienation and rebellion. The black-jacketed urban gang member represented a different social phenomenon than the middle-class girl who squandered her allowance, disobeyed her parents, and

Two teen-age Brooklyn gang members preen themselves at New York's Coney Island during the summer of 1958.

idolized celluloid antiheroes like Marlon Brando or James Dean. The teen-age craze for rock 'n' roll music was far more widespread than adulation for, or even interest in, the writings of Jack Kerouac and the other beats. Yet according to social psychologist Kenneth Keniston, the various "youth sub-cultures" shared at least one characteristic, namely, "a lack of deep commitment to adult values and roles." "They expect little in the way of personal fulfillment, growth, creativity from their future roles in the public world," Keniston wrote in *The Uncommitted: Alienated Youth in American Society.* "Essentially, they recognize that adulthood is a relatively cold, demanding, specialized, and abstracted world where 'meaningful' work is so scarce they do not even ask for it."

However accurate Keniston's assessment may have been, by the time his study was published in 1965 the title seemed inappropriate. For if the teen-agers of the late 1950s were uneasy about approaching adulthood and unwilling to commit themselves to predetermined roles and goals, the young adults of the early 1960s displayed a penchant for idealism that was equally striking. While the forms of that idealism varied, all drew at least some inspiration from the same source: the new president of the United States, John F. Kennedy.

The Kennedy years

To many Americans, the election of Kennedy in 1960 heralded the beginning not only of a new decade, but of a new age. Handsome in appearance and stylish in manner, the youngest man ever elected to the presidency and a gifted speaker, he seemed in many ways the antithesis of his immediate predecessor. From the outset, moreover, he made it clear that he intended to promote fresh ideas and encourage change, to establish new goals and cross a "new frontier." To tap the wellsprings of national idealism, he offered the challenge of commitment, urging the American people to "ask not what your country can do for you; ask what you can do for your country." To affirm the aspirations of blacks, he held out the promise of presidential leadership in the struggle for equal rights. And to win the allegiance of the American intelligentsia, he brought into his administration men and women of ideas—"the best and the brightest," as journalist David Halberstam later called them—in unprecedented numbers.

Yet for all that was new and different about the Kennedy administration, there was also much that was unchanged and old. In foreign policy as well as in domestic policy, the imperatives that had guided the actions of President Eisenhower continued to circumscribe the decisions of President Kennedy. A self-avowed "idealist without illusions," Kennedy strongly endorsed the U.S. commitment to "contain" international communism. During the 1960 election campaign, in fact, his stance on foreign policy issues was virtually indistinguishable from that of his opponent, Richard Nixon, who had served for eight years as vice president under Eisenhower. In his inaugural address, the new president called upon the nation to "pay any price" and "bear any burden" to "assure the survival and success of liberty." And in the years that followed, he made good on that promise by resisting Communist pressure in Berlin, Cuba, and Indochina.

In some ways Kennedy had little choice but to embrace the cold war policies of the past. A careful reader of public opinion polls, he knew that most Americans regarded the Communist threat as "the most important problem" facing the nation in the early 1960s. He also knew that if he showed any signs of "weakness" toward the Communists he would be attacked not only by the opposition Republican party, but also by conservative southern Democrats and many influential organs of the national media. Above all, he knew that any Democratic president who "lost" a nation, and particularly an Asian nation, to communism would risk losing the White House as well.

Political considerations alone, however, did not determine the course of Kennedy's foreign policy. He was himself both a product of and spokesman for the postwar consensus and therefore a committed cold warrior. The same was true of his chief advisers, many of whom were directly linked to the foreign policy establishment that had originally drafted the doctrine of containment. McGeorge Bundy, Kennedy's special assistant for national security, had first made his mark in the late 1940s by editing the memoirs of Henry Stimson, the secretary of state under Hoover and secretary of war under Taft and Roosevelt. His brother, William Bundy, the deputy assistant secretary of state for international security affairs, was the son-in-law of Dean Acheson. Secretary of State Dean Rusk had served as assistant secretary of state for Far Eastern affairs under Truman and Acheson and had been recommended to Kennedy by another establishment figure, former Secretary of Defense Robert J. Lovett. Averell Harriman, "ambassador at large" in 1961 and subsequently assistant secretary of state for Far Eastern affairs (1961–63), had been the director of economic aid to Europe under the Marshall Plan. Two other of Kennedy's many advisers, Walt W. Rostow and Arthur Schlesinger, had worked for the Office of Strategic Services (the forerunner of the CIA) during World War II.

The Kennedy administration did institute some important changes in the conduct of American foreign policy. In response to the Soviet vow to support "wars of national liberation" in the Third World, the U.S. sharply increased economic aid to developing nations and, at the same time, improved the military's capacity to wage limited war. Fearing that local crises might escalate into a direct confrontation between the United States and either China or the Soviet Union, further recognizing that local Communist insurgencies could not be "deterred" by sheer nuclear might, the administration abandoned the so-called doc-

"The best and the brightest." President Kennedy confers with advisers on the White House portico during the Cuban missile crisis, October 1962. From left, National Security Adviser McGeorge Bundy, the president, Chairman of the Joint Chiefs of Staff, General Maxwell Taylor, and Defense Secretary Robert McNamara.

trine of massive retaliation in favor of a strategy of "flexible response." As President Kennedy told Congress in March 1961:

Our defense posture must be both flexible and determined. . . . We must be able to make deliberate choices in weapons and strategy, shift the tempo of our production, and alter the direction of our forces to meet rapidly changing conditions or objectives at very short notice and under any circumstances.

Heeding the advice of military adviser (and subsequent JCS chairman) General Maxwell Taylor, Kennedy and his defense secretary, Robert S. McNamara, moved away from the "New Look" posture of the Eisenhower years and began to shore up the military's conventional forces. Army expenditures and manpower levels rose steadily over the

next few years, particularly after the Berlin crisis in the summer of 1961. In addition, efforts were made to modernize the army by developing special "counter-insurgency" units, like the Green Berets, and new tactics, like "airmobility," achieved by the use of helicopters. While the means changed, however, the ends remained the same: to confront the Communist challenge whenever and wherever it appeared and thus to protect the interests of the "Free World."

In his domestic policy no less than in his foreign policy, Kennedy at once followed and broadened a path that had been forged by his predecessors. Like Roosevelt, Truman, and, to a lesser extent, Eisenhower, he accepted as axiomatic the responsibility of the federal government to insure economic growth. Yet he also recognized that if prosperity were to bring genuine social progress, the persistent problem of poverty in the midst of bounty would have to be addressed. In formulating his economic policy, Kennedy relied heavily on the judgment of professional economists steeped in the theories of what was commonly called the "New Economics." Joining the government at a time when unemployment was close to 7 percent and overall economic activity sluggish, these "new economists" believed that they could simultaneously stimulate growth, reduce unemployment, and keep inflation at a minimum by carefully manipulating the levers of federal fiscal policy. Specifically, they contended that the government could increase aggregate demand and induce full employment either by cutting taxes or through deficit spending. Disagreements arose, however, about which of the two options to pursue. One group, led by J. K. Galbraith, favored spending more money to meet the vast need for public services and, concomitantly, to redistribute wealth toward the less well-off. Another group, led by Walter Heller, the chairman of Kennedy's Council of Economic Advisers, wanted a tax cut, largely for political reasons. Since many congressmen believed that economic health required a balanced federal budget, Heller argued, a cut in taxes was more likely to gain approval than any increase in public spending of adequate magnitude. Moreover, Heller maintained, a measure of redistribution of wealth could be effected by closing tax "loopholes" that favored the wealthy.

In the end, Heller and his allies won. In 1962 an initial tax cut was introduced in the form of an investment credit and liberalized depreciation allowances for businesses. A second general tax cut was proposed in 1963 and then enacted in 1964 under President Johnson. Lost in the political shuffle, however, were the tax reforms that Heller had advocated to accompany the cuts. As a result, while the economy took off, chalking up a record fifty months of unbroken expansion between the last quarter of 1960 and the second quarter of 1965, the distribution of national income remained the same as it had been since the late 1940s. By 1965, Americans in the bottom half of the scale received only 23 percent of total national income, a gain of one percentage point since 1945, while the share of those in the top tenth remained exactly what it had been at the end of World War II, 29 percent. Total national wealth was increasing, and so were most individual shares. But the relative difference in the size of the portions was becoming greater and, to some, more noticeable.

Black revolution

No Americans were more acutely aware of these imbalances than blacks. As President Kennedy himself pointed out in a nationally televised speech on June 11, 1963, blacks had "twice as much chance of becoming unemployed . . . one-third as much chance of becoming professional(s) . . . [and] about one-seventh as much chance of earning $10,000 a year" as whites in the United States. The relative economic distance between the two races, more-

over, was not diminishing but growing in the early 1960s. In Kennedy's view, it was these glaring inequities that had fueled the fight for equal rights and raised that struggle to the level of a "moral issue . . . as old as the scriptures and . . . as clear as the American Constitution."

But as Kennedy himself well knew, the black civil rights movement posed more than a moral challenge to the existing order; it also represented a thorny political issue that required cautious handling. Although a timely telephone call to the wife of the jailed Dr. King during the 1960 election campaign had helped Kennedy win widespread black support, once he took office the new president moved slowly into the minefield of equal rights for blacks. Elected by a precariously narrow popular margin and confronted by a skeptical if not hostile coalition of Republicans and southern Democrats in Congress, he realized that on the issue of civil rights he could move only as fast as the public would allow. To meet the escalating demands of blacks for racial justice, Kennedy was forced to rely on executive and judicial action rather than legislation, but even then it was difficult to keep up with the accelerating pace of events.

Under the direction of the president's brother, Attorney General Robert F. Kennedy, and his able assistant for civil rights, Burke Marshall, the Justice Department consistently backed black efforts to break down the barriers of segregation in the South. In the area of voting rights, the department filed forty-five suits in three years to protect would-be black voters from intimidation, racially biased literacy tests, and poll taxes designed to keep them from exercising their franchise. In transportation, the government sent 500 federal marshals into the Deep South in the spring of

1961 to protect "freedom riders" protesting bus terminal segregation and worked to outlaw all forms of racial discrimination in public facilities that touched upon interstate commerce—including airports, rail and bus stations, hotels, and restaurants. In education, the Kennedy administration pushed ahead with primary and secondary school integration and in October 1963 ordered federal troops into Oxford, Mississippi, to insure the right of James Meredith, a black air force veteran, to attend the University of Mississippi.

In two other crucial areas of racial discrimination—jobs and housing—there was little progress, and by early 1963 the leaders of the civil rights movement were becoming increasingly impatient with the Kennedy administration. "This administration," said Martin Luther King, Jr., "has outstripped all previous ones in the breadth of its civil rights activity. Yet the movement, instead of breaking out into the open plains of progress, remains constricted and confined. A sweeping revolutionary force is pressed into a narrow tunnel." As black discontent grew, so did southern resistance. Tensions peaked in April 1963, when King initiated a campaign to end discrimination in

Under the orders of police commissioner "Bull" Connor, police use their dogs to threaten black demonstrators in Birmingham, Alabama, April 1963.

shops, restaurants, and employment in Birmingham, Alabama. Practicing the tactics of "nonviolent direct action"—"sit-ins" at lunch counters, "kneel-ins" in all-white churches, and peaceful protest marches—the demonstrators were repeatedly harassed, attacked, and jailed by local law enforcement authorities under the direction of police commissioner Eugene "Bull" Connor.

Recorded by network television cameras and dozens of newspaper correspondents at the scene, the sight of policemen using electric cattle prods, fire hoses, and snarling dogs against unarmed demonstrators caused a surge of indignation throughout the country. The month-long Birmingham campaign stirred the consciences of many white Americans and brought increased support for the civil rights movement. A month later, when Governor George Wallace of Alabama tried to block the admission of two black students to the state university by standing in the doorway of the administration building, the president ordered in federal troops and then went on television to make a "moral" appeal to the nation. "The time has come for this nation to fulfill its promise," Kennedy said, and then called for enactment of the most sweeping civil rights legislation in American history.

The president and the leaders of the black community realized that the proposed civil rights bill faced stiff opposition in Congress. Many political observers, in fact, doubted that it could be passed unless Kennedy won a second term in office. Undaunted, the leaders of the major civil rights groups—Roy Wilkins of the NAACP, Whitney Young of the National Urban League, James Farmer of the Congress on Racial Equality (CORE), John Lewis of the Student Non-violent Coordinating Committee (SNCC), and King of the Southern Christian Leadership Conference (SCLC)—planned a "March on Washington" to lobby for the new bill. The Kennedy administration, fearing that a mass protest might endanger the bill's chance of passage, at first tried to stop the march. But after realizing that it could not be prevented, the president put the prestige of his office behind the demonstrators while urging them to maintain tight discipline.

"We Shall Overcome . . ."

The march for "Jobs and Freedom" was scheduled for August 28, 1963. With more than 100,000 people expected to arrive in the capital, federal and local authorities prepared for the worst. On the morning of the march, caravans of cars and more than 1,500 chartered buses and trains streamed into Washington from all over the country. Within hours a crowd of approximately a quarter of a million people filled the grassy area of the Mall around the Washington Monument and overflowed across Constitution Avenue onto the Ellipse, the oval-shaped park near the back of the White House. Joining the representatives of the major civil rights organizations were numerous white clergymen from the South as well as the North, a few labor union officials, and thousands of other supporters of the cause who had no tie to any formal group. As the temperature climbed toward eighty-five degrees and the appointed noon hour approached, the wave of marchers moved down the Mall to the Lincoln Memorial, blacks linking arms with whites, old men in black parson's suits with young men in their "freedom uniform" overalls. They chanted "Freedom! Freedom! Freedom!" and sang "We Shall Overcome," the unofficial anthem of the civil rights movement. Many carried placards that appended an emphatic "*Now!*" to the conventional themes of the day—"We Demand Voting Rights—*Now!*"; "We March for Jobs for All—*Now!*"; "We Demand Decent Housing—*Now!*"

At the Lincoln Memorial the crowd listened patiently for hours as speaker after speaker echoed the demand for an all-out federal commitment to the cause of equal rights. The finale came when Dr. King rose to announce that "1963 is not an end, but a beginning. There will be neither rest nor tranquility in America," he predicted, "until the Negro is granted his citizenship rights. The whirlwinds of the revolt will continue to shake the foundations of our nation until the bright day of justice emerges. I have a dream," King intoned,

It is a dream deeply rooted in the American dream. I have a dream that one day this nation will rise up and live out the true meaning of its creed: "We hold these truths to be self-evident, that all men are created equal."

The public response to the March on Washington was overwhelmingly positive. Not only had the day passed without any incidents of harassment or violence, but the spectacle of so many people—white and black—joined together in peaceful protest seemed to augur a happy future for the entire civil rights crusade.

Nevertheless, in the weeks and months that followed, the civil rights bill languished on Capitol Hill. Leading the opposition were the southern Democrats, many of whom were prepared to fight the bill by every means at their command, which were considerable. As representatives of a virtually one-party region, where reelection was often automatic, their long experience in Congress had made them masters in the arts of obstruction, while their seniority had given them the chairmanships of powerful committees. The Senate Judiciary Committee, headed by arch-segregationist James O. Eastland of Mississippi, kept Kennedy's bill bottled up throughout the summer and early fall but finally accepted a compromise version at the end of October. The bill was then scheduled to undergo further scrutiny in the House Rules Committee, whose chairman was another outspoken opponent of integration, eighty-year-old Congressman Howard W. Smith of Virginia. On November 21, 1963, the Rules Committee received the civil rights bill and began deliberations. The next day the deliberations were halted by the news that

March on Washington

On August 28, 1963, a quarter of a million people—black and white, young and old—converged upon Washington, D.C. for the March for Jobs and Freedom, an effort to hasten the passage of a new civil rights bill. Throngs of demonstrators marched, cheered, and sang and listened intently to the words of the civil rights leaders who addressed the crowd. Despite concern that so large an assemblage—the largest peaceful demonstration to date—would become unruly, the event proceeded smoothly. This dramatic display of racial harmony and earnest dedication to end discrimination proved to be a high-water mark in the movement for civil rights.

Left. *Marchers gather along the mall stretching from the Washington Monument to the Lincoln Memorial where speakers addressed the crowd. Above. "I Have A Dream": The march climaxes with Martin Luther King's stirring address from the steps of the Lincoln Memorial.*

Above. Weary marchers, black and white, refresh sore feet in the reflecting pool.

Left. Union contingents, religious groups, and individuals from all over the country march down Constitution Avenue. Above. A young marcher.

President John F. Kennedy had been killed by an assassin's bullet in Dallas, Texas.

LBJ and the "Great Society"

The chief task facing Lyndon Baines Johnson in the aftermath of the Kennedy assassination was to affirm his own legitimacy as president of the United States. "Every president has to establish with various sectors of the country what I call 'the right to govern,'" he later wrote in his memoirs. "For me that presented special problems . . . since I had come to the Presidency not through the collective will of the people but in the wake of tragedy." There were other "special problems" as well. Irrationally but symbolically, the fact that he was a Texan counted against Johnson, since many people could not help but associate him with the site of his predecessor's death. As a southerner, he was further tainted by suspicions that he would compromise away the substance of the civil rights bill, despite his rather liberal record on issues of race. Perhaps most of all, however, his lack of Kennedy's polish and grace made it difficult for him to project the same image of confident presidential authority that had so typified the previous chief executive.

Nevertheless, in the days and weeks following the assassination, Johnson showed himself to be equal to the challenge. While the nation still reeled in shock and disbelief, he resolutely took command of the government and induced a sense of direction. To ease the widespread atmosphere

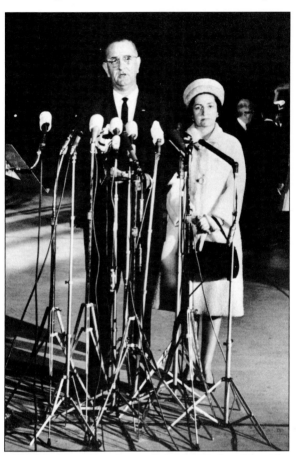

The new president, his wife Lady Bird at his side, addresses the nation upon arriving in Washington on November 22, 1963.

of crisis and to allay suspicions that Kennedy's murder had been part of a conspiracy, he promptly appointed a commission headed by no less than the chief justice of the Supreme Court, Earl Warren, to investigate the assassination. To demonstrate that he was a worthy heir to the Kennedy legacy, he cajoled most of Kennedy's chief advisers into staying on with his administration and pushed ahead with Kennedy's legislative program. First on the agenda was the tax cut, which he shepherded to final passage in the Senate. Then, drawing upon a lifetime's familiarity of the levers of power in Congress, he turned his attention to the civil rights bill. "The way that fellow operates," said Senator Richard Russell of Georgia, a leader of the opposition, "he means business. He'll get the whole bill." And he did.

Yet for all his successes, Johnson still needed, or rather desperately wanted, something more. To establish beyond question his "right to govern," he would have to win reelection the following November and win it decisively. Thus, in the spring of 1964, he launched his campaign with the announcement of his intention to build a "Great Society" beyond the borders of Kennedy's New Frontier. Adopting an idea that had been embraced by Kennedy shortly before his death, Johnson announced an "unconditional war on poverty" as the cornerstone of his new program. Most of Johnson's aides enthusiastically endorsed the idea, but one of his good friends, a speech writer and public relations expert named Horace Busby, sounded a note of caution. The president should beware of the effects of a poverty program on "the American in the middle—the man who earns $3,000 to $9,000." He wrote:

America's real majority is suffering a minority complex of neglect. They have become the real foes of Negro rights, foreign aid, etc., because, as much as anything, they feel forgotten, at the second table behind tightly organized, smaller groups at either end of the U.S. spectrum.

Lyndon Johnson was an astute enough politician to understand that danger. The people Busby was talking about were the very people who had kept him in public office all those long years. But he also knew that any president who succeeded in wiping out poverty would himself make an indelible mark on American history. His model was not Jack Kennedy, but Franklin Roosevelt, the man who had used the power of the federal government to lift up those who were downtrodden and forgotten. The creator of the Great Society could expect to be remembered as a great president.

Throughout the summer and fall of 1964, Johnson expanded upon his vision of the coming new order, appending to his poverty program proposals for medical aid to the elderly, for increased federal aid to primary and secondary education, for better natural resource conservation, and for more federal housing. At the same time, he tried to minimize the other major issue in the campaign, the war in Vietnam. To keep public attention focused on

Monday, November 25, 1963. The funeral cortege bearing the body of John F. Kennedy solemnly proceeds down Connecticut Avenue in Washington, D.C., on its way to Arlington National Cemetery.

domestic affairs and to neutralize Goldwater's fervent anticommunism, Johnson's campaign staff urged him to assume a posture of "tough restraint," an attitude modeled on President Kennedy's performance during the Cuban missile crisis of 1962. The more Goldwater harangued the president with calls for interdiction of supply routes and the bombing of North Vietnam, the more reasonable Johnson seemed as an advocate of using "great power with restraint." In speech after speech he stressed the same themes: a determination not to escalate or widen the war by bombing the North or by sending "American boys . . . to do what Asian boys ought to be doing to protect themselves" in tandem with an equally firm resolve not to "yield to Communist aggression."

There was an obvious tension between those two positions, but Johnson, and with him the vast majority of Americans, ignored it. If it came to a choice between escalating the war in Vietnam or "yielding to Communist aggression," between risking American lives in a distant Asian conflict or altering the long-standing foreign policy of the United States, which would the president choose? Throughout 1964 the answer seemed in doubt, as the situation in South Vietnam steadily deteriorated and Johnson authorized contingency plans to step up military pressure, including bombing, against North Vietnam. Long before Lyndon Johnson finally acted on those plans, however, he had already made his decision. In a meeting with Henry Cabot Lodge less than forty-eight hours after Kennedy's assassination, he had discussed with the ambassador to South Vietnam the need to plan for the future. In the course of their conversation he had revealed the extent to which he was, and would continue to be, a prisoner of the past. "I am not going to lose Vietnam," Johnson said. "I am not going to be the President who saw Southeast Asia go the way China went."

At 1:40 A.M., November 4, 1964, Lyndon Baines Johnson went on national television to thank the American people for their "mandate for unity." "I ask all those who supported me and all those that opposed me to forget our differences, because there are many more things in America that unite us than divide us." It was Johnson's greatest moment. He had just ridden to victory on the crest of a national consensus that had been building for nearly twenty years and now stood at high tide. He had established his "right to govern," and he was determined to govern well. The tragedy of Lyndon Johnson, if tragedy it was, is that by the time he reached that long-anticipated goal, he had already set in motion forces that would ultimately shatter the consensus, divide the nation, and deprive him of his most cherished prize.

The president and first lady, celebrating November's Democratic landslide victory, begin the first dance at one of five balls held on LBJ's inauguration night, January 20, 1965.

Suburban Frontier

American life was transformed during the 1950s by a sweeping migration from central cities to their surrounding rings—the suburbs. The suburban population increased nearly 50 percent that decade, almost equaling that of the central cities by 1960. One major developer, William Levitt, gave his name to this transformation when he constructed sprawling "Levittowns" of inexpensive, mass-produced homes in New York, Pennsylvania, and New Jersey. The new subdivisions fostered a new style of life for middle Americans, one built around children, the shopping mall, and the commuter train.

The first Levittown, built in the late 1940s in Hempstead, Long Island, became home for more than 17,000 families.

Inset. *Early residents of the new town pose outside their house in 1948.*

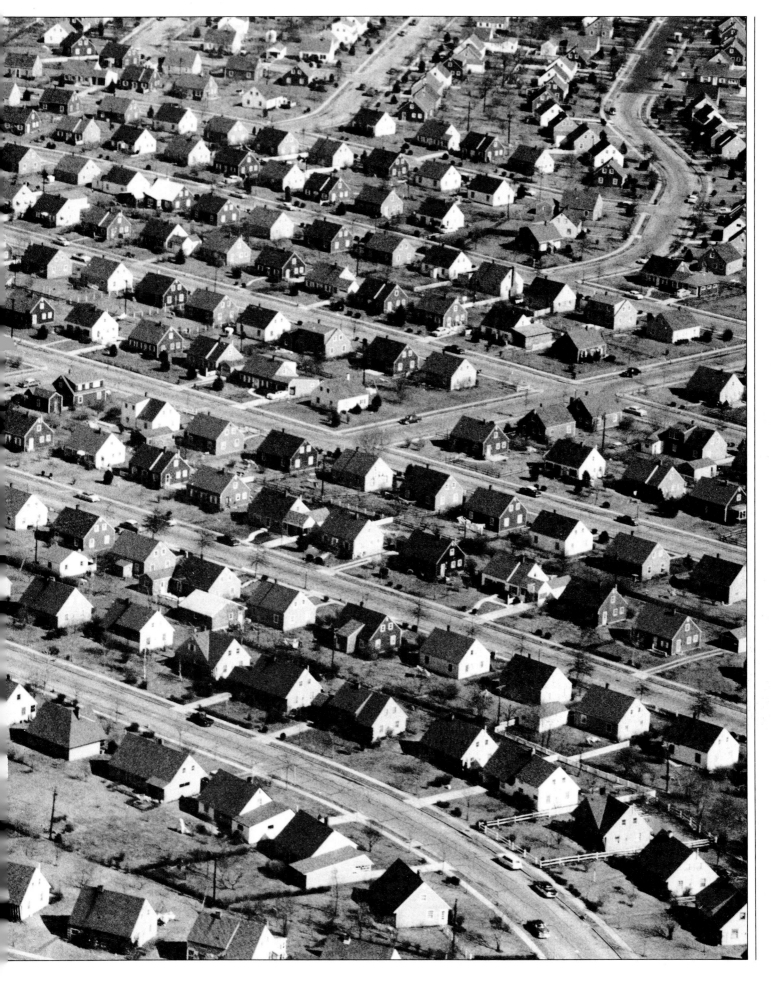

49

The Road Out

To meet the increased demand for transportation to work, to school, and to new suburban shopping malls, automobile manufacturers stepped up production and offered more models and styles of passenger cars than ever. Record numbers of new cars rolled off the assembly lines and into the suburbs via 41,000 miles of new expressways financed by the 1956 Interstate Highways Act. By 1960 nearly nine out of ten suburban families owned a car. Between 1945 and 1960 the number of two-car families rose by 750,000 yearly, and the number of car registrations increased from 26 million in 1945 to 60 million in 1960.

Ford engineering high command and staff present the Falcon at Dearborn, Michigan, in mid-1959. Ford manufactured more than 400,000 Falcons in 1960.

Inset.A new freeway goes up in San Francisco in 1958.

Baby Boomers

During the two decades following World War II each year set a new record for births. New York subway signs celebrated the baby boom: "Your future is great in a growing America. Every day 11,000 babies are born. ... This means new business, new jobs, new opportunities." It also meant an unprecedented focus on children. Archetypal suburban families were appearing on television's popular comedies: "Father Knows Best," "Ozzie and Harriet," "Leave It to Beaver." More parents than ever joined PTAs while their offspring joined scout troops, little leagues, and other activities organized for suburban youth.

School shortage. Children in a San Francisco suburb line up for school outside rented new bungalows converted to temporary classrooms, 1954.

Inset. *Little Leaguers in Manchester, New Hampshire, 1954.*

Weekend Rites

"No man who owns his own house and lot can be a Communist," remarked suburban pioneer William Levitt. "He has too much to do." Keeping suburban lawns green and trimmed, equipping the household with up-to-date efficiency gadgets, and participating in neighborhood social life and church activities busied the leisure hours of suburbanites. While many found better lives in the suburbs, others criticized suburbia's stifling conformity and sense of complacency, which sociologist David Riesman compared to a fraternity house "in which like-mindedness reverberates upon itself."

All eight members of the Joe Powers family pitch in to wash the family station wagon, Port Washington, New York, 1958.

Inset. *A back yard barbecue in Santa Barbara, California, 1960.*

Crisis

(1965-1966)

Few American presidents have enjoyed a more
auspicious beginning to a new term in office than
Lyndon Johnson did in January of 1965. He had
won reelection with a popular landslide, and his
party now held an overwhelming majority in
Congress, with 68 Democrats in the Senate and
295 in the House. The economy was growing at
the stunning rate of 5 percent a year, and his economic advisers were telling him that there was
no reason to believe the pace would slacken in
the future. The social reform agenda that he had
laid before the nation had been well received,
and he was confident that his latest Great Society
programs would soon be implemented. During
his State of the Union message on January 4, the
House chamber had echoed with applause,
cheers, and even some stamping of feet as he
committed himself and the federal government to
provide aid to education from preschool through
college, to rebuild the nation's blighted cities, to

provide medical aid to the elderly, to beautify the country's public lands and parks, to establish a national arts foundation, and to cut excise taxes. "This, then," he had concluded, "is the State of the Union: free, growing, restless, and full of hope."

Only one gray cloud hung over the horizon as Johnson embarked on his voyage to the Great Society: "that nagging little war in Vietnam," as *Newsweek* called it at the time of the inauguration. The war was going badly. After enduring five coups the preceding year, the South Vietnamese government was as far from achieving stability as it had ever been, the Vietcong were steadily gaining strength in the countryside, and Hanoi was stepping up the pressure by infiltrating its own regular troops into the South. In his State of the Union message the president had scarcely mentioned Vietnam, noting only that "our goal is peace in Southeast Asia" and "what is at stake is the cause of freedom." But however much he tried to ignore the issue, he knew that the American people were becoming increasingly troubled by it. The most recent polls, in fact, showed that fully 50 percent of the public believed that the Johnson administration was "handling affairs in South Vietnam" poorly, although the same surveys also reflected much disagreement over what course the president should pursue.

One week after Johnson's inauguration, on January 27, a memo arrived on the president's desk from Special Assistant McGeorge Bundy. Outlining views shared by Defense Secretary Robert McNamara, Bundy told the president that American policy in Vietnam could lead only to "disastrous defeat," and that "the time has come for harder choices." With the election behind him and the threat of a decisive Communist victory [in Vietnam] imminent, Johnson would have to choose between "escalation and withdrawal," between using "our military power to force a change in Communist policy" and deploying "all our resources along a track of negotiation, aimed at salvaging what little can be preserved." Secretary of State Dean Rusk, Bundy noted, still favored a middle course, since he believed the consequences of both alternatives "are so bad that we simply must find a way to make our present policy work. This would be good if it was possible," Bundy concluded. "Bob [McNamara] and I do not think it is."

In response to the memo, Johnson sent Bundy to Saigon to get a firsthand look at the situation. On the night of February 6, while Bundy was still in Vietnam and before he had filed his report, a Vietcong mortar unit attacked an American advisers' barracks at Pleiku in the central highlands, killing 7 and wounding more than 100 Americans. The president's reaction was unhesitating. "We have kept

our gun over the mantel and our shells in the cupboard for a long time now," Johnson said to his advisers. "And what was the result? They are killing our men while they sleep in the night." He immediately ordered a retaliatory air strike on targets in North Vietnam. It was not the first time the U.S. had engaged in such "reprisal" bombing of North Vietnamese territory: that had happened after the Gulf of Tonkin incidents the preceding August. Moreover, the plans for the operation, code-named Flaming Dart, had been drawn up months before. Johnson's decision nevertheless marked a major turning point in the American commitment to Vietnam. By the time Bundy returned to Washington with his recommendation to pursue "the most promising course available"—a policy of "graduated and continuing reprisal"—he was preaching to the already convinced. During the next few weeks the president abandoned the "tit-for-tat" rationale for the bombing in favor of a continuous air war against North Vietnam, ordered the first American combat troops to South Vietnam, and thus set his Vietnam policy on a collision course with his dream of the Great Society.

Preceding page. A poster at Madison Square Garden, New York City, announces one of the first major demonstrations against the Vietnam War in December 1965.

"Selma!"

The Vietnam War was not the only battle heating up in the early months of 1965. On Sunday, March 7, the day before the first two combat battalions of U.S. Marines landed on the beaches of Da Nang, South Vietnam, a group of about 500 blacks gathered along U.S. Route 80 on the outskirts of Selma, Alabama. Organized by Dr. Martin Luther King, Jr., who had left the night before to rejoin his congregation in Atlanta, they were about to embark on a fifty-mile protest march from Selma to Montgomery, the state capital, to cap off a voter registration drive that had begun two months before. Carrying satchels of provisions and bedrolls, the marchers proceeded a few hundred yards and then found their path barred by more than 150 local policemen and state troopers, 15 of them mounted on horseback. Dallas County Sheriff James G. Clark warned that they had "two minutes to turn around and go back," but the marchers stood silently and did not budge. Moments later, the phalanx of helmeted troopers moved in with tear gas, clubs, whips, and cattle prods—the horsemen mount-

Equipped with gas masks and truncheons, Alabama troopers charge into civil rights demonstrators attempting to march from Selma to Montgomery, Alabama, on March 7, 1965.

ing, in the words of one journalist, "what amounted to a Cossack charge"—and drove the demonstrators back into the city. More than 50 were seriously injured.

Coming at the end of an ugly campaign that had seen thousands of civil rights workers, including King himself, repeatedly harassed and jailed, Selma's "Bloody Sunday" triggered an uproar unprecedented in the annals of the civil rights movement. Across the nation clergymen, governors, state legislatures, and labor unions thundered denunciations. University campuses seethed. In Detroit, New York, Chicago, and Los Angeles, thousands joined "indignation marches" that snarled traffic for hours. There was also a major demonstration in Washington, D.C., though attention there focused on fourteen youths who contrived to stage a sit-in in the corridors of the White House itself. "Unless Selma is expunged by a mighty national act of repentance and reparation," wrote Walter

Lippmann, "how shall Americans look themselves in the face when they get up in the morning?"

For the next two weeks the Selma struggle dominated the national news as hundreds of civil rights supporters converged on the so-called "capital of the Black Belt" and challenged the authority of Alabama Governor George Wallace, Sheriff Clark, and their posse. The violence escalated. On the night of March 9, after a federal injunction forced King to postpone a second march attempt, a white Unitarian minister from Boston was murdered outside a Selma café by whites shouting "nigger lover" as they beat him with iron bars. Outraged, President Johnson summoned Wallace to the White House and informed him that if the National Guard were not called out, federal troops would be sent in to protect the marchers. Several days later, on March 15, in an impassioned address to a joint session of Congress, the president appealed for passage of a voting rights bill that would break the back of the southern resistance, concluding with the emphatic declaration that "We *shall* overcome." The next day, as if to underscore their defiance, mounted policemen brutally dispersed a group of 600 students staging a sit-in in front of the Montgomery State House. By that point LBJ had had enough. With the march now scheduled to begin on Sunday, March 21, he placed the Alabama National Guard under federal control and directed the secretary of defense to use whatever federal forces he might deem necessary to curb "domestic violence."

Army helicopters circled overhead and soldiers lined the road as 3,200 marchers listened to Dr. King before setting off on Jefferson Davis Highway on the morning of March 21. "Walk together, children," King told the crowd, "and Alabama will be a new Alabama, and America will be a new America." Walk they did. Although a court order permitted only 300 marchers to make the entire journey, by the time King entered Montgomery his army of supporters was more than 30,000 strong. Stopping at the steps of the Alabama state capitol, where the delegates of six states had met in 1861 to form the Southern Confederacy, the festive throng sang and listened to speeches culminating in King's rhythmic peroration. "How long?" he asked again and again, and each time he provided the answer: "Not long, because no lie can live forever. . . . Not long, because the arm of the moral universe is long and it bends toward justice."

It was, in many ways, King's most triumphant moment. For nearly ten years his stature and authority as the leading spokesman of the civil rights movement had steadily grown. He had brought unity to the movement, providing it not only with his own stirring rhetoric but, more important, with clearly defined goals and tactics. He had joined the

This time with National Guardsmen guaranteeing safe passage, marchers again begin the five-day journey from Selma to Montgomery on the morning of March 21, 1965.

Selma campaign only weeks after receiving the Nobel Peace Prize and watched as once again his supporters adhered to his creed of "non-violent direct action" in the face of sometimes savage physical force. Now, as he stood in the spot where the president of the Confederacy had taken his oath of office, he could gaze upon the faces of thousands of Americans—black and white, clergy and laymen, Hollywood celebrities and just ordinary folk—and believe that it would not be long before they all reached the Promised Land.

But as King himself realized, the impressive show of solidarity in Montgomery was in many respects a mirage, obscuring divisions within the civil rights movement that had been deepening for several years. The sources of those divisions were manifold. In part they were regional, reflecting the growing shift of attention and activity away from the struggle against *de jure* segregation in the South to the fight against *de facto* segregation in the North, and away from the demand for equal legal and constitutional rights to the demand for equal social and economic status. In part they were generational, pitting younger civil rights activists who were impatient with the slow pace of progress against older leaders who counseled moderation in the interest of maintaining a broad base of support. And in part they were ideological, arising from increasing doubts about the adequacy of the movement's goals and the ef-

fectiveness of its tactics. While the vast majority of blacks still embraced integration as their ultimate objective, the proponents of black separatism were capitalizing on growing mistrust of the white liberal establishment. Even more ominously, an increasing number of blacks were openly questioning, and in some cases rejecting, the belief that black aims could best be served by a strict commitment to nonviolence and a reliance on white-dominated political institutions.

Although barely noticed at the time, signs of change within the civil rights movement had been evident since the summer of 1963. It was then, for instance, that the moderate NAACP decided at its annual convention to launch a campaign against *de facto* segregation in northern school districts, and the Big Five leaders chose to make the March on Washington a protest for "Jobs *and* Freedom"— for equal economic opportunity as well as for equal rights. On the eve of the march, moreover, tensions erupted among the movement's leaders over the decision of James Farmer, the outspoken national director of CORE, not to attend the Washington demonstration, and over a belligerent speech drafted by John Lewis, the young chairman of SNCC. "We will not wait for the president, the Justice Department, nor the Congress," Lewis wrote, "but we will take matters into our own hands and create a source of power outside the national structure."

We will march through the South, through the heart of Dixie, the way Sherman did. We shall pursue our own scorched-earth policy and burn Jim Crow to the ground, non-violently.

Even though Lewis was ultimately persuaded to tone down his rhetoric on the occasion of the march, the sentiment that lay behind his words persisted.

From the fall of 1963 through the summer of 1964, both the incidence and militancy of black "direct-action" increased markedly. In the North, a rash of school boycotts during the academic year was followed by a summer outbreak of riots in Harlem, Rochester, Philadelphia, and four other cities. In the South, the Council of Federated Organizations, an operating coalition of major civil rights groups, launched a new voter registration drive that culminated in the Mississippi Summer Freedom Project. Dominated by SNCC and CORE, and recruiting hundreds of white university students from across the country, the project brought youthful idealism face to face with the entrenched power of southern racism and rapidly turned into a nightmare. By the time it was over, 3 civil rights workers had been killed, 80 beaten, 3 wounded by gunfire in thirty-five shootings, and more than 1,000 arrested; thirty-five churches had been burned and thirty homes and other buildings bombed. Rifts had developed between young black and young white activists, and both had been radi-

calized by the inability, or unwillingness, of the federal government either to provide them with adequate protection or to bring to justice those who had committed acts of violence against them.

"How is it," one project volunteer had asked a Justice Department official during a spring orientation session, "that the government can protect the Vietnamese from the Vietcong, and the same government will not accept the moral responsibility of protecting the people of Mississippi?" By the end of "Mississippi Summer" that question, and the connection it implied, was gaining force not only among young blacks in the South but also among young whites headed back to the campuses of the North, Midwest, and West.

Something still might have been salvaged from the project had the Democratic party been willing to seat the sixty-eight delegates of the newly formed Mississippi Freedom Democratic party at the presidential nominating convention in August. But that was not to be. Fearful that acceptance of the rival delegation would cause the South as a whole to bolt and perhaps precipitate a "white backlash" across the country, President Johnson scrambled to work out a compromise that would at least preserve a veneer of unity during the convention. Despite the entreaties of King and other moderate black leaders, who had already agreed the month before to a moratorium on major

Opposite. *A scene from SNCC's early days in the rural South: SNCC members conduct voter registration in a church in the Mississippi Delta, 1962.* Left. *By the mid-sixties, the group that took much of its early inspiration from Martin Luther King had moved north into the cities and, as this window from its Philadelphia headquarters attests, had begun to raise the radical cry of "Black Power."*

civil rights activity through the November elections, the MFDP steadfastly refused to modify its demand for full accreditation and ultimately left the convention in protest. What embittered the MFDP most of all was not simply the refusal of the president and the Democratic establishment to recognize their claims, but also the reluctance of the reigning black leadership to push the issue of racism to the forefront of the national agenda. The affair fueled suspicions within the MFDP that moderate liberals, black as well as white, no longer represented a solution to the problem facing black Americans but were themselves part of the problem.

Then came Selma where, King later wrote, "the paths of Negro–white unity that had been converging crossed . . . and like a giant X began to diverge." Long before King announced his plans to go to Selma, SNCC had been operating its own voter registration drive there, and many members therefore resented what they regarded as "de Lawd's" attempt to reap the harvest they had sown. Critical at the outset, SNCC workers became even more contemptuous of King after he declined to participate in the first aborted march to Montgomery and then refused to violate the court injunction barring the second march attempt two days later. By the time the third, successful march began on March 21, SNCC had officially withdrawn its support, and its break with the moderates was all but complete.

Thus, while public opinion surveys taken in the wake of the bloody Selma campaign showed white support for black civil rights at an all-time high (with 76 percent of all Americans favoring federal voting rights legislation), a split had developed within the leadership of the black community that would widen over time. Convinced of the futility of King's conciliatory approach, both SNCC and CORE adopted increasingly radical postures, challenging not only the willingness of white America to accept blacks within the framework of the ruling consensus, but the liberal tenets of the consensus itself. In dozens of heated staff meetings held during the summer and fall of 1965, the shift from reformism to revolution in both groups manifested itself in decisions to qualify and then repudiate the commitment to nonviolence, to limit white participation in each organization, and to oppose the Vietnam War. All three positions reflected a growing drift toward separatism, based on the belief that the plight of blacks in America could only be remedied by blacks, working with blacks, for blacks. What was needed, the leaders of SNCC and CORE concluded by the spring of 1966, was not a further extension of black rights, but "Black Power."

In Washington, the emergence of the black radicals did not go unnoticed. Determined to preserve the biracial coalition that had provided his mandate to build the Great Society, President Johnson decided in the spring of 1965 to expand and intensify the government's commitment to the cause of racial equality. In a major speech at Howard University on June 4, 1965, Johnson went further than he or any other president had ever gone before in calling for an end to "the one huge wrong of the American nation." He declared that "white America must accept responsibility" for the black man's "long years of degradation and discrimination." He talked of the "ancient brutality, past injustice, and present prejudice" that for blacks "are a constant reminder of oppression" and for whites "a constant reminder of guilt." Most striking of all, he strongly implied that mere equality of opportunity for blacks would not be enough: The goal was equality of condition—"not equality as a right and a theory, but equality as a fact and result." To blacks in the South, the president promised rapid passage of the new voting rights bill. To blacks living in the ghettos of the North, he vowed to "increase, and accelerate, and broaden" the war on poverty to which nearly $800 million had already been committed. And to whites he issued a tacit warning: The alternative to black "despair," he pointed out, was "destructive rebellion against the fabric of society."

As if to fulfill the president's grim prophecy, two months after his Howard University speech and only days after he signed the Voting Rights Act, the most destructive civil disorder in American peacetime history tore through the heart of the city of Los Angeles. Touched off by the arrest of three young blacks on the night of August 11, 1965, the riot began in the ghetto of Watts and quickly engulfed the surrounding black neighborhoods of the city's central district. At its height, more than 10,000 rioters rampaged through the streets amid cries of "Burn, baby, burn!" and "Selma!" overturning cars, setting fire to buildings, looting stores, exchanging gunfire with law enforcement officers, and hurling stones at firefighters. By the time the National Guard restored order on August 17, 34 people had been killed (25 of them black) and more than 1,000 wounded or injured; nearly 4,000 had been arrested; and nearly 1,000 buildings had been looted, damaged, or destroyed.

The same frustration and rage against injustice that led blacks to risk their lives marching through the hostile countryside of Alabama ignited the flames of Watts. The tactics differed, however, because the problems facing blacks in Los Angeles were in many ways different from those confronting blacks in the South. Forced to live in segregated ghettos with inferior housing, deprived of decent schools and confined to largely menial jobs, the blacks of Watts, like blacks in other major urban centers of the North and Midwest, were less concerned with insuring their legal and constitutional rights than with expanding their opportunities for economic and social advancement. Hostile relations with the primarily white Los Angeles police force, the lack of an adequate public transportation system, and the repeal of a state fair housing law the year before further heightened their sense of isolation and oppression. By resorting to violence, they thus served notice that their plight could no longer be ignored,

Looters comb the riot–torn streets of Watts in August 1965.

neither by the moderate black leaders of the civil rights movement nor by the white majority that dominated the society in which they lived. "I had a dream, I had a dream," mocked one Watts resident as Martin Luther King surveyed the wreckage left by the riot. "Hell, we don't need no damn dreams. We want jobs." "Well, it cost $200 million and thirty-four folks were killed," said another. "I hope whitey got the message."

"Whitey" did get a message but unfortunately not the one that the rioters may have hoped. Shocked by what seemed to be nothing more than an intolerable orgy of violence and destruction, many white Americans quickly concluded that blacks simply wanted too much too fast. It was one thing to stage peaceful marches for political rights in the alien and archaic Deep South; it was quite another to pillage and burn in a major American city. "They say 'Freedom Now,'" said one Philadelphian, expressing at once the outrage and fear felt by many other whites, "but freedom for what? To loot, rape, and murder?" In the wake of Watts, the "white backlash" began in earnest, and with its arrival "the orderly struggle for civil rights," as President Johnson called it, came to an end. What remained to be seen in the years ahead was whether the racial crisis on the one hand and the growing concern over the Vietnam involvement on the other could be resolved without tearing apart the "fabric of society."

Students in revolt

On September 4, 1964, an ad hoc committee of civil rights activists assembled on the sidewalk along Bancroft Way in Berkeley, California, to organize a demonstration against the *Oakland Tribune* for racially discriminatory practices. To passers-by who happened to take notice, it was hardly a novel sight. For several years the Bancroft strip had been used by a wide variety of political, social-action, and religious groups to pass out leaflets, recruit members, and solicit funds. Throughout the summer, and particularly during the Republican convention in San Francisco in July, it had been the site of animated rallies and political debates over the issues and candidates in the upcoming presidential election. Although some UC Berkeley administrators had expressed concern about the increasing intensity of political activity along the strip, no effort had been made to regulate the area until an executive of the *Tribune* called on September 4 to protest the fact that the picketing of the newspaper's offices had been organized on university property.

Ten days later, the university shut down the strip, claiming that it was enforcing a "historic policy." Challenged by a united front of campus organizations broad enough to include Youth for Goldwater, the administration modified its policy a week later to allow certain authorized groups to set up tables on Bancroft Way but continued the ban on speeches, fund raising, and recruitment. The stu-

dents responded by defying the new rules. On October 1 a former graduate student named Jack Weinberg was working at the CORE table when he was confronted by university officials. Told that if he were a student he was violating university policy and if not that he was trespassing, Weinberg said nothing. A short time later the campus police arrived. "Will you come peacefully," they asked, "or if not we'll take you." At that point someone in the gathering crowd shouted, "Take all of us!" While the policeman went to get help, Weinberg launched into a speech. "This is a knowledge factory," he declared. "If you read Clark Kerr's book, those are his words. . . . This is mass production; no deviations from the norm are tolerated." Then, in response to a heckler, he elaborated:

We feel that we, as human beings first and students second, must take our stand on every vital issue of discrimination, of segregation, of poverty, of unemployment.

Moments later the police arrived, seized Weinberg, and attempted to take him away in a waiting car. Schooled in the tactics of passive resistance, Weinberg went limp. So did most of the young people in the crowd surrounding him and the car. For thirty-two hours they stayed there, as speaker after speaker climbed onto the roof of the police car to denounce the university's "historic policy" and debate what should be done next.

Thus began what would become known as the Free Speech Movement, a revolt against the very "multiversity" whose virtues had been so ably extolled by University of California President Clark Kerr. Like most seemingly spontaneous rebellions, it had been long in the making. Intellectually, its roots could be traced to the critique of American higher education most clearly articulated in the Port Huron Statement of 1962, the founding manifesto of the Students for a Democratic Society. "We are the people of this generation," the document began, "bred in at least modest comfort, housed now in universities, looking uncomfortably to the world we inherit." The sources of their discomfiture, the authors went on to explain, were twofold. On the one hand, there were the pressing and perplexing issues of race and peace—"the permeating and victimizing fact of human degradation, symbolized by the Southern struggle against racial bigotry" and "the enclosing face of the Cold War, symbolized by the presence of the Bomb." On the other hand there was the university. Rather than addressing the problems of contemporary society, American universities had become bastions of "cumbersome academic bureaucracy" employing "social and physical scientists" who work "for the corporate economy" and "accelerate the arms race"—"a part of the hierarchy of power rather than an instrument to make men free." To reform society, the leaders of the SDS therefore concluded, they would first have to reform the university, breaking through "the crust of apathy . . . and inner alienation that are the defining characteristics of American college life"

FSM

The Free Speech Movement gripped the University of California's Berkeley campus in late 1964 and early 1965, when students struck (below) and conducted other forms of protest against university policy. Among FSM's leaders was Mario Savio, shown at left being hauled away from a climactic meeting between the UC president and students on December 7, 1964.

Right. *The revolt's beginnings. UC Berkeley students surround a besieged police car as speakers decry university policy on the night of October 1, 1964.*

Below. *A Berkeley faculty member attends a student rally during the final stages of the controversy over student rights. Faculty support for FSM played a crucial role in resolving the dispute.*

Inset. *Folk singer Joan Baez sings at a rally in support of student protesters on the steps of Sproul Hall, the university's main administration building.*

to "create a sustained community of educational and political concern."

Transforming the university into a base for political action, however, proved easier said than done. Although the first two SDS conferences of the 1962–63 academic year concentrated on the issue of university reform, most of the organization's energy was channeled into off-campus social action projects. Like many other youthful idealists of the era, members of SDS were especially active in the crusade for black equality. Working mainly in the urban ghettos of the North, where they established a variety of community action programs, they underwent the same process of disillusionment with what they perceived to be an indifferent white liberal establishment as those who participated in the southern civil rights movement. They also learned the same tactics. By the summer of 1964, the summer of the Mississippi Freedom Project, SDS was still an organization dedicated to social reform. But more radical impulses were already beginning to be felt within the councils of its leadership. Then came Berkeley.

The opening act in a drama that would be replayed on countless university campuses across the country in the next ten years, the Berkeley revolt in many ways established a prototype of student protest. Calling attention to the larger moral dimensions of a local issue, borrowing the "direct-action" techniques of the civil rights movement, and enlisting the support of sympathetic liberal faculty members, a relatively small group of hard-core activists succeeded in mobilizing a broadly based challenge to the university administration. Students staged sit-ins, invaded the main administration building, got arrested, went on strike, sang folk songs, and created slogans identifying the target of their protest: "My Mind Is Not the Property of the University of California"; "I Am a UC Student: Do Not Bend, Fold, Spindle, or Mutilate"; and "You Can't Trust Anyone Over Thirty." Administration attempts to end the rebellion through a combination of compromise and coercion, including the threat to expel two prominent demonstrators who had already been promised amnesty, succeeded only in adding fresh recruits to the legions of the Free Speech Movement.

After more than two months of inconclusive political wrestling, President Kerr announced in early December that he would speak to the entire university community in the outdoor Greek Theater. On the morning of December 7, more than 18,000 people were in attendance as Kerr—a man who, ironically, had once been accused by the House Un-American Activities Committee of being pro-Communist *because* of his campus free speech policies—talked of the need to "move ahead productively and in peace" using "the powers of persuasion against the use of force." Then, after Kerr concluded his address, FSM spokesman Mario Savio stepped forward to announce that a mass rally would be held later to discuss the situation. Before Savio had a chance to utter a word, however, two police-

men grabbed him around the throat and pinned his arms behind him. When thousands of students surged toward the stage, Kerr told the policemen to release the student leader and allowed him to make his announcement.

A more symbolic illustration of the mutual misunderstanding and opposing interests that separated the students and administration at Berkeley would have been hard to imagine. To the advocates of "free speech," by resorting to force when "the powers of persuasion" failed, the administration exposed the university for what it really was: an illiberal, essentially repressive institution unwilling to tolerate dissent. To the defenders of the "multiversity," the students' reliance on "mob action" to realize their goals posed a threat to everything the university stood for: the free pursuit of learning within an ordered environment. Ultimately it was left to the faculty to decide, and on December 8 they voted overwhelmingly in favor of the students. By a vote of 824 to 115, they acceded to all of the major demands of the Free Speech Movement, eliminating all restrictions on campus political activity that did not also apply to the community at large.

On February 15, 1965, two weeks after the Berkeley student newspaper announced that the Free Speech Movement had "for all practical purposes dissolved," a new issue came to the fore. "The campus and the entire nation has recently been immersed in conversation about the confusing situation in North and South Vietnam," reported an editorial in the *Daily Californian*. "Student groups have conducted marches, pickets, rallies, and debates on the subject." What occasioned the sudden burst of student anxiety over the war was President Johnson's decision the week before to launch reprisal bombing raids against North Vietnam. Up to that point student protest against American involvement in Vietnam, at Berkeley and elsewhere, had been minimal and infrequent. Even the SDS leadership had vacillated on the issue, seeing it as only one of many concerns that merited their attention. Now, however, a new sense of urgency gripped the youthful activists of the burgeoning "student movement." As the president began to escalate the U.S. military commitment to South Vietnam, they decided that they would escalate their opposition to the administration's policy.

During the next five weeks several hundred Berkeley students, led by veterans of the Free Speech Movement, staged three protest marches on the Oakland army terminal. At the end of March they followed the lead of the University of Michigan and joined more than 100 other campuses by conducting "teach-ins" to discuss the war and its implications. In the spring the Vietnam Day Committee was formed at Berkeley, and on May 21, 15,000 students attended a rally to protest the war. In early August the VDC organized several unsuccessful attempts to block troop trains passing through Berkeley, and a new slogan appeared on campus: "Make Love Not War."

In some ways the emergence of the antiwar movement

The Gentle Protesters

Even before students picked up their antiwar banners and began marching, thousands of older men and women were challenging U.S. involvement in Vietnam. These older protesters made up what was traditionally known as the American peace movement, and some of them had been around for a long time.

American pacifists began organizing during the early nineteenth century when citizens were first required to fight for the state. Some pacifists opposed war on religious, others on philosophical, grounds. All hoped that by standing up for their consciences they would convince others to do the same. Antiwar sentiment intensified during the First World War when organizations such as the Protestant Fellowship of Reconciliation (FOR) and the Quaker American Friends Service Committee (AFSC) were founded to win rights for conscientious objectors. During World War II pacifist groups again affirmed their opposition to war, despite the unpopularity of such a position. And as early as 1954, the AFSC spoke out against U.S. intervention in Southeast Asia.

Among the most prominent traditional pacifists was A.J. Muste, a long-time leader of the FOR and founder, with Bayard Rustin, of the radical pacifist *Liberation* magazine. Forced to resign from his post in a Congregational church because of his pacifist beliefs during World War I, Reverend Muste devoted his career to the pursuit of peace abroad and social reform at home. He helped form the American Civil Liberties Union in 1920, was active in the labor movement of the thirties, and taught Gandhian passive resistance to Martin Luther King in the fifties. In the early sixties Muste was in the forefront of the emerging opposition to American policy in Southeast Asia, which he condemned not only for moral reasons but also on the more pragmatic grounds that the United States

should not get "bogged down" in a war it "cannot win."

By basing his appeal on practical as well as principled considerations, Muste hoped to enlist the support of a new breed of peace activist that had first appeared in the late 1950s: the antinuclear arms protester. Stirred to action by the accelerating arms race between the U.S. and the Soviet Union, yet liberal rather than radical in outlook, the "ban the bomb" crusaders hoped to form a mass movement that would lobby the government for a total halt to the production and proliferation of nuclear weapons. In 1957 they established the Committee for a Sane Nuclear Policy, or SANE, to coordinate their efforts on a national scale. "Sociologically, SANE recruited from the business and professional middle class," recalled its director, Sanford Gottlieb. "These were issue-oriented, educated, middle-class people. They were concerned about nuclear weapons, nuclear testing, fall-out, and related issues." Perhaps the most famous of SANE's 25,000 members was Dr. Benjamin Spock, the pediatrician turned peace activist who joined the organization in 1962. "I thought of all the children who would die of leukemia and cancer," Spock said, "and of the ultimate possibility of nuclear war."

SANE often found itself in alliance with the Women's Strike for Peace, a loose coalition of some 50,000, mostly middle-aged, suburban women who advocated no specific program of action but whose goal was "universal, general, and complete disarmament." With no leaders, no membership lists, and no dues, WSP did not consider itself so much an organization as a "great communication system" that kept its adherents informed about the most vital issue of the time.

Ironically, the signing of the limited nuclear test ban treaty in 1963 deprived the "ban the bomb" movement of much of its original impetus, and for a time SANE functioned as little more than a "mailing list" organization. The movement was revivified, however, by growing American involvement in Vietnam, which many antinuclear protesters perceived as only a variation of a common militaristic trend in postwar American foreign policy.

Although antinuclear activists joined traditional pacifists in vigorously opposing the Vietnam War, the two groups

differed in the means of their protest. In the interest of appealing to a broad spectrum of public opinion, the leaders of SANE tried to keep their organization respectable by screening radical elements from demonstrations and by refraining from illegal activity, including nonviolent direct action.

Not so the traditional pacifists. Using techniques they had first brought to the civil rights movement, they engaged in various forms of civil disobedience, including pickets, sit-ins, vigils, and refusal to pay income taxes that finance war. Groups like the American Friends Service Committee, the War Resisters League, and the Catholic Worker movement placed special emphasis on resistance to the military draft, providing counseling on conscientious objection, and, in some instances, supporting actions such as draft card burnings. Unlike some of the student protests, however, pacifist opposition was never violent.

The traditional pacifists' more radical stance made it easier for them to work with student antiwar activists; SANE members had a harder time reconciling their efforts to reform but leave intact the existing social structure with the radicals' desire to create a whole new society. SANE's insistence that Communist-affiliated groups be excluded from demonstrations led SDS and SANE to stage two separate antiwar rallies in Washington in 1965. The tension continued into 1967, when for similar reasons SANE's national board of directors refused to endorse the giant Spring Mobilization To End the War in Vietnam. Many of SANE's local chapters, however, marched under the SANE banner anyway. For the most part the various antiwar groups, young and old, liberal and radical, worked together trying to bring an end to the war.

The older protesters provided a firm foundation for the antiwar movement, for they, unlike the students, could not be easily dismissed by the nation at large. By providing leadership and direction for people who had never before signed a petition or marched in a rally, this small but vocal minority helped create a truly broad-based antiwar movement in the United States. Their firm commitment to resisting the war brought them to the forefront in the beginning and sustained their opposition to the end.

at Berkeley could be seen as a direct outgrowth of the Free Speech Movement. Not only did both draw on the same people, tactics, and, in the case of many FSM leaders, experience in the civil rights movement, but the entire Berkeley campus had been politicized by the confrontation with university authorities the preceding fall. There was, however, one major difference. Rather than directing their protest against the university, antiwar activists decided, at least initially, to use the university as a base for their dissent. The same was true on other campuses as well. Although student demonstrations against administration policies continued to take place at dozens of colleges and universities, in ever-increasing numbers students were leaving the campus and taking to the streets to protest against the war.

Organized by the SDS, the first major student demonstration against the war took place in Washington on April 17, 1965, when 20,000 protesters gathered to decry the introduction of American combat troops in Vietnam the month before. Soon they were swelling the ranks of other, more broadly based antiwar organizations, like the National Coordinating Committee To End the War in Vietnam, and lending their support to liberal, middle-class peace groups like SANE.

The motives of the protesters varied greatly. For the self-avowed apostles of the "New Left," like the members of SDS, opposition to the war became a matter of ideological principle. Seeing the American prosecution of the war as but one manifestation of a society gone wrong, they condemned the government's policy in Vietnam in the same way and for many of the same reasons that they denounced the inadequacy of the government's response to the problems of race and poverty at home. "What kind of system is it that justifies the United States or any country seizing the destinies of the Vietnamese people and using them callously for its own purpose?" asked SDS President Paul Potter during the April 17 rally in Washington.

What kind of system is it that disenfranchises people in the South, leaves millions upon millions of people throughout the country impoverished and excluded from the mainstream and promise of American society . . . and still persists in calling itself free and finding itself fit to police the world?

For others, the problem was not so much with the system as a whole as with the particular policies of the Johnson administration, and their opposition to those policies was not so much ideological as moral. This was especially true of religious leaders who joined the antiwar movement and pacifist groups like the American Friends Service Committee. Still others objected to the war on more pragmatic grounds, believing that it was a waste of the nation's resources and doubting the military's capacity to bring the war to a successful conclusion.

Yet if the reasons for opposing the war differed, the object of much early antiwar dissent was the same. As more and more young men headed off to fight in a place that many could not even locate on a map, protest against the war increasingly took the form of protest against the Selective Service System.

Deciding who fights

On May 2, 1964, more than 1,000 students gathered before the United Nations building in New York City to denounce the "imperialist" policies of the United States government. Chanting "We Won't Go," they listed the places they would not serve if inducted into the American armed forces: Cuba, the Dominican Republic, and Southeast Asia. Twelve of the students then stepped forward, held their draft cards aloft, and burned them.

As a gesture of defiance against the Selective Service System, it was not without precedent. Seventeen years before, on Lincoln's birthday in 1947, between 400 and 500 men had publicly destroyed their draft cards to protest President Truman's decision to reinstitute conscription. The action of this later "May 2nd Movement" was, nonetheless, replete with a special symbolic significance. For 1964 was the year when the first great wave of the postwar "baby boom," the children born in 1946, reached the age of eighteen, the year when more than 1.7 million young men performed a rite of passage prescribed by law and signed up for the draft. The vast majority of them, of course, never gave it a second thought. Most simply regarded registration as a civic duty, and even those who did not knew that the chances of being drafted were not great. With the pool of potential conscripts rapidly expanding and call-ups holding at about 6,000 to 7,000 a month, and with a wide range of deferments and exemptions available, it seemed likely that fully two-thirds of all registrants would reach the ceiling age of twenty-six without ever serving in the armed forces—as long as the nation was at peace.

All that changed in March of 1965. To meet the needs of the expanding American military effort in Vietnam, the Selective Service System began issuing its "greetings" at a rapidly accelerating pace. Operating through a network of some 3,700 local draft boards, the SSS sent out 13,700 induction notices in April and another 15,100 in May. In July the number climbed to 27,400, and by December it was over 40,000.

Protest mounted. In addition to the mass demonstrations staged by students and prominent peace groups, which typically targeted the draft as the most visible symbol of the government's war policy, draft card burnings, sit-ins, and picketing of local draft boards became increasingly common. Congress quickly responded by toughening the penalties for such acts, making violations of Selective Service laws punishable by a fine of up to $10,000 and five years in prison. Draft card burners in particular were promptly and severely punished, although hundreds of other antidraft demonstrators were also arrested for of-

Seeds of division. During an early antiwar rally involving 700 people in Manhattan on May 1, 1964, a counterdemonstrator makes known her feelings. Others picketed the protest with signs reading "Castro Must Go" and "Can the Commies."

USA
LOVE
IT
OR
LEAVE
IT

Above. Demonstrators march against the draft in Boston, 1965.

Police haul away protesters staging a ``sit-in'' at a Selective Service office in Ann Arbor, Michigan, on October 15, 1965.

"We Won't Go!"

Choosing as its symbol the Greek letter omega (also the symbol of the ohm, the standard unit of measurement of resistance to the induction of electric currents), the draft resistance movement steadily gained momentum after the introduction of American combat troops in Vietnam in March 1965. All told, during the course of the war more than 200,000 young men were accused of draft offenses, although only 4,000 ultimately served time in prison. At left, draft card burners recoil from the spray of a heckler's fire extinguisher at an antiwar rally sponsored by the War Resisters' League, the Catholic Worker, and the Committee for Non-Violent Action in Union Square, New York City, on November 6, 1965. After allowing a prowar spokesman to state his views, the men shown here burned their draft cards before a crowd of 1,500, including FBI photographers.

fenses ranging from interference with the operation of a draft board to wearing a jacket emblazoned with the motto: "Fuck the Draft." In the meantime, the Justice Department undertook a nationwide investigation of the antidraft movement, based on speculation that many of the protests were incited and controlled by Communists.

For all the attention they attracted, however, those who publicly defied the draft remained a distinct minority. However strongly they may have felt about the war, the majority of draft-age males found it easier, or more prudent, to avoid conscription rather than resist it. One option was enlistment. As in the past, many young men signed up because they thought they would be drafted anyway, and they wanted to cut themselves a better deal. Of the half-million men who volunteered for the service between June 1965 and June 1966, for example, 180,000 enlisted after they had passed their preinduction physicals. Rather than enter the army or Marine Corps, where the chances of going to Vietnam were much greater, many chose to join the air force or the navy. As one newly recruited sailor explained: "There ain't no Vietcong submarines." Draft-motivated enlistments were even more common in the National Guard and the reserves, despite the commitment to six years of service.

Others, however, preferred to take advantage of the intricate system of exemptions and deferments designed to channel the nation's youth in socially useful ways. Although President Johnson revoked the exemption for married men in August 1965, local boards were still allowed to exempt men with families on the grounds of hardship as well as men deemed to possess critical occupational skills. Local discretion was also the rule in the case of many deferments. College students, for example, were eligible for II-S deferments until they fulfilled their degree requirements or reached the age of twenty-four, whichever came first. But it was up to their local boards to decide on an annual basis whether they were making satisfactory progress toward a degree. Initially most boards followed past policy and simply granted a deferment to anyone who could prove that he was enrolled full time in an accredited college or university. In early 1966, however, the SSS decided to reinstitute the Selective Service College Qualification Test, making students ranking in the lower levels of their class eligible for the draft. Despite a nationwide outburst of student protest against the SSCQT, more than 750,000 students took the test in 1966 in the hope of retaining their student deferments.

As the war continued and antiwar sentiment became more widespread, the means of evading, avoiding, and resisting the draft became more sophisticated. Aided by a network of draft counseling centers and lawyers specializing in the complexities of draft law, an ever-increasing number of young men brought legal challenges against the Selective Service System. While many of the issues were strictly procedural in nature, involving the technical-

ities of individual cases, others were not. A series of court rulings between 1967 and 1970, for example, stripped away the power of local boards to punish draft offenders and protesters by revoking deferments or accelerating induction. The most celebrated such case involved nine University of Michigan students who were reclassified I-A, the highest category of draft eligibility, after they were arrested for participating in a sit-in in December 1965.

At the same time, the courts progressively expanded the definition of "conscientious objection" in response to a flood of suits filed by men who opposed the Vietnam War on moral grounds. Although long-standing draft policy held that only members of such "historic peace churches" as the Mennonites, Quakers, and Jehovah's Witnesses were eligible for consideration as conscientious objectors, in 1965 the Supreme Court ruled, in the case of the *United States v. Seeger*, that neither membership in an established church nor belief in God were requirements for CO status. Rather, wrote Justice Thomas Clark, "a sincere and meaningful belief which occupies in the life of its pos-

SELECTIVE SERVICE CLASSIFICATIONS

I-A	Available for military service.
I-A-O	Conscientious objector available for noncombatant military service only.
I-C	Member of the armed forces of the United States, the Coast and Geodetic Survey, or the Public Health Service.
I-D	Member of reserve component or student taking military training.
I-O	Conscientious objector available for civilian work contributing to the maintenance of the national health, safety, or interest.
I-S	Student deferred by statute (high school).
I-Y	Registrant available for military service, but qualified for military service only in the event of war or national emergency.
I-W	Conscientious objector performing civilian work contributing to the maintenance of the national health, safety, or interest.
II-A	Registrant deferred because of civilian occupation (except agriculture or activity in study).
II-C	Registrant deferred because of agricultural occupation.
II-S	Registrant deferred because of activity in study.
III-A	Registrant with a child or children; registrant deferred by reason of extreme hardship to dependents.
IV-A	Registrant who has completed service; sole surviving son.
IV-B	Official deferred by law.
IV-C	Alien.
IV-D	Minister of religion or divinity student.
IV-F	Registrant not qualified for any military service.
V-A	Registrant over the age of liability for military service.

sessor a place parallel to that filled by God" was sufficient, provided that the applicant otherwise fulfilled the criteria for conscientious objection. Subsequent court decisions further broadened and secularized the "sincerity" doctrine, making it increasingly difficult for local boards to establish fixed standards. One study of the draft found, for instance, that among the three boards in Lake Charles, Louisiana, "one gave CO exemptions to almost every applicant, another gave them to no one, and the third looked at the merits of the case." In another case, a Samoan was granted conscientious objector status after convincing his California draft board of his belief that if he killed anyone, his pagan god would make a volcano erupt in punishment. All told, more than 50,000 men were classified as conscientious objectors during the course of the Vietnam War (compared with 7,600 during the Korean War). Depending upon the dispensation of their individual cases, some were required to perform public service jobs in lieu of military service, while others were inducted into the military as noncombatants.

By far the most popular way of beating the draft, however, was flunking the preinduction physical. Once a young man became eligible for the draft, he was required to report for an examination to determine his physical, mental, and moral fitness for military service. If he passed he would then be classified I-A and become immediately eligible for induction. If he failed he would be classified IV-F, permanently exempting him from military service, or I-Y, making him available for military service only in time of declared war or national emergency.

While it is reasonable to infer that the majority of IV-F exemptions during the Vietnam War were granted for legitimate reasons, cases in which individuals contrived to fail their physicals were legion. Some jabbed pins into their arms to simulate the "tracks" made by heroin addicts or artificially raised their blood pressure with caffeine and other drugs. Others aggravated sports injuries such as bad knees or, like one University of Michigan student who ate three large pizzas every night for six months, made sure that they exceeded the military weight limit for their

The possibility looming over them of losing their student deferments if they score low, UCLA undergrads register their protest while taking the Selective Service College Qualification Test in the spring of 1966.

height. And still others went to further extremes, as in the case of one draft prospect who faked a gastrointestinal ulcer by drinking a pint of his own blood and then vomiting in the presence of a military doctor.

Not all of these ruses worked. As time went on military physicians became more alert to feigned illness and injuries and took added measures to detect them. At the same time, however, civilian doctors became more willing to search for some identifiable infirmity, such as a heart murmur, and to attest to it by writing to the draft authorities. "The traditional doctor-patient relationship is one of preserving life," explained one physician. "I save lives by keeping people out of the Army."

With a third of all potential draftees deferred or exempted every year, with more than a quarter disqualified from military service or qualified only in the event of a national emergency, and with another 5 percent serving on the home front in the reserves and National Guard, the obvious question is, who did get drafted? Who was the soldier of the Vietnam War?

He was decidedly not, to begin with, representative of the increasingly well-educated, affluent, and suburban-bred postwar "baby boom" generation. On the contrary, the typical draftee of the Vietnam era was far more likely to come from a working-class family, to live in a city or small town, and to have no education beyond a high-school diploma. As one 1968 study of deferment policies and income levels showed, the likelihood of military service clearly diminished as income and education increased. A high-school dropout from a low-income family, for example, had a 70 percent chance of serving in Vietnam, as compared with 64 percent for a high-school graduate and 42 percent for a college graduate. In a survey of 100 draftees in his district, a Wisconsin congressman found that all came from families with an annual income of less than $5,000. Largely ignored by the draft resistance network, unable to afford the lawyers and doctors fees that aided their more well-heeled peers, poor and working-class men were, as Dwight Eisenhower once put it, "sitting ducks for the draft." "Factory neighborhoods, slums (and) Negro ghettos," concluded one study of the Vietnam-era draft, "were the draft boards' happy hunting grounds."

Once in Vietnam, moreover, army draftees faced a much higher chance of seeing combat and consequently suffered a significantly higher casualty rate than those who enlisted voluntarily. As William K. Brehm, assistant secretary of the army for manpower and reserve affairs, explained in 1970:

The popular jobs are the ones for which people enlist. They don't enlist for the hard-core combat skills. That is why draftees tend to populate the hard-core combat skills: 70 percent of the infantry, armor, artillery are draftees.

As a result, during the five years following the introduction

of American combat troops in Vietnam, draftees composed 39 percent of the army's in-country enlisted and officer force yet accounted for nearly 55 percent of all battle deaths. Overall casualty rates (killed and wounded) for draftees during the same period were 54.7 percent higher than for regular army volunteers.

The corresponding figures for black soldiers were even more disproportionate, particularly during the early years of the war. Between 1961 and 1966, for example, only 8 percent of all American military personnel were black, yet blacks accounted for 16 percent of combat deaths. In 1965, 23.5 percent of all army enlisted men killed in action were black. In response to outcries from the black community, the Pentagon in 1966 put pressure on the military to reduce the black casualty rate, so that by the end of the war the Defense Department could statistically demonstrate that the overall proportion of black combat deaths, 12.5 percent, mirrored the black proportion of the national population. Such figures, however, concealed not only the excess share of dying suffered by blacks during the first years of the war, but also the fact that during the period in which the American ground war was at its height, 1965 to 1970, black casualties ran 30 percent ahead of their numbers in Indochina.

In part the racial inequities of the Vietnam War, like the class inequities, could be attributed to the workings of the Selective Service System. Proportionally, blacks were overrepresented at the lower income and educational levels that made up the bulk of the draft pool and grossly underrepresented on local draft boards. (In 1967, only 1.3 percent of the 16,632 board members nationwide were black, and seven states had no blacks at all on their boards.) Draft policy was not the sole source of discrimination. With the introduction of Project 100,000 in 1966, the Johnson administration magnified the social imbalances of the Vietnam army already insured by the SSS. Billed as a Great Society program, the project was ostensibly designed to "rehabilitate" what Defense Secretary Robert McNamara called the "subterranean poor." With lower military standards for induction, it was argued, young men who had previously failed to meet the armed services mental or physical requirements would be able to learn new skills, gain self-confidence, profit from veterans benefits, and generally enhance their prospects for the future. Blacks in particular were supposed to benefit from the project, according to Assistant Secretary of Labor Daniel Patrick Moynihan, because the army offered a "world away from women . . . and the strains of the disorganized and matrifocal family life" that Moynihan held responsible for the problems of many young black men.

For all its high-minded purposes, however, Project 100,000 quickly developed into a vehicle for channeling underprivileged youths from the streets of America's cities to the battlefields of Vietnam. Carefully assigned to designated "poverty areas," black recruiters hung around

Newly arrived inductees await further instructions at Fort Jackson, South Carolina, 1966.

street corners, hamburger stands, and basketball courts looking for potential recruits. Using the language of the streets, they would "rap with the brothers" and try to convince black mothers that if their sons enlisted they would get "valuable training." Most recruiters were well aware, however, that anyone who had previously failed to score the minimum 31 out of 100 on the armed forces written test was most likely to be given a rifle and sent into combat. And in certain instances, Project 100,000 was accepting men who had scored as low as 10. In the end, 354,000 men entered the military under the program. Forty-one percent were black. Forty percent were assigned to combat roles. Although the Defense Department later denied that casualty rates for project men were disproportionately high, a Pentagon survey in 1969 found that their "attrition-by-death" rate was nearly twice as great as that of Vietnam-era veterans as a whole.

The "credibility gap" emerges

Despite the fact that tens of thousands of young men were going off to war, despite mounting protests against their going and complaints from some quarters about who was going, public opinion polls taken in 1965 and 1966 indicated that a majority of Americans supported the war effort in Vietnam. Within that majority there were substantial disagreements over the best way of prosecuting the war, with varying pluralities favoring administration policy (commonly phrased by pollsters as "continuing military action but remaining ready for negotiations"); further escalation; or an all-out effort, including a declaration of war, to end the conflict quickly. But on the whole most Americans seemed to accept the government's contention that the war was necessary, that the nation could afford it, and that eventually it would be won.

With some exceptions, the major news media echoed the same message. For like the government they reported on and the public they informed, most journalists in the early 1960s were still strongly influenced by the assumptions and imperatives of the ongoing Cold War. They tended to accept the need to contain international communism as a responsibility imposed on the U.S. as leader of the "Free World" and to interpret the growing American involvement in Southeast Asia within that context. As UPI correspondent Neil Sheehan later recalled, when he first arrived in Vietnam in 1962 he was firmly convinced that the United States was helping the non-Communist Vietnamese to "build a viable and independent nation-state and defeat a communist insurgency that would subject them to a dour tyranny." Fred Friendly, the president of CBS News in the early 1960s, put it somewhat differently. The journalist, he said, "went into Vietnam the same way he went into World War II and Korea—'as a member of the team.'"

Once in Vietnam, however, the handful of reporters who formed the Saigon press corps in the early 1960s— Sheehan, Peter Arnett and Malcolm Browne of the Associated Press, Charles Mohr of *Time*, François Sully of *Newsweek*, Homer Bigart and then David Halberstam of the *New York Times*—did not remain "members of the team" for long. Disparities, and at times outright contradictions, arose between what they were told at official briefings and what they learned from their own contacts or saw with their own eyes. Fearful that American violations of the 1954 Geneva agreements might be discovered and reported in the press, U.S. officials in the early 1960s simply evaded questions dealing with the apparent build-up of American war materiel. When the aircraft carrier U.S.S. *Core* docked in the Saigon River in early 1962, for example, the inquiries of reporters were met with an official "no comment."

As the U.S. commitment grew and the American presence became more visible, new fictions were created and the deceptions multiplied. Officially the Americans were only "advising" the Vietnamese, yet reporters saw them fighting and dying. Battles in which correspondents in the field watched ARVN units go down to defeat, like the one at Ap Bac in January 1963, were described by U.S. spokesmen as victories. President Ngo Dinh Diem, whom many reporters found to be a repressive despot completely out of touch with the aspirations of his people, was touted by the U.S. Mission as a strong and popular leader. "No responsible U.S. official in Saigon ever told a newsman a really big falsehood," asserted John Mecklin, who became head of the U.S. Information Service in Saigon in 1962. "Instead there were endless little ones."

The cumulative effect of those "endless little" falsehoods was to create a "credibility gap" between the U.S. officials and the American press corps in Saigon that would widen over time. Force-fed overly optimistic accounts of progress and subjected to repeated censorship efforts by the Diem regime, most Vietnam field reporters became increasingly disillusioned with the war effort. After the assassination of Diem and the collapse of his regime in November 1963, the tensions between the Saigon press corps and American officials in Saigon eased temporarily. But by then a permanently adversarial relationship had already been established. Not only did the coup confirm reporters' suspicions about official American policy statements and vindicate their judgment of Diem, but it also indicated that the Vietnam War was rapidly becoming an American war. Skeptical in the past, many correspondents now began to question whatever they were told by U.S. officials in Saigon and to file reports that often contradicted what the Johnson administration was saying back in Washington.

In many instances the dispatches from Saigon also contradicted stories on the war written by Washington reporters. Lacking the alternative sources and firsthand information available to their colleagues in Vietnam, the members of the Washington press corps had to rely on the

Let the Reader Beware

If the Vietnam War were as much a battle for "hearts and minds" as a contest for territory, that war was surely fought in the United States as well as Vietnam. Both official policymakers and their critics based their strategies, in part, on perceptions of public opinion about the conflict in Southeast Asia. Demonstrations, petitions, and letters to newspaper editors—antiwar and prowar alike—could only gauge the opinion of the most vocal segment of the country's population. Despite its flaws, only public opinion polling could tell contemporaries, as well as historians, what the "great silent majority" was feeling.

But polling was, and remains, a controversial and often misunderstood method to measure public opinion. To put it simply, opinion polling is a curious mixture of science and art. To the extent that polls are based on a scientific methodology they have a proven record of reliability. But where the science ends and the art begins they are filled with ambiguities.

Public opinion polling is at its scientific best in what professionals call the "design of the sample" or how the interviewees are selected. The Gallup organization, a pioneer in the field, has consistently employed the most sophisticated techniques in designing a sample. Technically a Gallup sample is called a "stratified random sample" because it does not choose its 1,500 interviewees completely at random but only after dividing the popu-

lation into segments (or, "stratifying the population") and then choosing proportionally from among those segments according to the most recent census data.

Gallup begins by dividing the country into eight geographic regions and then further dividing the regions into seven categories of localities based on population size. At this point Gallup randomly designates some of these localities as the site of the interviews. These localities are selected according to population and geography in proportion to their representation in the national population. Further refining selects randomly a few city blocks or subdivisions within the localities.

In each of these small areas an interviewer is given a predetermined path and asked to conduct an interview at each household along the way until he or she has reached a set number of interviews. Most interviewing takes place on weekends or evenings when adults are likely to be home. Other steps are taken to insure that the respondents are as typical as possible of the area. For example, corner houses, which are typically more expensive, are passed over.

In-depth studies have proven that the sample design employed by Gallup is, indeed, reliable. In the jargon of the profession, the "sampling tolerance" is "plus or minus three percentage points at the 95 percent confidence level." That means that if a poll were taken 100 times, in 95 cases the results would fall within three percentage points of the first sample.

If the design of the sample has become a highly scientific endeavor, the actual interview remains a finely tuned art, the most important part of which is the framing of the questions. Polling organizations are very sensitive to this issue and have been among the pioneers in showing the difficulties that arise by small changes in the wording of a question. In 1948, for example, one sample of French citizens was asked whether they supported "communism" while another sample was asked if they supported "the Communists." The latter drew 50 percent more support than the former, presumably because "the Communists" represented a native French political party with a long history, while "com-

munism" seemed to be a foreign ideology based in Moscow.

Framing the proper question became particularly important during the Vietnam War. Pollsters had long known that by asking interviewees whether they supported the president or the administration that a certain percentage of the population will automatically say, "yes." Known as the "president's followers," they will decide the question on the basis of "support for country." The results can sometimes be quite startling. In May 1966, before President Johnson began to bomb Hanoi and Haiphong, a Harris poll showed that the country was evenly divided when asked whether the "administration is more right or more wrong in not bombing" those two cities. One month later, after the bombing of those cities began, 85 percent thought "the administration more right." In this case it appears that 35 percent of the population was simply prepared to support whatever course the administration chose.

In the Nixon administration this problem became even more acute as President Nixon attempted to rally the country to his policies by invoking patriotic support for the office of the president. The result was that pollsters often found blatantly contradictory answers to their questions. In late 1970 pollster John Kraft found that three-quarters of the population "supported the president's policies" in Vietnam, while the very same majority also supported the policy alternatives advanced by his critics such as Senators Charles Goodell and George McGovern.

Such ambiguities have made the interpretation of poll results a riddle for the most knowledgeable readers. Often the trend found when a question is repeated over several months or years is more important than the actual result. If opposition to presidential policies increases from, say, 20 to 40 percent over several months, is it more significant that opposition has doubled or that the majority continues to support the president? In the end each reader can only interpret the results for himself, but perhaps a warning should be published with the results of each poll: Let the reader beware.

government, and especially the Pentagon, for their information on the war. As a result, their assessments of the situation in South Vietnam tended to reflect the official optimism of the Kennedy and Johnson administrations, increasingly expressed in the "hard," quantitative language of weapons captured, kill ratios, defection rates, and hamlets pacified. "We were largely at the mercy of the administration then," recalled the late Peter Lisagor, Washington bureau chief of the *Chicago Daily News.* "We had no touchstones on the war. And we were less skeptical on the war than we were on other things. There was a tendency to believe more because they were supposed to have the facts and you didn't, and we were inclined to accept an official's word on something as cosmic as war." "[S]kepticism came slowly and disbelief even more so to the bulk of the Washington press corps," wrote Jules Witcover of the *Los Angeles Times* Washington bureau.

The doubts expressed by the young reporters based in Vietnam, moreover, were often dismissed by older news hands at the Pentagon as the product of inexperience, a judgment that many government officials were quick to reinforce. Pentagon officials constantly sniped at the Saigon press corps and repeatedly took steps to counter the impact of what General Earle Wheeler, chief of staff of the army (and later chairman of the Joint Chiefs of Staff), described as "irresponsible, astigmatic and sensationalized reporting" from Vietnam. Pressure could be brought to bear in a variety of ways. In 1964, for example, the Defense Department initiated Operation Candor, a program that offered U.S.-based journalists two-week tours of the war zone at government expense. After being guided through carefully selected "secure areas" and attending countless military briefings, many of the visitors returned home persuaded that "real progress" had been made and said so in their columns. In other instances reporters unearthed apparently ground-breaking stories, such as *Time* correspondent Frank McCulloch's discovery in early 1965 that American combat troops would shortly be deployed to Da Nang, only to have their accounts silenced by "the highest source in the land." "For years the press corps in Vietnam was undermined by the White House and the Pentagon," contended John Shaw, also a *Time* correspondent in Vietnam. "Many American editors ignored what their correspondents in Vietnam were telling them in favor of the Washington version."

Shaw's conclusion undoubtedly was colored by the experience of one of his predecessors as *Time*'s man in Saigon, Charles Mohr. A man largely devoid of ideological passions, Mohr initially supported the U.S. war effort but also perceived that the fighting was going badly for the South Vietnamese. He began to file very thorough but also very pessimistic accounts of the actual progress being made in the war. In August 1963 he turned in a devastating assessment, which began with the statement "The war in Vietnam is being lost," and then proceeded to out-

line what he termed a "first-class major foreign policy crisis." Mohr's conclusions proved completely unacceptable to Otto Fuerbringer, the managing editor of *Time* and an ardent cold warrior. Fuerbringer ordered the dispatch rewritten, and the magazine published an optimistic piece that concluded that "government troops were fighting better than ever in South Vietnam." Several weeks later, Fuerbringer dictated a scathing indictment of Vietnam field reporters that appeared in the news weekly's "Press" section. The article accused the Saigon press corps of "helping to compound the very confusion that it should be untangling for its readers at home" and portrayed the journalists holed up in a hotel bar, nursing collective grievances, and concocting stories based largely on hearsay. Saigon reporters were outraged, and Mohr, who took it as a direct attack on his reportage, promptly resigned from the *Time* staff.

Coverage of the Vietnam War became much more extensive and complex after the introduction of U.S. combat troops in 1965. The *New York Times* led the way by adding two new full-time correspondents to what had formerly been a one-man bureau. *Newsweek* and *Time* soon followed suit. By the end of the year there were 131 accredited American media representatives in Saigon; by December 1966 the number was 175. As the American press and television contingent grew and the fighting heated up, reports from Vietnam increasingly focused on battlefield action involving American soldiers. Larger questions of American policy and South Vietnam politics, while not ignored, began to receive less attention than such statistical yardsticks of progress as enemy body counts.

Many of the new Vietnam correspondents, moreover, arrived with the same preconceptions and predispositions as their predecessors had had, including a willingness to trust information provided by official U.S. spokesmen in Saigon. Only gradually did the "credibility gap" reassert itself. As Frank McCulloch, the *Time* bureau chief in Saigon from 1964 to 1966, later explained, each correspondent typically passed through five "stages" of disenchantment during his or her stay in Vietnam. In most cases the correspondent arrived with a sanguine belief that the United States was engaged in the vital task of saving a grateful people from the grips of Communist tyranny. About three months later, McCulloch estimated, that initial attitude yielded to the realization that the American mission was more difficult than first assumed and that somehow it was being fouled up. In stage three, which usually came six to nine months later, the reporter laid the blame for the lack of progress on the Vietnamese. By the time the reporter began his or her second year in Vietnam and entered stage four, he or she had usually concluded that the U.S. was losing the war and the overall situation was much worse than it had previously seemed. Finally, McCulloch said, the correspondent admitted that the American effort was not working at all, that Americans

Left. Peter Arnett of the Associated Press argues with a U.S. military policeman who has just ordered him to leave a Buddhist demonstration in Saigon in April 1966.

Below. Members of the Saigon press corps meet in an office at UPI in the fall of 1963: Ray Herndon of UPI (left), Neil Sheehan of AP (rear), David Halberstam of the New York Times (right), and an unidentified photographer.

should not even be in Vietnam, and that they were doing more harm than good.

But that came later. In 1965 and 1966 most members of the Vietnam press corps did not reach stage five. Even those who filed some of the more pessimistic reports, like Charles Mohr, never questioned the legitimacy of the U.S. presence in Vietnam, only whether the war was being fought effectively. "Everyone thought I . . . was against the war," recalled Mohr. "I just thought it wasn't working. I didn't come to think of it as immoral until the very end."

A two-front war

The American ground war in Vietnam was nearly a year old when President Lyndon Johnson went before Congress on January 12, 1966, to reaffirm an article of faith shared by most members of his administration. "I believe," the president said, "that we can continue the Great Society while we fight in Vietnam," and the congressmen applauded. At the time, he had every reason to think he was right.

Stimulated by the Kennedy-Johnson tax cuts, the American economy in early 1966 was in the midst of one of the biggest booms in the nation's history. Unemployment, which had hovered around 7 percent five years before, was down to 4.5 percent. With American industries pumping away at nearly 90 percent of capacity, a ten-year high, the question was not whether, but when the "full employment" level (of only 4 percent unemployed) would be reached. The gross national product, which had stood at $500 billion in 1961, now exceeded $685 billion. Inflation had not risen over 2 percent in

A mother and her children shop at their A&P in Fairfield, Connecticut, in 1966.

the previous three years. The predictions of the "new economists"—the claim that through "fine-tuning" of federal fiscal policy they could expand the economy, reduce unemployment, and still keep prices stable—seemed to have been borne out.

There were, however, a few disturbing signs. As a result of the sharp and unanticipated increase in military expenditures during the second half of 1965, demand had begun to outstrip supply, spurring a rise in prices. As living costs rose, workers began to demand higher wages in excess of productivity increases, in turn raising production costs and leading producers to set higher prices. The inflationary snowball had begun to roll.

According to the theories of the "new economists," the threat of inflation could have been countered in one of two ways: either by cutting federal expenditures or by raising taxes. President Johnson thus faced a dilemma. Having already committed the country to a war that by the end of the fiscal year would cost $14 billion (as compared with a mere $100 million the previous fiscal year), he could either cut back on his Great Society programs to finance the war or he could ask for a tax hike only two years after putting through a major tax cut. Not surprisingly, the president found both alternatives unpalatable. The former meant reneging on a promise that lay at the very heart of his presidency; the latter, while it would provide for both guns *and* butter, was bound to be unpopular and to face stiff Congressional opposition in an election year.

In the end, the escalating costs of the Vietnam War would force Johnson to pursue both courses of action but not until it was too late to reverse the effects of spiraling inflation. In January 1966 he still held out hope that some middle course could be found, that somehow he could continue to wage his two-front war against poverty at home and communism in Southeast Asia without directly asking the American people to pay for it. In asking Congress for additional appropriations "to carry the new burdens" imposed by the war, he therefore also requested, and quickly received, a modest increase in excise taxes.

It was hardly enough. By the end of the year he was forced to admit there had been a "$10 billion error" in his projections of the cost of the war. The rate of inflation, moreover, was now running at nearly 3 percent. The following month, January 1967, he put before Congress a request for a 6 percent tax surcharge, only to withdraw it when the economy began to show signs of slowing down. Finally, in August 1967, he went back to Congress, this time asking for a 10 percent surcharge. By that point, however, opposition to the president's Great Society programs had grown strong enough to enable Congressional conservatives to demand a *quid pro quo*. If the president wanted a tax increase, said Wilbur Mills, the powerful chairman of the House Ways and Means Committee, he would first have to commit himself to deep cuts in social programs. After delaying that painful yet inevitable decision for nearly two years, Johnson reluctantly agreed to trim social spending.

Support for the Johnson administration's domestic policies had, in fact, steadily eroded since the summer of 1965.

New Chevrolets move along the assembly line at a General Motors plant outside Detroit in 1965. The automobile industry was only one part of the U.S. economy to enjoy the midsixties boom.

Urban riots, the growth of black radicalism, and the perceived excesses of federal "community action" programs, all contributed to an increasingly widespread feeling that the president's Great Society programs were not working or simply that the government was going too far, too fast. It was a sentiment that manifested itself in a variety of ways. Public opinion polls, for instance, reflected a sharp drop-off in white support for Johnson's handling of the racial issue between April 1965, in the aftermath of Selma, and late August 1965, after Watts. The shift was especially striking among white blue-collar workers, 41 percent of whom told Gallup pollsters that they thought the Johnson administration was moving "too fast" in the late summer, as compared with only 27 percent the previous spring.

Among local elected officials across the country, the new mood found expression in a steady stream of complaints about the uses to which federal poverty money was being put. Although some Great Society programs, like the Head Start preschool plan, were successful and highly praised, other schemes, like the decision to fund the Blackstone Rangers, a black Chicago street gang, provoked a great deal of public criticism. In Congress, opposition to the president's social reform agenda took the form of artful foot-dragging on a variety of new proposals, including an open-housing bill that would have facilitated desegregation of exclusively white communities.

By the fall of 1966 many political pundits were predicting that the "backlash" would result in a repudiation of Johnson's Great Society in the November Congressional elections. "The belief of many politicians and analysts," wrote Tom Wicker, the Washington bureau chief of the New York Times, on September 7, "is that while people may talk about Vietnam and inflation, they worry more about Negroes moving into the block, taking over their jobs and making their streets a battleground. Thus the white backlash . . . may become a major element in American politics this year." Although a record voter turnout on election day resulted in clear-cut Republican gains in both chambers of Congress, with the Democrats losing forty-seven seats in the House and three in the Senate, the extent to which the "backlash" actually materialized is difficult to assess. Ronald Reagan's victory in the California gubernatorial race, for example, was widely attributed to white outrage over Watts. Even more telling, a marked shift of ethnic blue-collar votes to Republican candidates in a number of major cities—New York, Boston, Philadelphia, Detroit, Chicago, and Los Angeles—seemed to indicate a rejection of Johnson's domestic policies, as did the victories of several outspoken opponents of open-housing legislation. On the other hand, as Time pointed out in its postelection coverage, seventeen out of the twenty-five congressmen deemed most likely to be unseated by the backlash were in fact returned to Congress. In Maryland, Democrat George Mahoney, whose campaign slogan was "Your Home Is Your Castle—Protect It," lost the race for

governor to Republican candidate Spiro Agnew, who supported a limited ban on housing discrimination. And in Massachusetts, Edward Brooke became the first black man to be elected to the Senate since Reconstruction.

If the election results were ambiguous with respect to domestic issues, they were even more so with respect to the other major issue of the day, the war in Vietnam. Despite mounting Congressional criticism of the president's handling of the war, from liberals who opposed further escalation as well as from conservatives who urged Johnson to go all-out to win, most Congressional candidates avoided making the war a central topic in their election campaigns. Only a few "peacenik" candidates, as Time dubbed them, entered the Congressional primaries, none of them won, and only in one case, the Berkeley-organized campaign of Robert Scheer, did a self-avowed peace candidate draw significant support. Nevertheless, wrote Andrew Kopkind in the New Republic, opponents of the war could find a "measure of hope" in the election of "a mini-block of 'peace Republicans.'"

[Senator Mark] Hatfield of Oregon, [Senator Charles] Percy of Illinois, and [Senator Edward] Brooke of Massachusetts will never bring about a reversal of US foreign policy but they all have serious doubts about Vietnam, and their presence in Washington will bolster congressional criticism. It will be harder next year for the Administration to get away with more escalation without cries from the Capitol.

Weighing the odds

Although the political landscape had changed markedly in the two years since Lyndon Johnson went before the American people to accept his "mandate for unity," the president remained confident that the growing crisis at home and abroad could still be resolved. In part his faith was simply a function of his character. Having committed himself to building the Great Society at home, and at the same time to winning the war against the Communists in Vietnam, he was determined to make good on both pledges. Yet in many respects it was a matter of plain old politics, an art in which Johnson was supremely skilled. From the outset he had recognized that "the aura and the halo" that surrounded him would eventually evaporate, that he would gradually lose his "power and authority . . . because that's what happened to President Woodrow Wilson, to President Roosevelt and to Truman and to Kennedy." As he confided to future Secretary of Health, Education, and Welfare Wilbur Cohen shortly after his inauguration in January 1965, "Something is going to come up, either something like the Vietnam War or something else where I will begin to lose all that I have now." The challenge, he told Cohen, was to accomplish as much as possible as quickly as possible.

And Johnson accomplished a lot. During his first eight-

White backlash. Young residents of Cicero, Illinois, an exclusively white suburb of Chicago, turn out in response to marches headed by Martin Luther King calling for open housing in the neighborhood in September 1966.

een months in office he managed to put through the tax cut, the Civil Rights Act of 1964, the Economic Opportunity Act, the Elementary and Secondary Education Act, Medicare, and the Voting Rights Act of 1965, to cite only the most notable achievements. It was, as Tom Wicker pointed out in early August 1965, a more substantial record of social legislation than most presidents compile in two full terms. If, by 1966, his political capital had begun to run out, in Johnson's view that was only to be expected. What it meant for the future, however, was that he would have to replenish the reservoir.

While the problems confronting the presidency in late 1966 may have been formidable, from Johnson's vantage point they were not insurmountable. Most of his opposition still stood on the periphery of the political spectrum, outside the mainstream of the national consensus, unable to mount a direct challenge to his leadership. Although the ranks of the antiwar protesters had grown markedly and their voices had become more shrill, they still represented a small minority of the American people. The same was true of the advocates of "black power," despite their increased visibility and the fear they seemed to instill in many whites. In Congress, the new conservative coalition was sure to cause Johnson problems on the domestic front, but with respect to Vietnam support for his policies seemed sufficiently firm. Even after the highly publicized Fulbright hearings in February 1966,* which openly questioned both the wisdom of the war effort and the president's authority to pursue it, no effort was made to tie Johnson's hands by refusing to appropriate funds for the war. Moreover, a vain attempt by Senator Wayne Morse to have the Senate repeal the Tonkin Gulf resolution had been crushed by a vote of ninety-two to five. Many Congressional critics of Johnson's war policy, in fact, favored a more aggressive military effort to defeat the Communists of Vietnam.

The key to President Johnson's future political fortunes, of course, was the outcome of the war itself. By the end of 1966 there were already 383,000 American troops in Vietnam, with another 42,000 scheduled to be deployed by mid-1967. The air war against the North was continuing at full throttle and, General William Westmoreland assured him, progress was being made. But how long it would actually take to win the war, no one could say for sure. That it eventually would be won, no one doubted—at least no one close enough to the president to influence his decisions. If the political deck was thus stacked against Lyndon Johnson, he did not yet know it. Instead he dealt his cards as he had dealt them in the past, carefully weighing the odds established long before by the framers of the postwar consensus, not fully realizing that that consensus was about to fall apart.

* See chapter seven of *America Takes Over*, another volume in THE VIETNAM EXPERIENCE.

For jobless young people (below), waiting to be interviewed for the Youth Corps in Newark, New Jersey, LBJ's Great Society offered an alternative to perennial unemployment. But in the midsixties, with the war in Vietnam beginning to drain funds from the war on poverty, government programs often failed to reach areas like East 100th Street, Harlem, New York, (left).

War Comes Home

More than anything else, the return of their dead from Vietnam awakened Americans to the costs of the war. The sight of flag-draped coffins arriving in towns across the country raised the inevitable question: "Why?"

One of those coffins bore the body of Private First Class Harold T. Edmondson, Jr., a nineteen-year-old native of Charleston, South Carolina, who had enlisted in the army after graduating from high school. Edmondson had hoped to be trained in the missile program but instead became a paratrooper, first serving in the 82d Airborne and then going to Vietnam with the 1st Brigade, 101st Airborne Division. He was killed in his first battle on January 30, 1966, in II Corps Tactical Zone along the east coast of Vietnam. His funeral, held in Mount Pleasant, South Carolina, on February 14, 1966, was captured on film by a passing photographer.

Family, friends, and an honor guard accompany the coffin of PFC Edmondson, killed in action in Vietnam.

During the funeral service a gravedigger brushes away a tear.

Above. Putting one son to rest, Harold T. Edmondson, Sr., tries to comfort another, Harold Jr.'s younger brother Kenneth. Left. "In the midst of life we are in death." A local bishop reads the prayer at PFC Edmondson's grave site in Mount Pleasant, South Carolina.

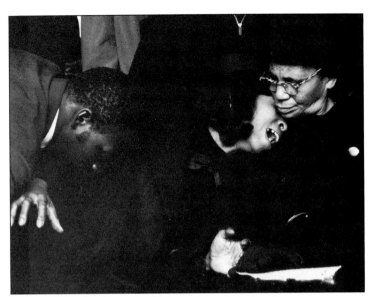

Edmondson's mother, herself a preacher, consoles his aunt while his brother folds the flag just presented to them.

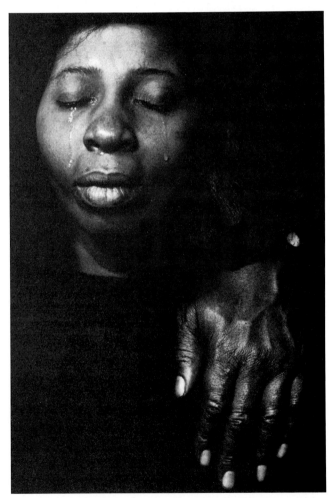

Above. *Ethel G. Scott, the deceased soldier's aunt, weeps at the grave side.* Right. *At the burial site, Edmondson's grandfather, George German, and another relative, Christina German, stand in silent mourning.*

Following page. *The young private's name is one among the more than 58,000 names of Vietnam War dead engraved on the Vietnam Veterans Memorial in Washington, D.C.*

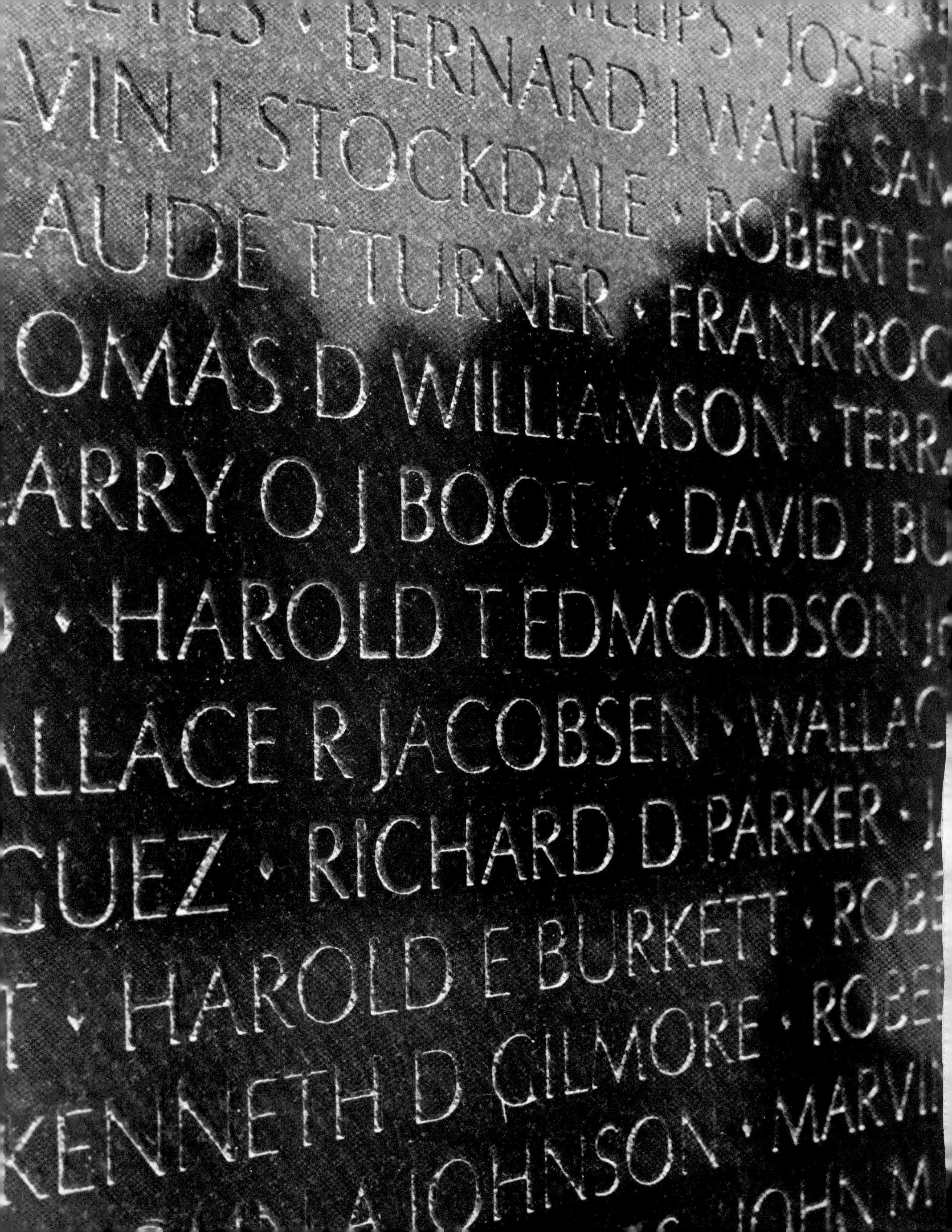

BERNARD J WAL

VIN J STOCKDALE

LAUDE T TURNER · FRANK ROC

OMAS D WILLIAMSON · TERRA

ARRY O J BOOTY · DAVID J BU

· HAROLD T EDMONDSON

ALLACE R JACOBSEN · WALLA

GUEZ · RICHARD D PARKER

HAROLD E BURKETT · ROBE

KENNETH D GILMORE · ROBE

JOHNSON · MARVI

Private First Class Harold T. Edmondson, Jr.,
1946–1966

Fragmentation

(1967-1968)

As with so many important events of what was to become the "student movement," it was neither planned nor predicted. Nor would it have been possible without an assist from policymakers in Washington. In early February 1966 General Lewis B. Hershey, director of the Selective Service System, announced that local draft boards would henceforth be free to draft previously deferred students who ranked in the lower levels of their college classes. The SSS would ask universities to report the class rank of their male students, information that would then be passed on to the local draft boards.

The SDS national leadership immediately announced a program of spring demonstrations protesting the new order. But the local chapter of SDS at the University of Chicago chose a different tack. Rather than focus their protest on the Selective Service System, they decided to challenge the role assigned to the university in Hershey's new plan. They organized an *ad hoc* committee,

Students Against the Rank, or SAR. SAR had but one demand: The university must end its policy of ranking students. By doing so, the university would be unable to provide the government with the required information.

From protest to confrontation

The students first tried conventional tactics. They held discussions with the administration, asked permission to state their arguments before the faculty (but were refused), and signed petitions. When all of these attempts failed, 400 students occupied the administration building, closing down its offices for five days before departing peacefully. It was the first closing of a university administration building since the Berkeley Free Speech Movement of 1964.

In the end, both the faculty and administration remained firm and SAR's demand was not met. However, similar sit-ins spread to many other campuses, including Cornell, Wisconsin, and San Francisco State, and earned the support of many faculty members. Within two years hundreds of colleges had abandoned the ranking of their students in order to keep the information out of the hands of Selective Service officials. The University of Chicago was one of them.

What was novel about the Chicago protest was that the local SDS chapter linked protest against the war to attacks on the multiversity. SAR listed three reasons for their protest: (1) "an immoral and discriminatory national policy"; (2) "the transformation of the university into a coding and classifying machine for the Selective Service"; and (3) the transformation of "a community of scholars into a set of madly competing factions" resulting from the scramble by students to earn high ranks. Taken together, the three reasons at once attacked the escalating war in Vietnam, the university's complicity in that war, and what was seen as the perversion of the original ideal of the university as an academy of learning into a multiversity.

The importance of this tactical innovation was not lost on the national leaders of SDS. The summer of 1966 witnessed the rise of a new movement that would persist for the rest of the decade: student power. For young student activists it was an auspicious time. The rise of a separatist "black power" movement had all but closed the civil rights movement to whites. The possibilities of expanding the power and influence of the "New Left" on many college campuses were obvious.

Newly elected SDS National Secretary Carl Davidson elaborated on the theory behind student power and its connection with a radical critique of American society in a manifesto entitled, "A Student Syndicalist Movement":

AID officials, Peace Corpsmen, military officers, CIA officials, segregationist judges, corporation lawyers, politicians of all sorts . . . where do they come from? They are products of the factories we live in and work in. . . .

They were shaped and formed on an assembly line that starts with children entering junior high school and ends with junior bureaucrats in commencement robes. And the rules and regulations of in loco parentis are essential tools along that entire assembly line.

In loco parentis. The Latin term, meaning "in place of parents," became a rallying cry for student power advocates. *In loco parentis* was the theory, adopted by most universities, that they became the guardians of the students enrolled on their campuses. Like parents, they could determine rules of social conduct. For generations students had bristled under regulations that determined when dormitories would be locked at night, when a woman could visit a man's room, and should they decide to sit on a dormitory bed whether their feet had to remain on the floor. For generations students had petitioned administrators and faculty to change these rules but to no avail. Now SDS was taking the lead, not in petitioning, but in demanding that these rules be changed as a matter of student rights.

Throughout the two years following the Chicago sit-in, student activists shrewdly combined the issue of university complicity in the war with campus questions concerning the quality of student life, both academic and social. At Penn State SDS challenged the concept of *in loco parentis.* At the University of Nebraska SDS led a left-wing student party that won on the platform of a student bill of rights. Increasingly students were demanding a restructuring of the university decision-making processes to provide a greater voice for students in the making of academic and social policy.

Under the banner of student power, protests and demonstrations spread throughout the country. One survey of 246 educational institutions of all types revealed that 90 percent experienced protests against university administration policies, and at more than 100 of these colleges and universities the protests involved over half of the student body. The most comprehensive survey of student activism was conducted by the Educational Testing Service. It found a dramatic increase in student demonstrations in the academic year 1967 from the level of 1964–65. Protests against university policy increased from 161 to 231, against racial discrimination on campus from 42 to 155. Direct actions against the war rose from 178 to 327.

Most dramatic was the increase in protest against university complicity in the war. No such protests were recorded in the academic year 1964–65, while three years later 602 campuses experienced demonstrations and protests on such issues as armed forces recruiting on campus, college involvement in the selective service process (including ranking of students), and Dow Chemical and CIA

Preceding page. *America at war with itself. Chicago's black ghetto erupts in flames following the assassination of Martin Luther King in April 1968.*

Students stage a sit-in in June 1966 at the uptown campus of City College of New York as a protest against the university for releasing their class ranks to draft boards. The sign in the foreground reads, "Don't Use Our Grades."

A Chorus of Protest

Some of the first cries against the war in Vietnam were set to music. In the latter half of the sixties, rock musicians drew upon the folk and protest song heritage to sing more socially conscious lyrics, with topics ranging from pleas for universal love and brotherhood to crowd-pleasing celebrations of drugs and defiance.

In 1963, while civil rights marchers were being repelled with firehoses and police dogs, Bob Dylan sang:

How many years can some people exist
Before they're allowed to be free?
The answer, my friend, is blowin' in the wind.
The answer is blowin' in the wind.

Dylan was the heir to the musical social commentary and protest legacy of Woody Guthrie, who had sung of the working man in the thirties, and more recently Pete Seeger, called one of the first "flower children." In the early sixties, other artists who sprang from the same Greenwich Village coffee houses as Dylan, such as Joan Baez and Peter, Paul, and Mary, sang similar themes of peace and social justice. The Byrds, a folk-rock quintet heavily influenced by Dylan, echoed an Old Testament passage put to music by Pete Seeger in "Turn! Turn! Turn!":

To everything there is a season . . .
And a time to every purpose under heaven . . .

A time of love, a time to hate
A time for peace, I swear it's not too late.©

Bob Dylan (with guitar) and Pete Seeger sing in support of the civil rights movement, 1962.

A hit in early 1966, "just as we were learning how to spell Vietnam," said one music critic, the song "simultaneously urged commitment and acceptance."

By mid-decade protest lyrics were finding a receptive audience across the country. Young people were becoming involved in a stylized subculture of music, clothes, and drugs. They were inspired by early folk artists and new directions in music by such artists as the Beatles, whose seminal 1967 album *Sergeant Pepper's Lonely Hearts Club Band* reflected various Eastern mystical and musical influences. Joining them were refugees from the "beat generation" of the fifties. The re-

sult was a lifestyle that became known as the "counterculture." For a group that had rejected many of the values of the older generation, it was not hard to accept new and diverse styles of music, especially those steeped in the expanding drug culture. *Rolling Stone's* Jon Landau wrote that among youth, "rock was not only viewed as a form of entertainment," but as "an essential component of a 'new culture,' along with drugs and radical politics." Many shared the alienation from the older generation expressed by the British band the Who, who sang in 1966:

Things they do look awful cold
Hope I die before I get old.©

From countercultural meccas like San Francisco's Haight-Ashbury district came a style of music known as psychedelia, a term meaning "mind expansion." With most of their fans—and quite often their members—high on marijuana, LSD, or other drugs, bands such as the Grateful Dead, the Jefferson Airplane, the Jimi Hendrix Experience, and the Doors played a freeform, loosely structured style of music that expanded the limits of rock as well as the minds of its listeners.

For music fans, "acid rock" was a means of escaping the world around them—a world whose wars and politics ran counter to their declared ideals of peace, universal brotherhood, and transcendent consciousness. Rock concerts became places for young rebels to congregate and "commune" with each other.

The festival at Monterey, California, in the summer of 1967, drew over 50,000 "flower children" and introduced such rising stars as Janis Joplin, Jimi Hendrix, the Buffalo Springfield, the Mamas and the Papas, and the Who.

Woodstock was the ultimate orgy of rock music and countercultural celebration (see picture essay, page 138). For three days in August 1969, between 300,000 and 400,000 people listened—or were just there—as musicians sang of the glories of peace, love, brotherhood, and

and most disillusioned songs ever composed in American music history. The Jefferson Airplane, who once followed the advice of Timothy Leary to "turn on, tune in, drop out," now exhorted youth to "Tear down the walls/We got a revolution." The time for action, they sang, was now.

Disillusionment with American institutions and social order developed throughout the decade. Graham Nash's "Chicago" was a bitter condemnation of the beating of protesters at the 1968 Democratic Convention.

had given rise to angrier and more bitter music. The counterculture was more disenchanted than ever, and its music preached both peace and confrontation. Ironically, perhaps the most fitting postscript to the era of American musical protest of the sixties came from a British band that had stopped touring America in 1966. John Lennon and the Beatles sang:

You say you want a revolution
Well, you know, we all want to change the
world . . .

Minstrels of the counterculture. Left. The Grateful Dead. Right. Country Joe McDonald at Woodstock, August 1969.

hallucinogenic drugs. Some lyrics reflected the increasing anger over Vietnam and the growing political tone of rock music. Country Joe and the Fish, a San Francisco group, sang sardonically:

Be the first one on your block
To have your boy come home in a box . . .
(And it's) one, two, three, what are we
*   fighting for?*
Don't ask me, I don't give a damn
The next stop is Vietnam.

Such a bitter chorus was not necessarily anomalous: By Woodstock, the disenchantment of the younger generation had been manifested in some of the angriest

In 1969 Creedence Clearwater Revival assailed the privileges of the upper class, especially in the draft, in "Fortunate Son":

It ain't me, it ain't me
I ain't no senator's son
It ain't me, it ain't me
I ain't the fortunate one.

After the murder of four students at Kent State University by members of the Ohio National Guard, Crosby, Stills, Nash, and Young sang angrily:

This summer I hear the drumming
Four dead in Ohio.

The growing death toll in Vietnam, the confrontations in Chicago and Kent State

But when you talk about destruction,
Don't you know that you can count me out.

In another version of "Revolution," however, Lennon says "in" immediately after that last line. The restlessness of the counterculture was revealed in an agonizing uncertainty as to the final solution. Revolution or universal love? The answer, to the minstrels of the age, was not as clear as the problem.

recruiting. Even a partial list of institutions experiencing the protests reads like a cross section of American higher education: Brown, Columbia, Cornell, Iowa, Iowa State, Missouri, Nebraska, SUNY-New Paltz, Northern Illinois, Old Dominion, Pomona, San Francisco State, Toledo, UCLA, Wisconsin.

In all, the Educational Testing Service found political protests on over 1,400 campuses across the nation during the school year 1967-68. This represented nearly half of America's 3,000 institutions of higher learning. These protests varied widely from peaceful assembly to illegal building occupations, but the overall pattern showed an unmistakable increase in student protest compared with just three years earlier.

Although ETS found that in more than half of the cases SDS had spearheaded the protests, the members of the organization remained a tiny minority on campus. SDS itself reported a membership of 25,000 students out of the nearly 6 million students enrolled in colleges throughout the country. The protests, however, revealed a troubling pattern that was to plague university administrators for the next five years. The ability of SDS to mobilize sizable minorities and, at times, majorities of students around particular issues was wholly out of proportion to their numbers. Many students were apparently sympathetic to the issues raised by SDS if not to the organization itself. Nowhere during the school year 1967-68 was this pattern more evident than at Columbia, a university that was to join Berkeley as the symbol of student protest.

The battle of Morningside Heights

For three years the tactics of the New Left had slowly escalated in intensity. In 1965 antiwar protesters generally limited their antiwar activities to legal marches and peaceful teach-ins. Soon students began to borrow from the tactics of the civil rights movement. Faced with police arrest after an illegal sit-in (usually at a draft center), demonstrators remained passive and limp. Suffering arrest still possessed the quasi-theological meaning expressed by Martin Luther King as "witness to evil."

The change was gradual and slow. At the October 1967 march on the Pentagon, the demonstration was deliberately split into two distinct "actions." The first was a peaceful assemblage at the Lincoln Memorial and the second a march across the Potomac River to the Pentagon, where half of the original crowd vowed to remain until arrested. Although a few extreme elements actually broke through National Guard lines to storm the Pentagon (and were quickly arrested), the rest of the 30,000 who gathered waited patiently until curfew to be placed under arrest. The ensuing violence of the night was almost entirely a result of the overreaction of the National Guard in making arrests. True to the tradition of the civil rights era, the protesters remained passive in the face of physical force.*

In the aftermath of the Pentagon protests, SDS leaders sensed a new and increased militancy among the nation's students. Later that fall Carl Davidson wrote a new SDS position paper entitled, "Toward Institutional Resistance," calling for "the disruption, dislocation, and destruction of the military's access to manpower, intelligence, or resources of our universities."

Among those who agreed with Davidson was Columbia University junior Mark Rudd. In the early winter of 1968 Rudd and his allies, known as the "action faction," gained control of Columbia SDS. By spring the action faction had planned a series of confrontations with the university administration. Defying a university ban against indoor demonstrations, SDSers staged a March rally inside Low Library to protest Columbia's participation in the Institute for Defense Analysis (IDA), a consortium of twelve universities that provided consulting services to the Defense Department. Six students faced disciplinary action. A few weeks later Rudd interrupted a memorial service for the slain civil rights leader Martin Luther King, yelling that the memorial amounted to "hypocrisy and an obscenity" in a "racist institution" like Columbia.

With the stage thus set, SDS called a rally for April 23 to join their two issues of the war abroad and racism at home. SDS demanded the end of the university's affiliation with IDA and a termination of the construction of a new gymnasium in Morningside Park, a city-owned plot of land in the adjacent Harlem neighborhood. SDS charged that the gym would not serve the ghetto inhabitants and was little more than a "land-grab" by the university.

The situation was already tense when 400 supporters of SDS appeared at the demonstration. They were joined by nearly 1,000 neutral onlookers and taunted by some 300 counterdemonstrators. More important, however, was the unexpected appearance of the Students' Afro-American Society. The SAS had previously played only an apolitical role in the affairs of Columbia and had never joined in the demonstrations of the white New Left. But in the aftermath of the King assassination they not only joined the protest of their white fellow students, but challenged them.

As the onlookers milled around at the conclusion of the SDS speeches, Bill Sales, a leader of SAS, took the podium and ignited the rally: "If you're talking about identifying with the Vietnamese struggle . . . you don't need to go marching downtown. . . . You strike a blow at the gym, you strike a blow for the Vietnamese people."

A brief game of cat and mouse between the administration and the demonstrators now began. Attempting to storm Low Library, which also served as the main administration building and housed President Grayson Kirk's private office, the students found the doors locked and well guarded. Veering northward, the students heeded the cries of, "To the gym! To the gym!" only to be met by city

* For more on the march on the Pentagon, see Chapter five of *Nineteen Sixty-Eight*, another volume in THE VIETNAM EXPERIENCE.

In April 1968, protesters march against Columbia University's construction of a gymnasium in Morningside Heights.

police at the construction site. But here the students served notice that Columbia would be different. Rather than peacefully await arrest, the students engaged the police in a brief but violent scuffle before retreating to the campus. Now crying, "IDA must go! IDA must go!" the students finally found themselves a step ahead of the administration at Hamilton Hall, an auxiliary administration building located near Low Library.

On the evening of April 23 black and white students huddled in Hamilton Hall, holding Acting Dean Henry Coleman and two others hostage overnight. But even before Coleman was released, the SAS had second thoughts, not about the building takeover, but about their white allies. Arguing that black students would lead the protest, and that white radicals could best support the black effort by opening up a separate front, the blacks ordered the whites out of Hamilton Hall. Rudd and company made their way into the now unguarded Low Library, establishing their headquarters in the office of President Kirk. During the next two days three more university buildings were occupied by white students, bringing the total number of squatters to nearly 700. All classes were canceled.

The faculty, meanwhile, attempted to mediate the dispute between students and administration. Its proposal, to halt construction of the gym at least temporarily and to establish a tripartite disciplinary commission consisting of students, faculty, and administrators (itself a major reform of university procedures), was rejected by both the students and the administration. The protesters and their allies now demanded total amnesty.

With the failure of the faculty intervention on April 29, President Kirk requested that the New York City police clear the seized buildings. After dispersing an angry Harlem crowd gathered outside, the police entered Hamilton Hall, where the black students permitted themselves to be arrested and removed peacefully.

Unbeknown to the white students, the SAS group occupying Hamilton Hall had made arrangements with the administration to leave the building peacefully. They had, in fact, spent much of the day planning the arrests with city officials. The white students, however, trusting the statements of SAS leaders who vowed never to relinquish the building until their demands were met, made preparations to resist.

Outside of Low Library allies and even opponents of the occupiers attempted to block the police as they entered the building. Students, faculty, and press alike were shoved aside, some pummeled with nightsticks and, in the opinion of doctors who treated them, perhaps even blackjacks, and thrown down the steps. Inside the building, the police dismantled the symbolic barricades the students had fashioned from office furniture and confronted the waiting protesters.

The students were divided about how to react to arrest. The majority wanted to maintain the civil rights tradition of passivity. The more militant, however, now believed this to be a sign of weakness and urged resistance to arrest, no matter how futile. In the end it made little difference. Nonviolent students were beaten and dragged down stairs. Those offering resistance were equally bludgeoned. All were carted off to waiting paddy wagons where they continued their protest, singing, pounding on the vehicle walls, and raising a new cry: "Strike! Strike!"

By sunrise more than 700 people had been arrested and more than 100 were injured. Still the disorder continued. Outraged students swelled the ranks of the protesters. The rest of the school year was disrupted by class boycotts, while faculty, students, and administration failed to settle the conflict. Amnesty for those involved in the initial protest became the most important issue. In mid-May students again occupied buildings on campus, and again Grayson Kirk turned to the New York City police.

The transition from confrontation to resistance was completed. Not only did the new occupiers of Hamilton Hall engage the police in hand-to-hand combat, but throughout the campus students hurled bricks and obscenities at the police, erected barricades, and broke windows. Nearly 500 members of the city's Tactical Police Force, later augmented by plainclothesmen, conducted a sweep through the campus, hurling tear gas canisters, clubbing fleeing students, and, in direct violation of their orders, entering two dormitories where they assaulted students at their desks.

Two weeks later the university held its annual commencement. A countercommencement attended by 2,000 formed the inevitable end to Columbia's violent and divisive spring.

The new student tactics at Columbia shocked the nation. *Fortune* magazine warned its readers that the new generation of student activists wanted a revolution, "not a protest . . . but an honest-to-God revolution." And Mark Rudd agreed. "We are out for social and political revolution, nothing less."

Many of Rudd's contemporaries would have disagreed with him. Lost in the headlines of the dramatic story at Columbia were the far more peaceful manifestations that typified the overwhelming majority of protests taking place that year at half of America's campuses. Equally lost was the other half of the campuses where satisfied stu-

dents continued their work without protest. Outside of the campuses, and generally disapproving of the student activists, were those American youths who never went to college. A survey conducted by Daniel Yankelovich in October 1968 revealed sharp disagreements between college youth and their noncollege peers. Only 17 percent of noncollege youth felt draft resistance was justified, compared to two-thirds of the students attending major universities. Three-quarters of noncollege youth opposed civil disobedience under all circumstances, compared to only one-quarter of the students at these elite colleges.

If these facts suggest that America's youth was as badly divided as their parents over the war and protest, there were other signs that the "student movement" had the potential of becoming a "youth movement." Young Americans not attending college were almost as likely (44 percent) as college students (50 percent) to agree that America's was a "sick society," a view increasingly shared by many in America's urban ghettos.

The cry of "black power" was born in the Deep South. But the concrete and debris of decaying urban ghettos proved to be as fertile to its growth as the alluvial soil of

the Mississippi Delta. In the South, the concept of black power was nurtured by such strong organizations as SNCC and CORE. Northern urban blacks, however, remained largely untouched by these organizations. They would give to black power a meaning that would drive many living in northern ghettos to reject the ideology of the biracial civil rights coalition that had been so carefully nurtured over a decade.

From Selma to Detroit

The first victims of black power in the North were those whites who had labored with civil rights organizations in the South. When not literally pushed out of separatist black organizations, they resigned because of hostility toward them. Lillian Smith, author of *Strange Fruit* and *Killers of the Dream* and a long-time CORE advocate, resigned her membership because she perceived in the organization a new element of "nihilists, black nationalists, and plain old-fashioned haters. . . . The new killers of the dream." Moderate black leaders also backed away. Roy Wilkins, head of the National Association for the Ad-

Above. *Members of the "majority coalition," which opposed the siege of Columbia's Low Library, scuffle with protest sympathizers. Inset. A student protester, John Kanliain, flashes a peace sign after being injured by police during the clearing of the library.*

107

vancement of Colored People, condemned black power as "anti-white power . . . a reverse Hitler . . . a reverse Ku Klux Klan . . . [which] can only mean death."

But black power activity rapidly spread north where the rhetoric of Stokely Carmichael was radically interpreted. Its most gruesome manifestation was the series of riots that struck northern cities from 1966 to 1968 and left their deadly legacy: 60,000 arrests, 10,000 injuries, and 250 deaths. Nearly 100,000 National Guardsmen were called into action in 1967 and 1968. Most important, riots left the ghetto dwellers with neighborhoods and livelihoods charred by the conflagrations.

The rise of the black power movement was, of course, not an outgrowth of the Vietnam War. The civil rights movement possessed a dynamic of its own that probably made the appearance of black power inevitable in any case. The war in Vietnam, however, had a dramatic impact both on America's black population, as well as on the movement whose goal was to make them equal citizens. Because the draft disproportionately affected Americans below the middle class, the war directly hit draft-aged

males of black families. Moreover, the rising costs of the war both drained financial resources from Lyndon Johnson's war on poverty and made many white Americans unsympathetic to large-scale spending on social welfare programs. As early as May 1965, Gallup polls showed that blacks were 50 percent more likely than whites to think that U.S. involvement in Vietnam was a mistake. Two years later that gap had widened to 60 percent. And by October 1968, when the Gallup organization asked Americans whether they were "doves" or "hawks," blacks (70 percent) were twice as likely as whites (35 percent) to label themselves doves.

The escalation of the war in Vietnam caused especially perplexing problems for Martin Luther King and other moderate black leaders. From the outset of the civil rights movement they had strongly supported American foreign policy. But by 1967, pressured both by his own constituency and by the retreat of the Johnson administration from the programs of the Great Society, King made a dramatic move: He broke rank. Speaking at New York City's Riverside Church, King blamed Vietnam for the failure of

Speaking Out

On April 15, 1967, New York's largest peace demonstration since the beginning of the war wound its way through the streets of the city from Central Park to the United Nations. The rally was made all the more significant by the vituperative denunciations of American involvement in Vietnam by major black leaders. SNCC leader Stokely Carmichael called America's Vietnam policy "brutal and racist" and attacked the draft, particularly as it affected blacks. Martin Luther King also denounced U.S. foreign policy and challenged the government to "honor its word [and] stop the bombing of North Vietnam." By the late 1960s, civil rights leaders stood divided over the direction of the black movement, but their shared objections to the presence of America—and particularly of black Americans—in Vietnam drew them together in opposition to the U.S. government.

progress in the war on poverty: "Then came the buildup in Vietnam and I watched the program broken and eviscerated." King, thus, in effect, rejected one part of the postwar consensus, that America had the ability and resources *both* to enforce a policy of containment abroad and solve its economic problems at home. King was preaching that America had been faced with a choice, and the Johnson administration had chosen military adventure abroad over equality at home.

King had come only very slowly and with grave misgivings to his criticism of the war. Black power leaders and organizations had no such compunction. At the same national CORE conference in July 1966 that officially adopted a program of black power, the assembled black leaders also passed a resolution calling for the withdrawal of American troops from Vietnam. Later that year SNCC joined CORE in its condemnation of American policy: "Vietnamese are being murdered because the United States is pursuing an aggressive policy in violation of international law." In the following year, sixteen members of SNCC refused draft inductions, citing Stokeley Carmi-

chael's complaint that the draft was "calculated genocide" against blacks.

Black power advocates came to view America's commitment to containment as but another manifestation of racism, at least as practiced in the Third World. The repudiation of containment thus joined the original impulse of the black power movement—a loss of faith that even unbroken prosperity would in itself bring full equality to American blacks.

The black power movement reflected the growing frustration of America's black citizens at the slowness of progress in the struggle for equality, particularly in northern ghettos. The majority of blacks continued to view integration and equality as their goals. But this commitment did not necessarily mean a rejection of black power. When coupled with long-standing grievances, the ideology of black power could erupt into a violent rejection of the American social and economic system. Such was the taut situation in Detroit as the summer of 1967 began.

Early on the morning of Sunday, July 23, 1967, members of the Detroit Police Department entered a "blind pig," an

Left. *Martin Luther King denounces American involvement in Vietnam before 100,000 ralliers outside of the U.N. Above. A group of protesters at the New York rally.*

after-hours bar illegally dispensing liquor on 12th Street in the heart of the city's west side black ghetto. The police found eighty-two guests present. Usually only a dozen customers or so frequented the bar. But that night friends were celebrating the safe return of two black servicemen from Vietnam. During the hour in which it took police to arrest the party goers, a crowd of about 200 assembled and began stoning the police cars and paddy wagons as they left the neighborhood. By 8:00 A.M. 3,000 people had gathered in the streets, and by late afternoon fire was raging in 100 blocks of the neighborhood. Looting and burning became so extreme that early in the evening President Johnson sent in the National Guard.

By midnight Monday, 4,000 persons were in jail. By Thursday, when the rioting was quelled, 2,700 regular army troops had been sent into the city.

What caused the riot? The *Detroit News* quoted "police and military officials" who pointed to "the vicious pattern of deadly sniping that prolonged Detroit's racial maelstrom." The police concluded that "there already is strong evidence to suggest a national conspiracy." They refused to issue any further elaboration. There were two problems with their theory: None of the alleged outside agitators was ever found, nor was sufficient evidence gathered to convict even a single sniper. The Kerner Commission, moreover, reported eight months later that of the forty-three persons killed during the riot, at most two or three *may* have been killed by rioters, none by sniper fire. The commission charged the police with the deaths of at least twenty people and the National Guard with another nine. Twenty-seven persons were arrested and charged with sniping, but in twenty-four cases the charges were dropped and none of the other three was convicted. The Kerner Commission concluded:

During the daylight hours of [Wednesday] July 26, there were 534 such reports [of sniper fire]. As they proliferated, the pressure on law enforcement officers to uncover the snipers became intense. Homes were broken into. Searches were made on the flimsiest of tips.

Subsequent investigation suggested that the police, themselves, were the cause of sniper alarms. Fearing sniper fire, they began shooting out streetlights. The wild firing in the air probably provoked residents to report the presence of snipers.

Godfrey Hodgson, a British reporter who witnessed the riot, concluded that the riot came about because blacks saw "an opportunity to defy a system of law and order which seemed to many blacks fundamentally biased against them." The arrest of the party goers at the blind

A street in Detroit's 12th Street ghetto area goes up in smoke during the first day of the riots, Sunday, July 23, 1967. By the time the riots were over four days later, fire damage had reached $45 million.

A lone policeman stands guard over a looted supermarket in Detroit during the riots.

pig was immediately followed by looting. Whites on the scene recalled a "carnival atmosphere" at the time. While blacks did not quite remember showing such feelings, many were certainly happy to take what they considered to be theirs. (In this they were joined by not a few poor whites from neighboring streets.) The police did little to stop the looting, fearing that "not one of our policemen would have come out alive," according to Police Commissioner Ray Girardin.

If economic grievances had propelled the original looting, deeper social grievances inspired the riot itself. There was no difference in unemployment rates between the black rioters and nonrioters. Half of the 83 percent of the arrested participants who were employed held the best of ghetto jobs—work in auto factories—and were members of the UAW. The rioters typified the 12th Street ghetto, a residential neighborhood where many inhabitants owned the homes in which they lived. As Rennie Freeman, a black organizer, put it:

Those rioters was running down the streets and I see these middle class people standing out on the porches giving the Black Power sign. You know, women in house dresses giving the fist. And it is clear that this thing about the lower class being disenchanted is bullshit. Negroes are disenchanted. . . . Everybody is pissed off.

Harvard sociologist Lee Rainwater put it more academically. The problem was a "caste system" that confined even relatively comfortable blacks to the ghetto. Rainwater concluded that even those "who by dint of their own efforts, manage to come reasonably close to an average American standard are still subjected to special disabilities and insults because of their confinement to a ghetto community."

The war in Vietnam no more caused the Detroit riot than it caused the rise of black power. But the war often was mentioned in comments from ghetto residents, and it helped to shape attitudes toward violence in general. Frank Ditto, a community organizer who moved to Detroit not long before the riots, told a television interviewer, "The way society looks at these things, we would say it's unfortunate, but the United States is dropping napalm bombs on women and children over in Vietnam and no one has anything to say about it."

The Kerner Commission was also interested in the connection between the war and the riot. It asked the ghetto inhabitants whether America was "worth fighting for." Of those who admitted participating in the riot, nearly 40 percent responded "no," compared with about 10 percent of the nonrioters. (Over 50 percent so responded in a poll of participants in a riot in Newark, New Jersey, in 1967.) One black told the commission, "If Negroes had an equal chance it would be worth fighting for." And a woman complained, "My husband came back from Vietnam and nothing had changed."

Back to "The World"

Poor blacks rioting. Affluent white students rioting. To many citizens, America at the beginning of 1968 seemed to be turning into a jungle. But some 1.7 million of their fellow citizens knew otherwise. They were Vietnam veterans and they had been to the real jungle. For most the transition to civilian life, even if it carried a heavy psychological burden, at least promised tangible economic rewards. The war they had fought overseas had brought the economy at home to a near boiling point; there seemed to be jobs for everyone. On January 1, 1968, only 2.4 percent of all Vietnam veterans were unemployed, compared to 3.9 percent of the population as a whole. But in comparison to their World War II and Korean War predecessors, this was about the only advantage Vietnam vets enjoyed, and even it was enjoyed unequally. Nearly one-half of all blacks reenlisted, most because they found few employment opportunities in civilian life.

For those wishing to attend school, veterans' benefits were pitiful. While America's veterans of the two previous wars received full tuition, book costs, and $75 per month, Vietnam veterans received only the $75 per month, until 1969, to cover all expenses, at a time when a private college cost $3,000 to $4,000 per year. In 1969 this stipend was raised to $165 per month, provided that the veteran was a full-time student. Even this sum was insufficient to fund an education at many colleges and universities, and the proviso that the veteran engage in full-time study severely limited opportunities to earn additional income.

There were early warning signs of a more severe problem. Marine First Lieutenant Leo Stover won a Silver Star in the Vietnam War and came home to find a good job as a flight engineer for TWA. One night after his return to the U.S., he nearly destroyed a cocktail lounge because other customers would not quiet down and allow him to hear a televised speech by General Westmoreland.

Many years later, Lieutenant Stover's outburst of violence would have been diagnosed as a classic example of PTSD, Post-Traumatic Stress Disorder. This psychological condition, however, was recognized neither by the government nor by mental health professionals until the 1980s. The national news media first began to inform their readers of the veterans' adjustment problems in 1968. In one area of crucial importance to veterans—higher education—no systematic study of the special needs of veterans was undertaken until 1971, when a group of psychologists and educators formulated a special program for veterans at Southern Illinois University.

If the typical veteran was often misunderstood by Americans, even more perplexing was a group of veterans who actually participated in antiwar protests. The Vietnam Veterans Against the War (VVAW) was formed in April 1967 when a half-dozen veterans, marching in uniform in a New York City antiwar demonstration, met by chance. However small a minority they were, they provided evidence of a new element in the ever-increasing circle of antiwar protesters in the country.

The veterans who returned in 1967 and 1968 had been among the first to be drafted after the commitment of American combat troops to Vietnam. Many, in fact, had volunteered for the peacetime army prior to 1965. They had accepted assignment to Vietnam, even if reluctantly, as a patriotic duty. The attitudes of their younger brothers and neighbors, however, had changed markedly by 1967.

In a 1981 survey of Vietnam veterans conducted on behalf of the Veterans' Administration, almost two-thirds of the Vietnam veterans who entered the armed forces prior to 1967 said that they had "positive" feelings upon enlisting or being drafted. For those entering after 1967, such feelings were expressed by a minority, 41 percent.

In the 1960s, as it is today, Somerville, Massachusetts, was a working-class suburb of Boston. The population was almost entirely white, with Irish-Americans predominating. It was ideal territory for armed forces recruiters. One survey of Somerville's veterans conducted in 1973 revealed that 84 percent had volunteered for service. But when asked why they volunteered, only 22 percent offered reasons classified as positive. Instead, men said they joined to "get away from home" or to "avoid trouble with the police." Others simply said that they were "sick of school" or wanted the "security of the job." But the most common response was "nothing else to do." Few of them considered other alternatives. One commented, "There was a time in my life when I said if they call me I won't go. But they caught me at a weak spot [with no plan]." But the usual explanation was less prosaic: "I'd lost my driver's license, everybody else went in, so that was it." The researcher concluded:

It was simply taken for granted that unless you could find an alternative, it would happen as inevitably as you would have to go on welfare if you couldn't find a job. Even if you aimed at going to college for an out, the army would likely get you while you were working to save to pay your tuition.

Boiling over

In the fall of 1967 political commentators could—and many did—predict with confidence that if Lyndon Johnson chose to seek reelection in 1968 the Democratic party would surely stand with him. It was not hard to figure out why. Despite growing economic problems largely induced by the war, especially inflation, America was riding the crest of a great wave of prosperity.

In early 1966 unemployment sank below the 4 percent level that economists defined as "full employment." By the end of 1967 the figure stood at 3.75 percent, and one year later it fell to its lowest level of that decade or the next, 3.3 percent. Even this figure was somewhat misleading since thousands of jobs went begging. In mid-1967 the Illinois

Department of Labor reported 75,000 openings for skilled laborers in the Chicago area alone.

The gross national product reflected the prosperity with an unbroken string of quarterly rises. Where the GNP had passed the bellwether $500 billion mark only in 1960, by mid-1966 it surpassed three-quarters of a trillion dollars.

But Lyndon Johnson had built a looming problem for himself and the country when he refused to press for the tax increase he needed in 1966. Wilbur Mills, chairman of the House Ways and Means Committee, simply said no, not in a Congressional election year. Mills said no again in 1967, not unless Lyndon Johnson made further cuts in his Great Society programs. That price was too high, so Lyndon Johnson watched as the economy began to burn. His Council of Economic Advisors had not been wrong. Inflation, first in evidence in 1966, persisted and soon broke into a gallop. A 3 percent rise in the consumer price index in 1966 was followed by another in 1967, and the CPI jumped 4.5 percent in 1968.

This inflation was one of three factors, all of them caused or intensified by the war in Vietnam, that caused the "dollar crisis" of 1968. A chronic deficit was affecting the U.S. balance of payments: More dollars were leaving America for foreign countries than were returning to the U.S. Previously other nations had been willing to accept dollars rather than gold as payment for debts. Now, speculating that the dollar would have to be devalued, they demanded more gold. As the laws of economics dictate, the increased demand for gold put pressure on its price to rise. But the U.S. was committed to keeping the price of gold at thirty-five dollars an ounce and not diminishing the dollar's value. Something had to give.

Inflation contributed to the deficit in the balance of payments by making foreign goods cheaper in comparison to American goods, causing Americans to import more goods than ever before. In addition, American industry was running near its capacity, at over 90 percent. Much of that capacity was for defense-related goods. Forty percent of the increase in the labor force from 1965 to 1968 was absorbed by defense expenditures. To satisfy their demands for consumer goods, Americans again had to turn abroad. Overall, imports rose 60 percent between 1965 and 1968, wiping out America's balance of trade surplus and leaving an overall deficit in payments.

Finally, the spending of the American treasury directly in Vietnam and the adjacent Southeast Asian countries that supported the U.S. effort created another hemorrhage of dollars, $1.6 billion worth annually. Together with the $2 billion estimated as the loss in the balance of trade attributable to the war, Vietnam was sapping $3.6 billion per year from America.

By late 1967, speculators sensed that the U.S. would have to raise the price of gold, so they began to hoard the metal. In late November, seven industrial nations agreed to support the value of the dollar at thirty-five dollars per

Alone in New York City's Central Park, a Vietnam veteran shows his opposition to the war after a demonstration on April 15, 1967, that marked the beginning of the Vietnam Veterans Against the War.

ounce of gold and speculation abated. Only four months later a new round of speculation forced the London gold market to close, and the U.S. dollar was in critical trouble.

Representatives of the industrialized countries met again in crisis but again could come up with only an interim solution. This one was more ingenious: A separate market was established for selling privately held gold at whatever price the market commanded. Central banks, however, still held to the value of thirty-five dollars an ounce in fixing the value of their currency. Since most of the speculation on gold centered on the central banks, the great gold rush ended—for the time being.

The other America

The dollar crisis had little or no meaning for poor Americans, and for them the tales of economic prosperity streaming from the television screen and radio might as well have been "The Adventures of Ozzie and Harriet." The prosperity of the early war years had, as predicted, trickled down the American economic pyramid, but a trickle was all. The basic distribution of income in the United States remained virtually unchanged between 1965 and 1968. During those years the poorest 20 percent of American families increased their share of the national wealth by only 0.2 percent to a still-abysmal 3.6 percent. Forty percent of the population still received only 10.6 percent of the nation's income in 1968. Meanwhile, the wealthiest 20 percent possessed nearly one-half of the nation's wealth, 43.4 percent. Their share had dropped less than 1 percent since 1965.

Blacks were the worst off. Over 27 percent of black families lived in what was officially declared to be poverty, compared to 11 percent of white families, and half of all blacks (49.3 percent) lived at the subsistence level of $5,000 per year or less. One-fifth of the white population lived at that level. Mindful of these facts, but not forgetting the plight of poor whites, Martin Luther King called for a new protest March on Washington, a "tent-in" in Washington, D.C. It was planned for the spring of 1968. His goal, he told followers, was "to cripple the operations of an oppressive society." It now seemed to Dr. King that his dream

could never be achieved within the framework of the post-war American consensus.

An assassin's bullet determined that Reverend King would never make it to Washington, but his successors in the Southern Christian Leadership Conference did. Unlike the King-led 1963 March on Washington, the Poor People's Campaign failed to stir the conscience of America. With the failure of his appeal to America, Dr. King's successor, Reverend Ralph Abernathy, chose to approach a narrower segment of opinion, the Democratic party, and to take his appeal to the Democratic Convention in Chicago.

The first casualty

Even before Lyndon Johnson announced the build-up of American ground forces in Vietnam, the Selective Service System had served as a ready target of protest for citizens disagreeing with American military policy. During the first two years of antiwar protest, the draft was the primary target of opposition. The tenuous public acceptance of the draft after World War II could be said to have been the

first victim of the Vietnam War. As *Newsweek* reported in mid-1967, "the draft was, in this century at least, grudgingly respected—until Vietnam revealed the inequities of a system geared only to Big War or Cold Peace. . . . Now resentment is the rule."

Until 1967 antidraft protest was used as a symbol of opposition to the entire war. But buoyed by reports that as many as 25 percent of all male college students would refuse induction, activists formed a national antidraft movement early that year. The new movement was designed to hinder the war effort. *New York Times* columnist Tom Wicker argued, "If the Johnson administration had to prosecute 100,000 Americans in order to maintain its authority, its real power to pursue the Vietnamese War or any other policy would be crippled if not destroyed." Led by Dr. Benjamin Spock and Reverend William Sloan Coffin, chaplain of Yale University, 320 educators and intel-

Resurrection City. Members of Martin Luther King's Poor People's Campaign protesting the plight of poor blacks and whites set up shelters on the Washington Mall in May 1968.

lectuals joined in signing a treatise entitled, "A Call to Resist Illegitimate Authority."

The new movement quickly attracted the attention of the Justice Department. It was one thing to protest the draft but another to counsel widespread draft resistance. One day in October 1967, Spock, Coffin, and three others urged their audience at Boston's Arlington Street Church to resist the draft. This was the opportunity the Justice Department was looking for. Ten weeks later the five were indicted on charges of conspiring to encourage others "to refuse or evade registration or service in the armed forces."

The trial of the "Boston Five" began on May 20, 1968, and lasted nineteen days. On June 14, after seven-and-one-half hours of deliberation, a jury found four of the five, including Spock and Coffin, guilty. The men appealed, and one year later, on July 11, 1969, the verdicts were overturned. In a decision that was to be repeated in many trials of war protesters, a U.S. Court of Appeals found the presiding judge to have handled the case improperly. So the "Call to Resist Illegitimate Authority" had overcome its first major legal challenge, and the draft resistance movement grew apace.

The president was not unmindful of the resentment the draft caused. Not only were antiwar activists opposed to the "illegitimate authority" of the SSS, but even those who supported the war were bothered by its patent unfairness.

With this in mind, President Johnson asked Congress to authorize him to make the selection of inductees on the basis of a lottery. He also requested that nineteen-year-olds, the youngest eligible, be drafted first, rather than "oldest first." In addition, he asked for abolition of deferments for graduate school students. Congress was badly divided among those who preferred the old system of virtual autonomy for local boards, those who opposed any draft at all, and those who wanted reform. In the end, Congress, in passing the Selective Service Act of 1967, rejected a lottery and the drafting of "youngest first" but empowered Johnson to abolish graduate student deferments. In addition, Congress granted automatic deferments to a student so long as he was making satisfactory progress toward a bachelor's degree. Previously, local boards were permitted, but not required, to do so.

The inequities in the draft system and the draft resistance movement, limited as it was, eventually provoked another crisis within the armed forces: a manpower shortage. The extensive granting of deferments and the unwillingness of a small percentage of eligible males to enter the armed forces under any circumstances meant that the armed forces had a narrow pool from which to fulfill their manpower needs. President Johnson's unwillingness to call up the reserves further limited the military's ability to draw upon the nation's substantial manpower potential.

The manpower shortage was a complicated matter. Only a few military specialties actually experienced a shortage of men. By mid-1967 the navy and air force to-

gether required an additional 9,000 to 10,000 pilots, and neither service believed it could erase its manpower deficit for at least a half decade. In general, however, the crisis was a result of the level of preparedness and the previous commitments of units already in existence. By early 1968 the JCS reported that the 82d Airborne Division was "the only readily deployable army division" based in the U.S. One brigade of that division was ordered to Vietnam in early February. The other four army divisions still based in the U.S. (down from the eight in 1965) were underequipped, many lacking the new M16 rifle. It was a fact, according to the *Wall Street Journal*, that no more than 250,000 men could be dispatched quickly overseas in an emergency.

Congress: the Vietnam debate

In early 1967 there were still eighteen months to go before the Democrats convened to select their nominee for the 1968 presidential election, but already it was clear that the Vietnam War would dominate the convention. Lyndon Johnson had forestalled any full-scale Congressional debate on the conduct of the war, but the traditionally unruly Democratic Convention would be much more difficult to orchestrate. This had been made clear in the expressed opinions of some of those in the newly elected Ninetieth Congress who took the oath of office in January 1967.

Those in the Eighty-ninth Congress skeptical of Johnson's policy had been reluctant to speak out. Republican Senator Thurston Morton could count only ten doves at the beginning of 1967, but one year later he told reporters that the number had increased to about twenty-five, including himself. Behind those twenty-five stood an uncounted number of additional senators, especially Democrats, who had reservations but, either out of party loyalty or fear of presidential retaliation, refused to break with LBJ and denounce the war publicly.

Congressmen, of course, were able to read public opinion polls as well as Lyndon Johnson. At the time of the November 1966 elections the polls suggested that a majority, even if a very slim one, still approved of the president's handling of the war in Vietnam. But by early January he had lost that majority. Throughout the year his support eroded, until July of 1967, when the percentage of disapproval of Johnson's handling of the war, according to pollsters, equaled the rate of approval he had received in the heady days of the build-up in 1965.

Other public opinion data confirmed the slide. One of the most important signposts was the Gallup poll of October 1967 when, for the first time, a majority of Americans (excluding those with "no opinion") believed that sending troops to Vietnam had been a mistake in the first place. What these public opinion questions failed to answer, however, was whether the growing frustration reflected a more "hawkish" or "dovish" America.

Other questions posed by pollsters help to suggest an answer. Gallup asked Americans whether they favored "increased attacks" (escalation), the beginning of withdrawal (deescalation), or keeping troop numbers at their present level. In November 1966 a majority, 55 percent, favored "increased attacks." The remainder were evenly divided between the two other options. By August 1967, however, while a majority still believed in "increased attacks," down five points to 50 percent, deescalation was now heavily favored over "present level" as a second choice, 32 percent to 10 percent.

Who were these people flocking to the ranks of the doves? In stark contrast to the conventional wisdom, it was *not* the well-to-do, well-educated who favored deescalation. By occupation, it was manual workers who most favored a troop withdrawal; by age, it was those fifty years and over; by income, those making under $5,000; and by education, those who had completed only grade school.

What differentiated these people from the antiwar activists was how they interpreted the problem of the war. The war forced both white and black activists to reconsider the entire basis of the American postwar consensus. The student movement and black power advocates rejected both pillars of the consensus: The policy of containment had led to an immoral war, and economic prosperity was not solving the country's social ills. Even for moderates like Martin Luther King the war seemed to invalidate one major tenet of the consensus: America could not both contain communism abroad as well as take care of its own pressing domestic problems.

But the masses of Americans who turned against the war in 1967 had a different understanding. In mid-1967, while a majority of Americans had in some way become disturbed by the war, more than two-thirds of those responding to a Gallup question still believed the "war in Vietnam is morally justified." Unlike the activists, their opposition was not ideological, but pragmatic. The war was too costly (70 percent of the country opposed a tax hike to finance the war) and it was dragging on too long (a majority thought the war was at a stalemate). Also it was preventing America from getting on with its important tasks: containing communism where it really counted (as, for example, in the Middle East) and addressing the problems at home. Equally important, *all* of America's afflictions seemed somehow to be caused or worsened by the war in Vietnam: demonstrating students, urban riots, dollar crises, a diminution of military force in readiness. If only the war would go away, people began to say, surely these other problems would as well.

If there was any man in the United States in the 1960s who could read the polls better than Lyndon Johnson it might well have been Allard K. Lowenstein. In 1951 he had been elected president of the National Student Association and ever since had attempted to harness the energies of youth into liberal politics. He was experienced in working on losing causes: Adlai Stevenson's presidential campaigns, Hubert Humphrey's attempt to upset John Kennedy as front-runner in 1960, the Mississippi Freedom Democratic party in 1964. But in 1967, at age thirty-eight, he undertook the most "hopeless" cause of all, to unseat Lyndon Johnson. More improbably, he intended to do so by forming an alliance between the long-haired, ideological opponents of the war on campuses and the patriotic manual workers whose quiet, pragmatic antiwar feeling the polls told him was growing. He had a goal, but no candidate, so his campaign took on the unglorious title of the Dump Johnson Movement.

A campaign in search of a candidate

The movement was hatched in August 1967, the product of a brainstorming session between Lowenstein and a handful of student leaders. They spent the next few months talking to prominent Democrats and liberal organizations known for their antiwar feelings and organized them into an *ad hoc* group called Concerned Democrats. Their schedule was already cast in stone: the primary elections scheduled for the next March in New Hampshire, April in Wisconsin, and then the Democrats' August convention to be held in Chicago.

Lowenstein scheduled a meeting of Concerned Democrats for October, then postponed it for two weeks because he still lacked that most necessary of commodities, a candidate. He felt that within two additional weeks he could find his man.

Senator Robert Kennedy had been his first choice, but Kennedy felt that his candidacy would inevitably turn the campaign into a vicious personality contest between himself and President Johnson. Kennedy told Lowenstein that another candidate could better focus attention on the war itself. George McGovern was not willing; he faced a difficult reelection campaign for his Senate seat in 1968. Eugene McCarthy also said no. Kennedy, he said, would be a far stronger candidate. But something about McCarthy made Lowenstein come back. The senator felt *so* strongly about the war. Lowenstein described the growing student base for an antiwar candidacy. Finally McCarthy asked, "How do you think we'd do in a Wisconsin primary?" Lowenstein had his candidate.

As late as December 27 McCarthy was still telling reporters that the New Hampshire primary was "not particularly significant." Only a month later the bloody Tet offensive fighting in Vietnam changed that. Thousands of students flooded into New Hampshire to campaign for McCarthy. It was a youthful campaign, where one of the most important tasks was to determine how many sleeping bags could fit on the floor of a church. Their motto was "clean for Gene" and many of the young canvassers had shorn their long hair in preparation for meeting the state's conservative voters. By election day, March 12, the students had visited more than half of the 120,000 homes in New Hampshire. They sought out the manual workers and farmers of New England, the people whose antiwar feelings had grown most substantially, according to Gallup. When the votes in New Hampshire were counted, McCarthy had lost to the incumbent president by only 230 votes out of 60,000 and had captured twenty of New Hampshire's twenty-two elected delegates.

For the previous six months Kennedy and his advisers had struggled over the question of the senator's entry into the race. One group of advisers, mostly men who had served on President Kennedy's staff, argued that 1972, not 1968, was Robert Kennedy's year and that it would be virtually impossible to unseat an incumbent president in a convention struggle. The other, younger group, comprised largely of Kennedy's staff when he had been attorney general, argued that the senator, as the most prominent antiwar Democrat, had a moral obligation to lead the opposition to President Johnson's policies. Failure to do so, they argued, would deplete the "moral capital" upon which any future presidential campaign of his would depend.

Eugene McCarthy's victory in New Hampshire ended the debate. It proved that President Johnson could be beaten in primary contests, and it also removed the charge that a Kennedy campaign would divide the party. The party was already divided. Knowing full well that his entry into the contest would raise charges that he was acting as an opportunist, Kennedy believed that only he possessed the "political muscle" to successfully challenge the incumbent. So on March 16, Robert Kennedy too joined the race, further splintering Lyndon Johnson's support.

Neither the style nor substance of Eugene McCarthy's campaign was likely to attract many black voters nor, over the long haul, a large following among blue-collar workers. But Kennedy was another story. Even the revelation that he had authorized the secret tapping of Martin Luther King's telephone would not turn blacks against the Kennedy campaign. Said a black barber in Watts, "It's like finding the woman you love in bed with another guy. It hurts. But you still love her."

The press described the Kennedy and McCarthy campaigns as "new politics," referring more to form than substance, but there was something radically different in what the insurgent candidates were saying. For the first time since 1948, Democratic candidates for national leadership were campaigning against the cold war consensus. In that, they were joined by another candidate, Governor George C. Wallace of Alabama.

The focus of the Kennedy and McCarthy campaigns was on the application of the consensus policy of containment in Vietnam. Wallace's efforts centered on domestic issues. To be sure, Wallace appealed to the public's frustration over the course of the war, but he appealed directly to those who urged more forceful action in Vietnam. At home he drew support from those tired and an-

The "new politicians." Senator Eugene McCarthy (left) addresses a university crowd in Appleton, Wisconsin, and Senator Robert Kennedy (above) reaches out to supporters in Sacramento, California, during the 1968 presidential campaign.

tagonized by riots and demonstrations. But the fluidity of American public opinion during 1968 was best attested by the upsurge of support Wallace received after the assassination of Robert Kennedy. Most observers have explained this phenomenon as an example of the irrationality of American voters, or perhaps more charitably, the emphasis on personality rather than issues. But there was a thread of logical continuity. The Kennedy and Wallace campaigns, and the McCarthy campaign as well, dramatized the deep fragmentation of American society. Americans were looking for someone, anyone, who could restore order to the chaos of American politics in 1968.

Lyndon Johnson might well have been able to survive the campaigns of his former Democratic supporters and win his party's renomination. The challenge of electoral politics still thrilled him. In early 1968 he began to prepare his reelection campaign, and when Kennedy entered the race in March, one reporter wrote that it had "caused Johnson's glands to race." He quickly convened his cabinet for a primary season pep talk and to lay plans for the campaign. But unbeknown to the president, at that very moment his most trusted advisers were about to shatter the last bastion of firm support for his war policies.

The wise men

At the end of World War II such men as Dean Acheson, Clark Clifford, Averell Harriman, and protégés of General Marshall, like Omar Bradley and Matthew Ridgway, had helped President Truman to forge his postwar consensus, educated Americans to the necessity of active involvement in world affairs, and shaped the policy of containment. Now, more than twenty years later, they were referred to in news accounts as LBJ's "Wise Men," and they had bad news for the president. In 1965 and again as recently as November 1967, they had strongly supported Johnson's commitment to Vietnam. He was faithfully executing the policy they had helped to shape. But on March 26, 1968, several of the wise men once again entered the Oval Office, this time to tell the president that the United States must "move to disengage." "We can no longer do the job we set out to do," Dean Acheson told the president. The verdict of the wise men was the final blow for Johnson. By March 1968, with peace no closer than it had been at the outset of his administration, the president realized that whatever mandate he once had was now gone, that his prospects for reelection were grim, and that his options for further action were few.

He nonetheless decided to make one final, bold bid for peace. In a nationally televised address on March 31, 1968, Johnson announced a unilateral bombing halt over the northern portion of North Vietnam and invited the North Vietnamese to begin negotiations toward a mutually acceptable settlement of the conflict.

What distinguished Johnson's newest peace offer from the others he had presented in the past was a dramatic gesture of good will and sincerity directed both to the American people and the North Vietnamese enemy. Surprising even his closest White House aides, Johnson concluded his speech: "I will not seek, nor will I accept" the nomination of the Democratic party for another term in office. With the incumbent missing from the scene, the Chicago conclave would surely feature a full-scale debate over the post-World War II consensus.

The media: from Saigon to Chicago

The free press, much like universities, is an institution in America whose function is to step back, cast its gaze upon society, and to report, comment on, and criticize what it sees. As such, the press often seems in quiescent times to be a disinterested, even imperious, observer. But it is also a part of the society that it is called upon to report. During times of rapid change or crisis these two realities often become confused or interchanged, not only to the public at large, but also to the media of the press themselves. The nation's universities quickly discovered after 1965 that they would be as much the object of America's crisis as its chronicler. The same was true of the national press. It, no less than society itself, was fragmented and looking to rediscover its purpose.

One manifestation of this fragmentation was the growth of the underground press. The alternative press that emerged after 1965 differed from its precursors, like *I.F. Stone's Weekly*, in two respects. First, Vietnam totally dominated its political concerns, and second, it consciously tailored itself to the new youth culture.

The *Berkeley Barb* was the first of a kind of "alternative" newspaper that proliferated all over the country. It began in 1965 as a newsletter for the University of California's Vietnam Day Committee. Its founder, Max Scherr, began publication because he assumed that there were many others like himself who were simply tired of walking to campus every day to learn what was going on among students. The *Barb* became immensely influential—and profitable as well. It mixed the latest news from Vietnam with service features for its readers, such as a column by "Dr. Hip Pocrates," who offered advice on such varying matters as contraception or what to do if one's dog swallowed a tablet of LSD. The *Barb* also served as a local bulletin board, providing information on how to get rides to a nearby rock concert or a political demonstration.

Ramparts magazine was another example of the alternative press. Founded in 1962 by Catholic laymen as an avant-garde literary magazine, two years later—just one month after the beginning of the Berkeley Free Speech Movement—it adopted a more political perspective. By 1968 it had startled many Americans with important revelations of questionable government activities. In April 1966 it exposed the fact that a Michigan State University re-

President Johnson is overcome with emotion after listening to his son-in-law's taped impressions of his tour of duty in Vietnam, in which he described the hardship of seeing casualties and losing men. July 31, 1968.

search group was actually employed by the Diem government in Vietnam. One year later *Ramparts* broke the story of CIA infiltration and financing of the National Student Association. In 1968 the magazine revealed CIA involvement in the assassination of Che Guevara and published parts of his diary.

Changes in the news media extended beyond the growth of an underground press. Reporting the war in Vietnam and its repercussions at home presented a challenge to the more established news media as well. This challenge was all the more stark in the context of the reporting habits that had come to dominate the established media in the first decades following World War II.

The 1950s become known as a decade of complacency, and that description fit few institutions in America as well as the press. Reporters by and large found little reason to doubt the integrity of government news briefings and reported events accordingly. As NBC News reporter John Chancellor recalled the era, "I could win debates by coming in toward the end and saying, 'Now I am going to read you official U.S. government figures.' And that would always stop everything because those were official U.S. government figures."

This attitude of complacency particularly characterized the coverage of international affairs. It was an age of consensus, of bipartisan foreign policy, and reporters did little to question or challenge for their readers the government's definition of the national interest. Maverick reporters who did so, like I.F. Stone, were generally dismissed as isolated iconoclasts. The result was that few reporters conducted independent investigations of foreign events and instead relied on the government's version. Most Americans thus remained ignorant, or learned only many years later, of the nature of their government's involvement in such events as the overthrow of governments in Iran, Guatemala, and the Congo.

The reporters covering the fighting in Vietnam in the early 1960s arrived in Saigon with most of the values of their colleagues at home. They broke from the mold, however, when the realities of the guerrilla war seemed to be at odds with official government pronouncements of progress. But no matter how critical they became of the American effort in Vietnam, there was one line that few ever crossed: doubting the wisdom of America's commitment to South Vietnam and the importance of the policy of containment. David Halberstam, then of the *New York Times*, was among the most consistent and vocal of those early critics. Yet when he returned to the U.S. in 1963 and wrote *The Making of a Quagmire*, a book documenting his disillusionment with U.S. policy in Vietnam, he still concluded

Above. *The cover of the March 1967 edition of* Ramparts *announces the magazine's exposé of CIA infiltration and financing of the National Student Association.*

that Vietnam "is perhaps one of only five or six nations in the world that is truly vital to U.S. interest."

With the deployment of American combat troops in 1965 this early criticism receded into the background. More and more reporters thronged into Saigon, and the number of accredited journalists in Vietnam rose from the handful of the early 1960s to over 100 by the end of 1965. They brought with them a confidence in the ability of American troops to get the job done. Frank McCulloch's timetable proved remarkably accurate. These new reporters found their confidence in the American effort gradually tested. When most had spent a year in Vietnam their optimism had vanished, to be replaced first by doubts about the effectiveness of American policy and then about the wisdom of the entire commitment to Vietnam. Unlike their colleagues in Vietnam in the early 1960s, they were willing to—and many did—cross the line to question where the national interest in Vietnam really lay.

In the process these reporters raised questions that have long characterized the relationship between the press and the government: Whom should a reporter trust? Should a journalist rely on official briefings? It was certainly easier. One need only attend the daily news conferences, add a little background information obtained over drinks with a well-placed official, and file a story. Or should a reporter find his or her own sources of information and trust them? They might not have the "big picture." They might have their own axes to grind. It was an informational minefield, but by 1967 reporters in Vietnam were increasingly trusting their own sources rather than the government line.

The battle of Con Thien in the fall of 1967* provided a classic example of the virtues of this aggressive reporting, as well as its limitations. The battle was literally discovered for the American people by John Laurence, then a twenty-seven-year-old correspondent with CBS News. Laurence had heard reports of heavy fighting near the DMZ and decided to hitch a ride out of Da Nang with some marines to see for himself. Other reporters would later charge that the marines and MACV had deliberately played down the battle in its initial stages because of heavy American casualties.

Departing Da Nang at 6:00 A.M., Laurence arrived by jeep at Con Thien six hours later. He was welcomed by a series of incoming North Vietnamese rocket barrages. The enemy artillery could not be seen from inside the camp because the guns were placed on the other side of the DMZ, firing over a series of hills. Laurence and his sound

* See *Contagion of War*, pg. 160 ff., another volume in THE VIETNAM EXPERIENCE.

A street vendor hawks the latest edition of Chicago's "underground" newspaper, the Seed *(left), one of many imitators of the Berkeley* Barb *(above). These newspapers combined news about radical politics with reporting on youthful lifestyles.*

man and cameraman spent much of their time inside bunkers, occasionally poking the camera outside to film the effects of the enemy rockets. Caught in a bunker during one barrage with the camp commander, Lieutenant Colonel Lee R. Bendel, Laurence captured on tape the chaos of the marine encampment.

The next morning Laurence was on his way back to Da Nang. His film was shipped via Saigon to New York and for the extraordinary length of four minutes was offered on the Monday night news, five days after it had been shot. Within hours the marine camp at Con Thien was besieged by reporters.

One month later the last of the reporters had left the marine encampment. MACV headquarters had declared victory and American newspapers dutifully reported the good news. "U.S. Guns Batter Reds at Con Thien," headlined the *New York Post*. "Reds Flee Gun Posts; Con Thien Siege Ends," the *Denver Post* reported. And AP quoted General Westmoreland's victory statement: "We made it a Dien Bien Phu in reverse."

Disrupting the harmony of this chorus was the voice of Charles Mohr of the *New York Times*. Mohr had checked his own by now well-developed sources (he was already a three-year veteran of Vietnam). He reported:

Aerial photos confirmed a limited withdrawal but did not necessarily prove that the bulk of the gun pits—most of which have never been located—were hit by B–52 bombing raids and United States artillery.

He concluded that "few sources believe that more than a respite has been gained."

On October 11 a laconic AP dispatch began, "Long-range Communist artillery and Red mortars opened up again yesterday and today on U.S. Marine positions south of the Demilitarized Zone" and never once mentioned the declaration of victory, barely one week old.

The Con Thien story was but one example of what reporters in Vietnam believed was the mismanagement of news in Vietnam by the MACV command. It was not that MACV's official versions contained lies, but rather that taken together they may have presented an inaccurate picture of the entire war effort. John Chancellor suggested, "The pieces [of information] were in the main true. The mosaic itself may have told a false story."

Thanks in large measure to the cooperation of MACV, probably unprecedented in the history of warfare, America's working press was able to present a wealth of information to the American public on the course and conduct of the war. Many of the subjects that were to become objects of passionate debate after the war were first aired during the conflict by the press. Differences between the marines and the army over American strategy in Vietnam were described by *Life* magazine in 1965. *Newsweek* discussed the strategy debate at the time of General Lewis Walt's retirement as head of the marines in Vietnam in

1967. Of greater significance was R. W. Apple's full-page article, "Vietnam: The Signs of Stalemate," which appeared in the August 7, 1967, edition of the *New York Times*. It was an exhaustive report describing the controversies over virtually every aspect of the war, from the deployment of American troops to the conduct of the pacification program to relations with the Saigon government.

But of these examples, only one, Apple's article in the *Times*, was prominently displayed. The truly national media outlets, the television networks, the weekly magazines, and the wire services, apparently believed that such stories were not of sufficient interest to their readers. Analyses of the complex controversies surrounding the conflict were either not presented or else "buried" at the end of flashier stories about combat operations or leading personalities. A 1967 CBS news documentary about the air war over North Vietnam was a good example of how the mass media avoided controversial issues. "Vietnam Perspective: Air War in the North" followed the flights of several combat pilots, concentrating almost entirely on the men's undeniable courage and a description of North Vietnam's air defenses. But was the air campaign over the North succeeding? Was it worth the cost? Viewers of the documentary had to turn elsewhere for answers to these questions. CBS failed to present an interview with an expert from the Pentagon or elsewhere to evaluate the effectiveness of the air war.

The CBS documentary highlighted another problem in the media's coverage of the war in Vietnam. The documentary was produced not by CBS reporters based in Saigon, but by the network's *CBS Reports* unit in New York. New York- and Washington-based reporters, including most of the nation's leading political columnists, did not have the benefit that their Saigon-based colleagues had of testing government statements of progress against the realities of combat in South Vietnam. Throughout 1966 and 1967 most of these domestic reporters continued to report and comment upon the war on the basis of the Johnson administration's optimism.

The *Washington Post* illustrated this division between Saigon and Washington reporters. While the young journalist Ward Just was filing a series of powerful stories from Vietnam in 1966 and 1967 for the *Post*, revealing the weakness of the American position, the newspaper's editorial page, under the editorship of James Russell Wiggins, consistently supported the administration's policies. Top administration figures—McNamara, Rostow, and Rusk—were readily available to take Wiggins's telephone calls and leak the latest classified statistics from Vietnam to him. In Walter Lippmann the *Post*, of course, had one of the most powerful antiwar voices in the country, but he was balanced on the editorial page by the opinions of Joseph Alsop. So pleased was Lyndon Johnson with the *Post*'s editorial direction that he once remarked that, "Russ [Wiggins] is worth two divisions to me."

It was against this backdrop of skepticism, confusion, and division within the media that a climactic confrontation took place in late 1967 and 1968. The media, the government, and events in Vietnam themselves all seemed to engage in a three-staged battle for the "hearts and minds" of the American public. In the end the American people, its government, and institutions would be shaken as never before in the course of this war.

The media, public opinion, and Tet

Concerned about the slow erosion of public support for his policies in Vietnam, Lyndon Johnson mounted in August 1967 a huge government effort "to get the message out" that the United States was winning in Vietnam. This government "success offensive" was nothing less than an effort to recapture public opinion.

The White House doled out to reporters a never-ending stream of previously classified statistics showing progress: progress in "kill-ratios," progress in pacification, progress in logistics. Hubert Humphrey, Dean Rusk, and Robert McNamara scrambled for television appearances and held private background chats with favored reporters.

By far the biggest stars of the success offensive, however, were the three major leaders of the war effort in Saigon: military commander William Westmoreland, Ambassador Ellsworth Bunker, and pacification chief Robert Komer. Bunker and Westmoreland shared a table one Sunday morning on NBC's "Meet the Press." Westmoreland spoke at a luncheon of the National Press Club. Their message, in Westmoreland's words, was, "I am absolutely certain that whereas in 1965 the enemy was winning, today he is certainly losing."

The men conducting the success offensive were given the access to press, radio, and television that high officials have always attracted. But the reporters in the U.S. covering the news had not learned the lessons of their colleagues in Vietnam. They still mostly trusted the assessments of the highest officials of the land and so, it seemed, did the American people. Approval of Johnson's handling of the war shot up 7 percent from August to November, according to Gallup polls. More important was the public's perception of American progress in Vietnam. Gallup gave those it polled three choices: "losing ground," "standing still," or "making progress." The contrast between July, before the "success offensive," and December, at its conclusion, was startling. "Losing ground" went down from 10 to 8 percent. "Standing still" lost thirteen points, falling to 33 percent. Those who believed the U.S. side was "making progress" rose from 34 percent in July to 50 percent in August. Then the enemy began its own battle for American public opinion.

Beginning on January 30, 1968, Communist forces attacked thirty-six of South Vietnam's forty-four provincial capitals, five of its six major cities, and countless military headquarters, airfields, and combat bases, all within forty-eight hours. The Tet offensive and the American-South Vietnamese response to it lasted through the end of March and resulted in an estimated 72,000 enemy soldiers killed, while the U.S. lost nearly 5,000 men and the South Vietnamese over 10,000 during that period.

Military historians and journalists will long debate the relationship between the actual events of the Tet offensive, the media coverage of those events, and public opinion. Was it a victory or defeat? A military victory but a psychological defeat for the U.S. and South Vietnam? Such questions in some way missed the main point. In the public mind what was being tested was simply the honesty of the administration and its success offensive. Whatever faults the media may have committed in reporting the initial impact of the enemy's Tet offensive, the evidence later suggested that their coverage was not what turned American public opinion against the war. Early polls showed, in fact, that the country, as it usually does during crises, turned for a time more hawkish. When asked to describe themselves as "hawk" or "dove," 4 percent more Americans opted for hawk at the end of February than in late January. But the bottom of support for the war was about to fall out. Only a month later hawk sentiment had dropped nineteen points, while those calling themselves doves increased sixteen.

The reason for this remarkable shift could be found by a later look at the "progress question" posed by Gallup's pollsters. Whereas making progress showed a clear majority over losing ground and standing still combined in December, by June the situation had been reversed. Making progress now stood dead last; it was a belief held by a mere 18 percent of the population. Losing ground had tripled its support to 25 percent of the responses. But most Americans had become convinced that the war was a stalemate. Fifty-two percent of those responding (and 47 percent of the total sample) believed that the U.S. and its allies were standing still.

During this crisis of confidence induced by the Tet offensive, journalists were not only reporting the raging battle in South Vietnam and the reaction to it in the United States, but also experiencing many of the same feelings as their fellow citizens. They too felt their confidence, which had heightened during Johnson's success blitz, shaken. As many reporters in Vietnam had already given up trusting official pronouncements of progress, top political reporters and editors at home now began to look at the war in a different light.

Walter Cronkite had gone to Vietnam in 1965, a self-described "containment man." According to journalist David Halberstam, "he did not like the brashness of the younger correspondents who sat at the military briefings, tearing into the military officers." While his junior colleague, Morley Safer, urged him to spend more time talking with younger officers, Cronkite trusted his contacts in the air force, some established during his days as a World War II combat correspondent, and was impressed by the air power America could bring to bear on the fighting. Until 1968 his reporting on CBS's "Evening News" reflected his confidence.

Two weeks after the beginning of the Tet offensive, Cronkite again traveled to Vietnam. He was upset by what he saw and heard. Returning to the United States he described the war as "mired in stalemate" but, equally important, announced his conversion to the belief of the Saigon-based reporters. Official statements could not be trusted: "We have too often been disappointed by the optimism of the American leaders to have faith any longer in the silver linings they find in the darkest clouds." Walter Cronkite's trust was a major casualty of Lyndon Johnson's success offensive and Cronkite's disaffection in turn seriously affected the president's morale. It was only a month later that LBJ chose to leave the presidency.

As luck would have it, the opening of the presidential primary season followed close on the heels of the enemy offensive. McCarthy's stunning showing in New Hampshire, Lyndon Johnson's "abdication," Kennedy's drive for the nomination and his assassination all set the stage for the Democratic party's convention in Chicago.

To Chicago would come most of the competing factions, the disaffected voices of a divided and fragmented nation. And there to bring this cacophonous chorus live to the American people were the television cameras. Long before the politicians and demonstrators packed their bags, network executives, reporters, and technicians set up their machinery, more than $40 million worth of electronic gear for coverage of the convention.

Chicago: preparations for battle

What the staffs of the television networks did not reckon on was a labor dispute. All of the equipment that the networks owned and with which they planned to bring the convention into the homes of millions of Americans was completely dependent on something they did not own, telephone lines. Only through telephone lines could they link their remote cameras and their transmission centers to send the sounds and images of Chicago instantaneously through the air. But Illinois Bell's electrical workers were on strike, and only two weeks before opening day it seemed that the convention might even have to be moved from Chicago. If telephone lines were not installed the convention could not be telecast. The Democratic party would rather move to another city than hold a convention that could not be televised to the nation, and Mayor Richard Daley of Chicago knew it. At the last minute he intervened and gained a special dispensation. The striking electricians would install sufficient lines to insure live coverage from the amphitheater itself, but the union would not install additional lines to allow TV to operate live cameras in other parts of Chicago. This meant that any other film or videotape footage shot in the city would have to be rushed to the amphitheater television transmission centers, developed and edited there, and then televised. There could be no live coverage away from the floor of the convention because everything else would require delays of two to four hours.

Reporters thought they saw an ulterior motive in Mayor Daley's compromise. The mayor's stated defense was that he had achieved as much as he could in negotiations with the striking union. But many reporters later felt otherwise, that Mayor Daley had other reasons for restricting television's ability to roam the streets of Chicago, because, in reality, there were two political conventions planned for Chicago that week. One was the official Democratic Convention that was about to nominate Hubert Humphrey for president. The other was pure street theater, Jerry Rubin's Youth International party, or "Yippies," who proposed to nominate as its standard bearer a pig named Pigasus. Mayor Daley did not take kindly to such competition.

Theodore White suggested in *The Making of the President, 1968* that only two kinds of people could take Jerry Rubin seriously, the police and television reporters. That was all Jerry Rubin needed. He worked with no organization, he possessed no activist base, and was, in fact, disliked by many of his former colleagues in the New Left for his monumental ego.

The Rubin style was one that Rennie Davis, a fellow organizer of the New Left, termed, "organizing with mirrors": Call a few press conferences, organize a party, plan an ingenious program of events, introduce a pig as presidential candidate, and the media, especially television, will project the illusion of organization.

Prior to the convention, Chicago's daily newspapers competed to print rumors about Jerry Rubin and his Yippies' plans. The *Chicago American* clearly won the contest. It estimated that as many as 250,000 protesters would attend. The *American* reported a rumor that had circulated in, of all places, the Cook County jail, that plans were afoot to assassinate Mayor Daley, Hubert Humphrey, and Eugene McCarthy. It also reported about "yippie girls who would act as hookers and try to attract delegates and put LSD in their drinks." A *Chicago Tribune* columnist wrote of reports that saboteurs would try to destroy the control tower at O'Hare International Airport.

Estimates of the number of demonstrators who actually "invaded" Chicago ranged from 5,000 to perhaps 25,000. Not all were Yippies. The Walker Commission, which later investigated what followed in Chicago, listed ten separate *types* of organizations that planned protest activities during the convention. After the Yippies, the most prominent youth groups were organized under the banner of the Mobilization Committee To End the War in Vietnam, headed by David Dellinger, a pacifist-activist since World War II. The Mobe also worked closely with SDS and its

Police seize Pigasus, the Yippies' presidential candidate, prior to the opening of the Democratic Convention in August 1968.

most prominent leader, the former University of Michigan student, Tom Hayden. In addition to the youth contingent, there were veteran middle-class protesters from such organizations as Women's Strike for Peace and the National Lawyers' Guild. Before the spectacle was over, others found themselves caught in demonstrations, sometimes willingly, often by circumstance—young McCarthy workers, passers-by, curious matrons from Chicago's suburbs, and inquisitive journalists.

Negotiations between protesters and city authorities did not go well. The police, believing the worst of Jerry Rubin's prophecies, refused to issue the demonstrators any of the permits required to mount peaceful marches, to hold rallies in the parks, or to sleep outside overnight.

This last restriction ignited the situation. Mayor Daley argued that citizens of Chicago could not sleep in the parks overnight, so why should demonstrators. His officials relented to a limited extent, making "arrangements" for demonstrators to sleep in Grant Park, across from the big Conrad Hilton Hotel, but not in Lincoln Park some three miles to the north. The distinction seemed arbitrary, and few things could mobilize the youth who had descended on the city as quickly as the exercise of arbitrary authority. They chose to challenge it.

The city of Chicago imposed a curfew for 11:00 P.M. at Lincoln Park on Sunday night, August 25, the eve of the convention. The 1,000 or so demonstrators who crowded into a part of the park refused to leave. The police quickly applied their clubs. Edwin Diamond, then an editor of *Newsweek,* watched the melee and later observed:

It became clear that cameramen were to be prime targets along with demonstrators: the police planned repression and they planned to keep it from wide public view by clubbing photographers, smashing cameras and confiscating films.

Once the violence began, Chicago's own news reporters changed their focus. They were among those who felt the blows of police clubs. As they had done on Sunday night, police again cleared Lincoln Park on Monday evening. The *Daily News* headlined its Tuesday edition, "Cops Attack 11 Newsmen." The overline read, "Daily News reporter clubbed." The story quoted one "veteran Chicago newsman" as commenting that it was the "most vicious behavior on the part of the police" he had witnessed in twenty-five years.

On the floor of the convention, reporters were also taking a beating, mostly metamorphically, but in some instances literally. Even before the convention opened the networks began competing with each other on potentially *the* story of the week: the "Draft Teddy Boom." As a means of bridging the irreconcilable views within the party, many Democrats had dreamed of the possibility of drafting Senator Edward Kennedy ever since his brother Robert's assassination. The "Draft Teddy Boom" was set off by the arrival of Kennedy's brother-in-law, Stephen Smith, in Chicago on Sunday and the almost simultaneous decision of Richard Daley to postpone a caucus at which Illinois delegates would select their presidential candidate. These two events inspired reporters and commentators to speculate that a move was underway to nominate the Massachusetts senator.

Whatever the possibility of this, it melted away shortly after noon on Tuesday when Smith left Chicago. There had been some fire below the smoke: Kennedy and McCarthy aides had talked but could not agree on the release of McCarthy's delegates to Kennedy for the first ballot. But lacking telephone communication with their downtown reporters, television news executives at the convention hall were unaware until several hours later that the Kennedy-McCarthy negotiations had broken down. So they filled the airwaves with rumors and shots of delegates marching in the convention hall with makeshift "Draft Teddy" posters. Later, television was charged with manufacturing the entire "boomlet" out of antipathy to Humphrey's candidacy. In reality the networks had extrapolated on the basis of true, but limited, information; had they been equipped at that time to communicate from hotel lobbies to broadcast studios, the Kennedy story may not have developed as it did.

When it came to live action at the convention scene itself, television was not wanting for material, some of it very close to home. On the second night of the convention, Dan Rather of CBS News was attempting to move about the floor when he was slugged and beaten by roving security men. Rather was not arrested and continued his duties, but Walter Cronkite commented from his anchor booth, "I think we've got a bunch of thugs here!"

To one sitting at home that Tuesday night in the summer of 1968, this is the spectacle that flickered across the television screen: The convention votes to split the Georgia delegation between the segregationist Governor Lester Maddox's supporters and those of the young black assemblyman, Julian Bond. Black delegates from the North walk out in protest when a nearly all-white Alabama delegation is seated. Television reports more clashes with the police in Lincoln Park, for the third straight night. Fist-fighting breaks out between the two parts of the Georgia delegation. The networks announce that tear gas is being fired on demonstrators downtown. It is past midnight before the Democrats begin to debate the party's platform. Finally, it is nearly 2:00 A.M. as the convention reaches its fever point, the debate on Vietnam. The doves are furious. The first full-scale debate on the war in Vietnam held by

any regularly constituted institution of American politics is to take place while two-thirds of the nation is fast asleep.

The New York delegation moves to adjourn the debate until the following afternoon. The chairman cuts off the delegation's microphone, illegally ignoring the motion. But the chairman cannot choke the microphones of the television reporters, so the doves take their case directly to the airwaves. Mayor Daley, never far from a small portable television near his seat, has had enough. Facing toward the rostrum he slashes a forefinger across his throat, the universal director's symbol to "end it." On that cue the convention chairman announces a recess. The most tumultuous night in the history of televised political conventions comes to a bitter end.

Storming the Bastille

Wednesday, August 25, was destined to be a long day for the delegates, the demonstrators, the police, Mayor Daley, Hubert Humphrey, and above all, the employees of CBS television. The day was substantially the same for employees of all the TV networks, but by coincidence, the way in which one of the world's most pervasive communications networks transmitted the news that day was meticulously chronicled by a writer, Thomas Whiteside, in the *Columbia Journalism Review*. Written from the vantage point of the CBS control booth at the convention, it provides an unusual glimpse into network decision making on what turned out to be a most controversial moment.

For CBS technicians the day began very early. The postponement of the debate on the Vietnam plank of the party platform necessitated an afternoon convention session, so the network's live coverage began at 12:30 P.M. The bitterness that had persisted ever since the convention's "call to order" was still evident. The debates on Monday and Tuesday had been only tactical skirmishes, tests of delegate strength, arguments over rules and procedures. Wednesday afternoon's debate on Vietnam was, in contrast, a matter of grave substance. It revealed just how deeply the consensus that had ruled American foreign policy since the mid-1950s had fragmented.

Paul O'Dwyer, candidate for the Senate from New York, asked the Democratic party to make a choice between financing the war and providing for the country's domestic needs. The "$30 billion that is wasted in that war," he argued, "could well be spent to relieve the burden and the problems in the inner city and poverty in our country areas." Senator Albert Gore of Tennessee hit at the very core of the war effort, the extension of the policy of containment to Asia, a decision made in the early 1950s. "That's when the foundations for the mistakes were laid," he said, reminding his audience that "it was Dulles [who] proposed that we maintain a military foothold on the mainland of Asia." Gore urged Democrats to reconsider those policies of twenty years: "What I am pleading for is for this Democratic party to recognize that we must declare our freedom from those mistakes."

The divisiveness seemed contagious, even reaching into the CBS anchor booth. When Robert Wussler, executive producer of CBS's convention coverage, criticized Walter Cronkite's choice of words, the anchorman, feeling that he was being censored, jotted a note, stood up, and prepared to remove his headset. The note read, "I quit." Jeff Gralnick, an associate producer seated next to Cronkite, reported to the executives in the control booth, "He's serious!" Cronkite's ruffled feathers were smoothed during a fortuitous commercial break and the anchorman returned to his duties.

On Wednesday evening the scene worsened. From the podium Iowa Governor Harold Hughes exclaimed, "Affluent as our country is, we do not have the resources to finance the machinery of ever-escalating war and at the same time to relieve the agony of the cities and repair the deep wounds of poverty and racism in our society." On the floor, correspondent Mike Wallace was assaulted by security guards but kept talking into his microphone:

"Now come the strong arms! The Chicago police, wearing hard hats." And then a last, "Oooh!" Wallace was thrown to the floor and taken briefly into police custody in the bowels of the amphitheater. The producer called for a comment from Dan Rather who had been struck the night before. "It's a roughhouse situation," he remarked from the floor. And then, just as San Francisco Mayor Joseph Alioto began to nominate Hubert Humphrey, Cronkite's voice returned with an air of urgency, "There has been a display of naked violence in the streets of Chicago."

While the convention delegates argued, far more turbulent activities had been taking place in downtown Chicago. The antiwar demonstrators planned for Wednesday night the culmination of their protest. A coalition of demonstrators, including some McCarthy workers who now realized that their candidate had no chance of being nominated, vowed to march three miles from downtown Chicago to the amphitheater to protest the nomination of Humphrey. The city had refused to issue a permit, so the crowd of 5,000 or more milled around in indecision in Grant Park across from the Conrad Hilton Hotel. That eve-

The omnipresent eye. ABC television cameramen (left) aim their lenses while John Chancellor of NBC News (kneeling at center) relaxes during a rare moment of order at the Democratic Convention in August 1968.

ning at approximately 7:15 some caught sight of Ralph Abernathy and his supporters from the Poor People's Campaign. Abernathy's group had a police permit to march legally to the amphitheater and, beckoned by shouts of "join us," most of the demonstrators crossed a small bridge to Michigan Avenue to join Abernathy and his group.

By 7:30 a crowd of approximately 4,500 demonstrators formed at the intersection of Michigan Avenue and Balbo Street. A subsequent U.S. Attorney's report described the crowd as a blend of "young and old, hippies, Yippies, straights, newsmen and cameramen." Two TV mobile units were there, trapped in the crowd. A phalanx of approximately 300 policemen faced this motley crew. After conferring with Abernathy the police made way for his Poor People's Campaign, led by their three mule-drawn wagons. The demonstrators cheered as they saw the line surge forward. But quickly the police closed ranks, stopping the rest of the demonstrators. Unable to see what had transpired ahead, they could not understand why their progress had been halted.

From the rear, the crowd began to push forward, shoving the front line of demonstrators to within ten feet of the police. Some demonstrators sat down in the street, an alternate tactic that had been discussed in the event that the crowd was not permitted to march to the amphitheater. The police ordered the demonstrators to disperse, but they refused. Police approached the crowd and began to arrest demonstrators in peaceful fashion. TV lights glared on the scene, and then a projectile hit a policeman on the head. Theodore White, an eyewitness who was admittedly hostile to the demonstrators, claimed later that nothing was thrown from the crowd. Rather, he saw something falling from a window of the Hilton Hotel directly above. Nevertheless, at precisely 7:55 P.M., the police retaliated and surged into the crowd with billy clubs swinging. Many protesters fell limp, but others fought back. "The whole world is watching! The whole world is watching!" some of them screamed.

At that moment only nearby onlookers were watching. The film from the disturbance was raced by courier to convention center, where more than two hours transpired before it was developed and edited. Thus it was nearly 11:00 P.M. when Walter Cronkite broke into the speeches nominating Hubert Humphrey to introduce the newsreel to his audience.

CBS technicians were prepared and spliced this two-hour-old film of violence into live action on the convention floor, showing Mayor Daley's angry face in the convention hall, then scenes from Michigan Avenue, then candid shots of the mayor, all against the backdrop of the soundtrack of the downtown riot. At the film's conclusion Dan Rather interviewed Mayor Daley, who assured the national audience that "the situation is well in hand." It seemed incongruous, but he was right. At the very moment that Daley spoke, peace had, in fact, temporarily returned to the streets (but it was only a few hours before violence broke out again, shortly after midnight).

Both the decision to interrupt the nomination of the man who was to be the presidential candidate of the Democratic party, as well as the manner in which the tape was played, reflected difficult, and unusual decisions for CBS producers. Although less is known about the decisions of the other two networks, the results were similar. Both NBC and ABC broke into the speeches nominating Humphrey in favor of showing the violence on Chicago's streets. All such editorial choices suggest a reporter's or producer's opinion about what news is important news, and the answers that the three networks arrived at that night said much about the fragmentation of American society in the year 1968.

On that night, at least, it seemed unclear to CBS whether one of the central events in America's democratic process was more important than political protest in the streets. Traditionally, the nation's political dialogue is carried on within a framework established by the two major political parties, but by the summer of 1968 millions of Americans had become disenchanted with that monopoly. The George Wallace campaign proved it and so did the coalition of street demonstrators and their supporters watching at home. The juxtaposition of Mayor Daley's face with scenes from the Michigan Avenue riot was an old trick of cameramen but one seldom used to embarrass prominent public officials.

In its convention coverage in general, and on Wednesday night in particular, television presented a picture of chaos, not order. If this was an unusual picture of American democracy, it was also a reflection of what American society was experiencing. What CBS and the other networks found out, however, was that many Americans did not like what they saw and they blamed the messenger.

CBS reported that overnight telegrams criticizing their reporting outnumbered favorable ones eleven to one. A scientific survey conducted by the University of Michigan two months later found that, when asked whether the police had used too much force in Chicago, only 19 percent said yes. Another 57 percent believed that either the right amount of force or not enough force (25 percent) had been used. Among demographic groups, the demonstrators were supported only by blacks and those with college degrees who were under the age of thirty. Not only had the demonstrators failed to storm the amphitheater; they had failed in their effort to gain significant public support for the antiwar cause.

Picking up the pieces

If opponents of the protesters and supporters of Mayor Daley were upset by CBS's coverage on Wednesday night, they had no cause for complaint on the following

Confrontation

The journalistic photographs on these pages provided Daniel Walker with some of the most vivid evidence for his report on the disturbances in Chicago during the Democratic Convention. Left. A police officer maces a woman outside the convention hall. He then maced the photographer to prevent him from taking more pictures.

Protesters begin a walk to comedian Dick Gregory's house on August 29, the final evening of the convention. Gregory had "invited" the protesters to his home to test "freedom of movement" in the city, but police quickly halted the marchers.

Above. *Chicago police turn on a newsman who had complained that the officers were hassling young people in a car.*

The Old Town area on Chicago's North Side was a site of frequent trouble during the convention. Above. Police corner a black youth in an alleyway before beating him to the ground on August 28. Right. Earlier that week officers club another youth in the area.

night. That night Walter Cronkite invited Mayor Daley to his anchorman's booth for an interview. Viewers might have expected a titanic confrontation between the most uncompromising politician in the convention hall and television's most prominent newsman, but Cronkite did not provoke one. He did not confront the mayor with videotapes of actual police violence and ask him to defend it. Instead, in David Halberstam's words, he "played straight man" to the mayor. Thomas Whiteside, in his chronicle of the event, was equally disappointed:

The Star [Cronkite] simply caved in under a Daley landslide of self-justification. The Mayor took charge of the interview and, unhindered, denounced the peace demonstrators and extolled the pure name of the city of Chicago and the Chicago police for the better part of half an hour.

Material dealing with the demonstrators was collected by the city of Chicago and fashioned into a one-hour-long television program that was offered to TV stations and broadcast by the impressive number of 142 of them around the country in September. The city's program seemed to capture all of the scatology and violence of the Yippies' language. But it developed that the film's makers had used a fake soundtrack to "prove" the verbal provocation. The city also displayed in the film a series of bizarre weapons with which the demonstrators allegedly intended to assault the police. One of the more exotic charges was that the demonstrators had planned to loose poisonous spiders on the police, and the film even showed a captured spider, but a Chicago news reporter later determined that it had been confiscated by the police from a railroad employee who had no known connection with the demonstrators. Despite the dubious devices employed by the film's makers, the city's account was widely hailed. Newspaper headlines blared: "Nation Sees 'Other Side' of Disorders" and "Daley's TV Riot Film Applauded."

Other accounts strongly disputed Mayor Daley's version of the events. Daley charged that the presence of television cameras provoked violence. Alvin Thaler, a CBS cameraman on the scene, believed that cameras actually *inhibited* violence. "Whenever we put our lights on, we reduced the amount of violence in front of us." His opinion was echoed by print reporters, who were not hampered by the electrical equipment of television and could wander freely. They reported much more severe violence on the side streets around Michigan and Balbo, where television crews had not penetrated. On one occasion Chicago police boarded a city bus in which long-haired youths were seated, blocked the exits, turned out the bus lights, and began to beat the riders. One policeman shouted, "You long-haired queer. We're going to stomp the shit out of you." The National Commission on the Causes and Prevention of Violence created a special Chicago Study Team headed by businessman Daniel Walker to investigate the disturbances in Chicago. The Walker Report tended to

agree with the accounts of news reporters. It found that "the many films and video tapes of this time period [Wednesday night] present a picture which does not correspond completely with the police view." The report concluded that the events of Wednesday night were best characterized as a "police riot."

Consensus or polarization

When the Democratic convention concluded on Thursday evening, the man left to contemplate the pieces of the shattered American postwar consensus was the party's presidential candidate. Hubert Humphrey, who had main-

A determined Hubert Humphrey addresses the crowd at a rally in Chicago after the Democratic Convention as Mayor Richard Daley looks on. Humphrey faced the difficult challenge of maintaining the mayor's good will while at the same time winning the support of those Democrats who had opposed the mayor's tactics during the convention, symbolizing the dilemmas facing Humphrey and the Democrats throughout the campaign.

tained a remarkable good cheer through all of his beleaguerment, decided to try to put the pieces back together, beginning with his acceptance speech. Acknowledging the divisions within his party and America at large, he pleaded, "I hope that you will also recognize the much larger areas of agreement" and called for the "paramount necessity for unity—unity in our country." Rejecting the belief of Democrats like Paul O'Dwyer of New York and Harold Hughes of Iowa, who argued that the Democratic party must find a new path, Humphrey reiterated his commitment to the old consensus. That consensus had served the Democratic party well, leading to its hold on the White House for fifteen of the previous twenty-three

years. Candidate Humphrey recited the past accomplishments of his party, intoning the names of Roosevelt, Truman, Stevenson, Kennedy. Then he came to Lyndon Johnson. The very mention of that name sent the convention hall into a raucous paroxysm of "boos" and "yeas."

In his attempt to win the election, Hubert Humphrey felt it was necessary to rebuild the old consensus or, at least, a semblance of it. Richard Nixon, the Republican nominee, looked at the prospect differently. In his mind the mechanics of reaching the number "270," the majority of votes required to be elected president in the Electoral College, did not require consensus. The polarization of American voters was perhaps a better way to victory.

Woodstock

"Chicago," announced *Rolling Stone* magazine, "was only the labor pains. The inheritors came to life outside the village of White Lake." White Lake, located near the town of Bethel, New York, provided the site for an event in August 1969 that was to be a fitting climax for the old decade and an auspicious announcement of the new. The Woodstock Music and Art Fair was four days of "sex, drugs, and rock 'n' roll" that became a metaphor for a generation. On the surface Woodstock was far from idyllic: rain, mud, broken portable toilets, scarcity of food and water, massive traffic jams, and three deaths. But it was also sunshine, sharing of whatever food and drugs were available, two births, and above all, music. More than any one thing, Woodstock was the utlimate battle of performers: the Grateful Dead, the Who, Janis Joplin, Sly and the Family Stone. The pictures on these pages provide a glimpse at the metaphor that was Woodstock, perhaps best put into words by one festival-goer from Montreal: "It's unreal. I'm wet, fed up, tired, and it's beautiful."

Right. *A half-million young people form New York State's third largest city for the weekend of August 15, 1969.*

Above. *Some of the crowd used great ingenuity to find refuge from the weekend's downpours.*

Inset. *The singing of Janis Joplin highlights the performances of Saturday evening.* Above. *The crowd displays a rapture of its own.*

Left. *The rock group Santana holds center stage on Saturday afternoon, the festival's second day.*

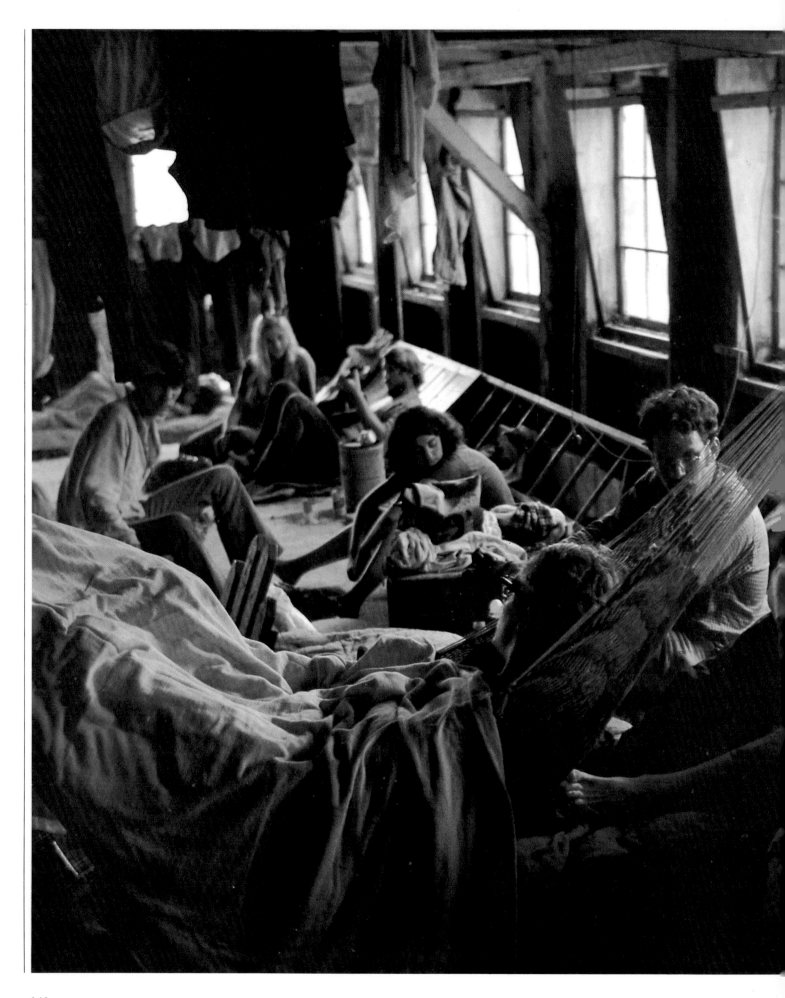

Left. *The festival-goers experienced two heavy rainfalls during the weekend. Forced to take shelter wherever they could find it, a few lucky ones seek protection in an abandoned farm shed.*

Inset left. *The amateurs had a chance to make music as well. Here a female flutist abandons her own music to dance to the rhythm of a conga drummer.*

Below. *At festival's end a young couple makes their bed amid mountains of trash and empty soda cans.*

Skinny dipping offered both a respite from the steamy August heat and the only means of washing. At Leon's Lake, a quarter mile from the stage, a crowd gathers (right) to bathe and socialize, while a young man (above) adorns himself with a garland of flowers.

Polarization

(1969-1972)

Shortly after midnight on Wednesday, November 6, 1969, Richard M. Nixon stepped before the television cameras to acknowledge his election to the presidency of the United States. Several years later, in his memoirs, Nixon described the bitter resentments he had felt over the course of the tough campaign, anger directed against Lyndon Johnson, against antiwar protesters, and above all, against the media. But on this night Richard Nixon put his anger behind him and recalled an incident from the campaign in a small Ohio town not unlike the one in which his father was born. A young teen-ager held up a sign for the passing Nixon campaign with a simple plea, "Bring Us Together." "That will be the great objective of this administration at the outset," Nixon said, "to bring the American people together."

He repeated the theme ten weeks later during his inaugural address:

The simple things are the ones most needed today if we are to surmount what divides us and cement what unites

us. To lower our voices would be a simple thing . . . .

We cannot learn from one another until we stop shouting at one another—until we speak quietly enough so that our words can be heard as well as our voices.

"For its part," the new president promised, "government will listen."

It was a welcome message. America had undergone a fragmentation during 1968 unparalleled since the Civil War. One commentator called it a "crisis of pluralism" and suggested that "clearly the daunting task of the American President in 1969 is nothing less than to heal a nation."

Richard Nixon's words were heeded. Hubert Humphrey, the defeated Democratic candidate, observed for several months a rare self-imposed silence. Even J. William Fulbright, the most persistent critic of Lyndon Johnson's war policies, lowered the volume of his complaints.

To be sure, there were others who ignored the president's plea. Within a month after Richard Nixon took the oath of office, National Guardsmen were called in to clear students from occupied buildings at the University of Wisconsin and Duke University. The Black Panthers initiated a "Free Huey" campaign to gain the release of their leader, Huey Newton, who had been convicted of a murder charge that was later reversed. And civil liberties lawyers announced a program for aiding servicemen resisting orders to go into combat. Groups such as these had long served notice that they no longer had faith in the American government. If the president were truly to "heal the nation" he could only do so by building a new consensus around which these dissidents could rally.

The strategy of polarization

Richard Nixon chose not to build a new consensus. He, in fact, may not have been capable of doing so, since he was in so many ways a creature of the old. It came as a surprise to many that Nixon's "hero-president" was the Democrat, Woodrow Wilson. Wilson had been both a theoretician and an early practitioner of the concept of the ascendancy of the executive branch and the active president asserting his will over Congress. As stated, Wilson's foreign policy goals were more ambitious than Nixon's. Not a mere "generation of peace" but an eternity of peace, a "war to end all wars," had been his dream. When Wilson, however, chose to ignore Congress, even to do battle with that coequal branch of government in his effort to realize his ideals, his second term ended in a stalemate between the executive and the legislature. It was an ironic choice of heroes that this new president had made, for he seemed almost compelled to repeat Wilson's mistakes.

In early June the president set out to prove that he, un-

like Lyndon Johnson, would not make himself a prisoner of the White House. He accepted two invitations to serve as commencement speaker on college campuses, one at the Air Force Academy and the other at General Beadle State College in South Dakota. The president's message was tough. He lashed out against "new isolationists" who urged "unilateral disarmament" on the American people. "Such a policy," he concluded, "would be disastrous for our nation and the world."

"Isolationist?" asked Senator Fulbright in disbelief. "This is nonsense. None of us is saying let's withdraw into our shell." The senator labeled the speech "demagogy." Another veteran dove, Senator Albert Gore of Tennessee, asked, "What and who is the president talking about? I know of no one in Congress who is advocating or who has advocated unilateral disarmament."

Nixon was using familiar tactics: Keep the opponents on the defensive; the best defense is a good offense. Critics described it as "stuffing straw men with outlandish notions." In any case, it may well have ended Nixon's five-month honeymoon with the Democratic-controlled Ninety-first Congress.

Richard Nixon's 1968 election had not been a victory for the Republicans. For the first time in over a century a newly elected president faced a Congress in which both houses were dominated by the opposition. Volatile as the politics of 1968 were, the composition of the House and Senate remained virtually unchanged. Vietnam had been a major issue in several key Senate races. Without exception the most vulnerable Democratic doves survived: Fulbright of Arkansas, Church of Idaho, McGovern of South Dakota, and Nelson of Wisconsin. And outspoken hawks like Republicans Marlow Cook, Edward Gurney, and Barry Goldwater were also sent or returned to Washington.

Continuing the pattern of the 1966 midterm elections, a handful of Republican moderates went to the Capitol. Ultimately these young senators, together with a group of veteran Republican moderates, canceled out the strength of many conservative southern Democrats and made it impossible for Nixon to control even his own party in Congress. The new Congress was polarized not so much around party lines as along ideological ones.

If the ideological confrontation had any unifying theme it was Congressional authority. Liberal Democrats and moderate Republicans began to question the postdepression trend toward a government dominated by the presidency, a presidency that not only was given free reign in the conduct of foreign policy, but that also established the agenda for domestic affairs.

The Ninety-first Congress first asserted itself over a crucial question of military policy: President Nixon's request to fund a modified antiballistic missile system. President Johnson had first proposed an ABM system in 1967 when secret intelligence sources told him that the U.S.S.R. was already preparing its own. His proposed "Sentinel" system,

American Gothic, 1968. A father and his two sons stand solidly behind government foreign policy in a New York City prowar parade in late 1968. The American flag became a symbol of the polarization of American society.

however, roused technical objections, including the opposition of Dwight Eisenhower. Nixon scaled down Johnson's proposal to a smaller ABM system, designed more for use as a "bargaining chip" in negotiations than to provide a full nuclear defense. Even that drew sharp Congressional criticism, but in the end the Senate split fifty to fifty in its vote on August 6, and Vice President Spiro Agnew cast the deciding ballot in favor of the missile system.

Earlier that spring the Senate Foreign Relations Committee had raised a more fundamental challenge to cold war policies. By a vote of fourteen to one it passed the National Commitments Resolution, which would have required the executive to gain legislative approval for any "national commitment by the U.S. to a foreign power." The resolution eventually passed the Senate but died from lack of action by the House. Although still unsuccessful, Congress was clearly beginning to reassert its constitutional prerogatives in the conduct of foreign affairs.

The imbalance between executive and legislative was never as great in domestic issues, and here Congress felt more at ease in challenging the ascendant presidency. The first real opportunity arose when President Nixon nominated in succession two southern judges to fill a vacancy on the Supreme Court. Clement Haynsworth and Harrold Carswell were each turned down by the Senate. The grounds for rejection differed in each case, but Richard Nixon sensed beneath the surface an attack on his presidential powers and unwisely defended at a news conference his "right" to "appoint" Supreme Court justices. His critics jumped to the defense of Congress. The president had obviously not read the constitution, they claimed. He only had the right to nominate justices; only the Senate could confirm their appointment.

The Haynsworth and Carswell nominations were symbolic of more than the clash between the president and Congress. After the Senate rejected Carswell, Nixon said:

I have reluctantly concluded that it is not possible to get confirmation for a Judge on the Supreme Court of any man who believes in the strict construction of the Constitution, as I do, if he happens to come from the South.

In his later memoirs, Nixon explained that the statement was intended as a punishment for those who voted against the Haynsworth and Carswell nominations. "I was determined," he wrote, "that they would at least pay a political price for it in the South."

The "southern strategy" was but one component of a policy that by the fall of 1969 became the full-blown practice of the politics of polarization. The administration's rhetoric, led by "point-man" Vice President Agnew, was designed not to bring Americans together, but to separate them: North from South, black from white, dissident from flag-waver. The administration did not deny that this was its goal. In fact, on October 30, 1969, Agnew admitted and justified the use of the politics of polarization:

If, in challenging, we polarize the American people, I say it is time for a positive polarization. It is time to rip away the rhetoric and to divide on authentic lines.

Why the politics of polarization? There were electoral considerations to be sure; the policy would reach a high point during the 1970 Congressional elections. But the more important reason was hidden in the minutiae of public opinion polls. By the fall of 1969 the number of "doves" on Vietnam had come to swamp the ranks of "hawks," leading 55 percent to 31 percent; the rest were undecided. Peace sentiment had actually increased more in the course of 1969—thirteen percentage points—than in the more volatile year of 1968 when it increased by only 7 percent. Above all, the politics of polarization was designed to separate the "pragmatic" peace movement from the Vietnam War's ideological opponents, to prevent a recurrence on a nationwide scale of the New Hampshire phenomenon, when manual workers and farmers had joined with student activists to topple a president. Agnew concluded his October 30 remarks:

When the President said "bring us together" he meant the functioning contributing portions of the American citizenry.

In the short run the administration's tactics seemed to pay off. The president received a surge of support following his appeal to the "silent majority" in November, and Vice President Agnew seemed to grow in stature and reputation throughout the country. But it remained a risky venture. In late November, *Time* magazine wrote:

What will happen in the longer haul is more problematical. . . . Not only is he [Nixon] stimulating dissent among many moderates and on the left by his new belligerence, he also risks stirring up the hard-line right. . . . He may exacerbate the tensions of a nation distraught and confused as it has not been since the Depression. The danger augurs ill for both his presidency and the American people.

The military under attack

The polarization of American civilian society found its parallel within the armed forces as trends in the breakdown of discipline that first began in 1967 and 1968 began to accelerate. The war in Vietnam certainly bore a portion of the direct responsibility. The widespread drug abuse problem began in Vietnam and was gradually carried—often by Vietnam veterans—wherever American troops were based. Racial problems were fueled by the blacks' war experiences. It was difficult for a black soldier to accept that while he could die alongside a white buddy in Vietnam, he could not live with him near some bases in Europe and the United States or get the same respect from his commanding officers. Finally, the wartime breakdown of command authority, the increase in combat refusals and officer fraggings, had a detrimental effect upon command relationships all over the world.

On the other hand, the indirect role played by the Vietnam War is for historians as difficult to unravel as the relationship between the war and the social and moral upheaval that accompanied it in civilian life. "Let's face it," said an army captain in Germany, "the big problem is the Army's not set up to change and yet society's going through tremendously accelerated change." Drug abuse in the army, for example, reflected a growing trend in society at large. Although new recruits made up less than half of the population at Fort Dix, they comprised 80 percent of the drug-related cases in the post infirmary. Sixty-five percent of army drug users in Germany in 1971 had started before induction. Whatever the cause, one thing was certain: The military was in trouble.

In the early seventies, increasing numbers of men were judged unfit for military service. Discharges based on misconduct, unfitness, and unsuitability rose to more than 30 per 1,000 in 1971 and 1972. The marines, traditionally known for their stringent discipline, led the way with 68.7 discharges per 1,000 in 1970 and a staggering 112.4 per 1,000 the following year in a corps-wide house cleaning undertaken as the marines left Vietnam. In addition to purging the men they did not want, the armed forces experienced increasing difficulties in keeping the men they did. In 1971 the army reenlistment rate was less than 4 percent. By 1970 the combined retention rate for all services was only half of that in 1966 and the lowest since the Korean War.

At the same time, many men were not waiting for the end of their hitches to leave. During the years 1969 to 1973 the number of discharges for desertion remained above the 5 percent level worldwide. At the peak period of such incidents an American soldier was going AWOL every two minutes and deserting every six minutes.

Nor were those who remained on duty always mentally present. Drug use and abuse skyrocketed in the early 1970s. Over 40 percent of the troops based in the U.S. or Europe used marijuana, almost equal to the 50 percent usage estimated for Vietnam. The use of psychedelics, such as LSD, by military personnel in the U.S. and Europe (over 30 percent) actually outstripped the problem in Vietnam. The use of drugs contributed to an increase in crimes—both on and off base—committed by those troops as drug addicts turned to crime to support their habits.

Drugs were not the only cause of criminal activity on the part of military personnel. Racial tensions provoked much more serious outbreaks of assaults and violence. At Camp Lejeune, home of about 30,000 marines, 70 percent of them Vietnam veterans, a clash in July 1969 between blacks and whites left one corporal dead and at least fifteen others wounded. In March 1971 racial fighting at the Bethesda Naval Medical Center became so severe that the base's enlisted men's club was temporarily closed. A Department of the Army report later admitted that the army had "a race problem of serious proportions both in the continental United States and overseas" and that "Negro soldiers seem to have lost faith in the Army."

Grievances of blacks in the armed forces were often justified. While they made up nearly 10 percent of all army personnel, they constituted only 3.4 percent of the officer corps and a bare 0.6 percent of officers ranking colonel or above. In addition, the military justice system was open to charges of racist practices. Arrested black soldiers were held in pretrial confinement an average of five days longer than whites in 1971 and 1972. Fifty percent of all soldiers held in confinement in 1971 were black. Moreover, punitive discharges as a result of courts-martial were given to blacks 33 percent more often than whites, and when sentenced to hard labor, the average black was given a full year longer than a white. So bad did racial tensions become that on some bases blacks began to wage a guerrilla war against whites. A barracks area at Fort Benning, Georgia, known as Kelley Hill, was the scene of many nighttime attacks upon white soldiers. A popular saying at the post was, "Kelley Hill may belong to the commander in the daytime, but it belongs to the blacks after dark." One noncom noted that his unit had split up into "two street gangs."

The military was becoming polarized not only along social lines ("juicers," or beer drinkers, versus "heads," or drug users) and racial lines (black versus white), but also on the major political question of civilian life: the war in Vietnam. To a large extent, the political beliefs and activities of young GIs reflected those of young civilians in the United States.

By 1971 there were at least 144 underground newspapers published on or near American military bases. Most did not go to the extreme of one West Coast paper, which advised soldiers, "Don't desert. Go to Vietnam and kill your commanding officer." But one had only to look at the names of some publications, such as *Left Face* (Fort McClellan), *Shakedown* (Fort Dix), and *Counterattack* (Fort Carson), to get an idea of their political stance.

In addition, antiwar coffee houses operated near as many as twenty-six bases, offering places for soldiers to meet, listen to rock music, and talk about Vietnam. Though the coffee houses really lay beyond their jurisdiction, the military used a variety of means—invoking violations of health regulations or citations as public nuisances—to get local authorities to close them. Nevertheless, in 1971, popular coffee houses like the Shelter Half at Fort Lewis and the Oleo Strut at Fort Hood were still in business.

Servicemen could also join organizations like the Concerned Officers' Movement to express their antiwar feelings. In May 1971 twenty-nine officers in COM at Fort Bragg signed their names to an antiwar advertisement in a local paper. When the army suggested that these men should resign from the service, the Pentagon intervened. It ruled that there was no violation of army regulations, so the dissenters were not disciplined.

Dissent in the Ranks

The trauma of the war in Vietnam greatly affected the morale of enlisted men in the armed forces after 1968, causing many of them to question the authority not only of their officers but also of the military system as a whole. As a result, the public caught a glimpse of military life seldom, if ever, seen before.

Above. *An active duty soldier with "new regulation" hair length distributes an underground GI newspaper at the entrance to Travis Air Force Base in northern California.*

Right. *A senior officer of the 4th Infantry Division, Brigadier General Dewitt Smith, pays a visit to an antiwar GI coffee house at Fort Carson, Colorado, to respond to his men's concerns about the "quality of life" at the base.*

In November 1970, Virginia Nasmyth poses in front of a billboard in Mission Valley, California, that publicizes the fate of her brother. Although Americans were divided over what action to take, all wanted the speedy return of the POWs.

The end of the draft

It was no wonder that when Richard Nixon asked Defense Secretary Melvin Laird to devise a "detailed plan" to phase out the draft and replace it with an all-volunteer army, leaders of the armed forces, long opposed to an all-volunteer force, reluctantly agreed. Nixon ticketed the end of the draft for July 1973, the date on which Congress would again have to extend the Selective Service Act. Starting in 1969, the president took a series of steps designed to reform the Selective Service System and then pave the way for the new volunteer forces.

In May 1969 Nixon asked Congress to authorize him to institute a lottery system for the selection of draftees and to induct nineteen-year-olds first, two measures that Congress had denied Lyndon Johnson in 1967. While Congress was debating, the president secured the retirement of General Lewis B. Hershey as director of the SSS. Replacing Hershey was no easy task. Football coaches John Pont of Indiana and Paul Dietzel of South Carolina both turned the job down. Finally a reluctant Curtis W. Tarr, assistant secretary of the air force and former president of Lawrence College, accepted the post.

In the meantime Congress passed the lottery bill, and the president scheduled the first drawing for December 1, 1969. In the glare of television lights in the tiny auditorium of the Selective Service Building, Representative Alexander Pirnie of New York pulled from the bowl the first of 366 blue capsules, each denoting a day of the year. The first date drawn was September 14, followed by April 24 and December 30. That meant that local draft boards would be required to choose first all eligible males born on September 14 when they made their selections in January 1970. If a local board had no eligible male born on that date, it would select those born on April 24, and so on, until it fulfilled its quota.

Under the new regulations a man would be eligible for drafting only for one year. If he were deferred at the age of nineteen he would keep his original number and his year of eligibility would begin when his deferment expired. During the course of 1970, men were drafted with lottery numbers as high as 195. In 1971, after new numbers had been drawn for the newly eligible, draft calls reached only to lottery number 125. The lottery itself did not change the social composition of those drafted since it did not affect deferments, but coupled with declining troop levels in Vietnam, it gave each eligible young man a better ability to predict whether he would be drafted.

In addition, Nixon radically changed the deferment picture for certain groups. By executive order he prohibited the granting of any new occupational and fatherhood deferments. He also asked Congress to authorize him to cancel undergraduate student deferments. Congress complied on September 21, 1971, and, the newly entering males in the college class of 1975 found themselves no longer exempt from the draft. But by that time, declining draft calls made the point moot. In 1971 draft inductees dipped below 100,000 for the first time since 1962.

Resistance to the draft, however, did not go away. On May 20, 1973, just weeks before the draft would expire, a Camden, New Jersey, jury found seventeen men and women, including four Catholic priests, not guilty of destroying Selective Service files—this in spite of the fact that the accused admitted having done so and were caught in the act by eighty FBI agents. The jury seemed to agree with the defendants' argument that their actions were justified as a protest against an "illegal and immoral war." It was the "first total legal victory for the anti-war movement in five years of such draft record incidents," according to one account. Father Edward Murphy, one of the acquitted defendants, said, "We finally got a jury that said, 'enough.'" And indeed, by 1973 virtually everyone in America had had enough. Still the draft would linger as a constant source of debate—for those who had fled the country rather than be drafted as well as for young people, barely old enough to remember Vietnam, who would five years later be faced with the demands of a new Selective Service System.

There was another group of men for whom draft resistance must have seemed ironic, if not embittering. They were "in exile" from their own country, not out of any philosophical commitment or opposition to the war, but because they had no choice. These men were the prisoners of war held captive by the North Vietnamese. When Richard Nixon took office on January 20, 1968, the Defense Department placed the official number of POWs at over 400; some of them had already been prisoners for more than five years. In addition, no one knew how many of the 1,300 Americans reported missing in action had joined them in captivity. The editors of *Look* magazine, critics of the war effort, echoed the sentiments of most of their countrymen when they wrote, "The welfare of these unfortunate men and the feelings of their families are matters of simple humanity—not politics." That universal concern, however, became caught in a bitter tug of war between Nixon and his critics, a battle brought on by the new administration's decision to bring the POWs into the public arena.

Under President Johnson, efforts to improve the treatment of POWs and to secure their release had been the province of the State Department. Because they believed that publicity over the POWs might make Hanoi more intransigent, Johnson administration officials worked quietly through diplomatic channels. But their success was very limited; the enemy had returned only twenty-seven POWs over a five-year period, mostly for propaganda purposes. Citing this failure, Nixon's Secretary of Defense Melvin Laird persuaded the White House to transfer authority for the POWs to the Pentagon. He then announced that the question of prisoners of war would become a public matter to be discussed openly.

Several intentions motivated the administration. Publicly, the White House hoped that the outcry would prod Hanoi to improve conditions for the prisoners and perhaps even force the enemy to release them. Privately, however, the president was also seeking to co-opt a potentially explosive issue in the face of growing discontent among the families of POWs.

On December 26, 1969, Nixon met with representatives of the newly organized National League of Families of Prisoners and Missing in Southeast Asia and promised them that any settlement of the war would have to include the return of their loved ones, at least those still alive. The administration provided substantial assistance to the league: free transportation to meetings, free telephone lines, and lists of potential donors to support League operations from Republican party lists.

The administration also used the POW issue as part of its policy of polarization and its attempt to silence war critics. The president cited the prisoners as a rationale for keeping troops in Vietnam: "As long as the North Vietnamese have any Americans as prisoners of war there will be Americans in South Vietnam and enough Americans to give them an incentive to release the prisoners."

Although Americans initially rallied to the administration's cause, the tactic eventually backfired. Critics of the war argued that only a total withdrawal of U.S. forces would bring the prisoners their freedom. They noted that, historically, captured troops were exchanged at the end of hostilities, not during them. "In the first Indochina war," the *New Republic* reminded its readers, "the Vietnamese freed French Union troops after the truce. Their release hinged . . . on the French decision to get out of the war."

The administration's POW campaign also caused a second problem. It convinced Hanoi that the prisoners constituted a powerful bargaining chip in negotiations. It could demand just what Nixon did not want: a unilateral withdrawal of U.S. troops in exchange for their release.

Even some of the POW families began to lose patience with Nixon's war policies, fearing that Vietnamization would bring the American troops home but leave their loved ones imprisoned in North Vietnam for an indefinite period of time. Mrs. Harold Kushner of Danville, Virginia, the wife of a captured air force doctor, organized some 350 members of the National League of Families into a splinter group called POW-MIA Families for Immediate Release. She charged the White House with "using the prisoner issue to buy time for the South Vietnamese government," and many members of the new group joined the peace movement. Eventually Mrs. Kushner seconded the nomination of George McGovern at the 1972 Democratic convention. And Mrs. James Stockdale, the wife of a navy captain who had been shot down and captured in 1965

and the league's founder, added, "If there's no progress by May [1972] we should make the POWs a major issue, even if it means becoming anti-administration and supporting a Democrat."

Thus by the presidential campaign of 1972 the return of the POWs had become one of the most vulnerable points in Richard Nixon's war policy. American troop strength was down to less than 50,000 men. Weeks passed without a single new American combat death. Richard Nixon was riding high in the public opinion polls and, according to those polls, most Americans felt they could, as the president desired, ignore the continuing war in Southeast Asia. But having raised the POW issue he could not now evade it. Henry Kissinger described in his memoirs how the POWs had put additional pressure on his negotiations: "At the outset it rallied support at home, although in later years it was turned against us, as the prisoners became an added argument for unilateral withdrawal." By the spring of 1972 ending the war meant little more to Americans than bringing the POWs home.

New York City "hard hats" take to the streets to counter the demonstrations of antiwar protesters on May 8, 1970.

In politicizing the issue of the release of the POWs, the Nixon administration made one important calculation: Millions of Americans would not respond by sorting through the arguments of hawks and doves but rather would rally to the cry of patriotic duty.

The hard hats

Among those groups whom the Nixon administration would count on, none was more important than America's blue-collar workers, a labor force comprised to a great extent of "hyphenated Americans," the ethnics. Patriotism was, indeed, a powerful emotion among them. At the outbreak of both world wars the loyalty of most ethnic groups was at some time questioned. They responded with voluntary military service and, in many cases, battlefield heroics. After World War II, "joining the Cold War consensus was the surest means of affirming their patriotism," Richard Polenberg, a leading commentator on ethnic politics, explained.

By 1969 these blue-collar workers found themselves in a deep quandary, perhaps expressed best by one who had lost a son in Vietnam. "It's people like us who give our sons for the country," he bitterly explained. "I hate those peace demonstrators. . . . The sooner we get the hell out of there the better." It was a familiar juxtaposition, frustration with the war coupled with a hatred of those who refused to support their country's policies. Such Americans were perfect targets of the politics of polarization.

A large proportion of ethnics and blue-collar workers opposed the demonstrations. As early as 1967, a prowar demonstration in New York City brought out, as the *Berkeley Barb* described it, "A hundred thousand workers [who] marched down Fifth Avenue . . . Seamen, Teamsters, Longshoremen, Auto Workers, Carpenters, Bricklayers, and many others." During the October 1969 antiwar Moratorium, New York Mayor John Lindsay ordered all American flags to be flown at half-mast. At one police station, the men raised their flag full mast and "ringed the flagpole in defiance," according to *Time* magazine.

The hardhat movement received its greatest publicity in May 1970, in the aftermath of the American incursion into Cambodia. On May 8 New York City construction workers assaulted student protesters, while, according to some reporters, the city police stood by idly. The hard hat became a symbol of patriotism. Two weeks later, Peter Brennan, president of the Building and Construction Trades Council of New York, helped organize a demonstration that attracted nearly 100,000 building tradesmen and longshoremen to a rally around city hall. Vice President Agnew praised "the impressive display in [sic] patriotism—and a spirit of pride in country that seems to have become unfashionable in recent years."

By the fall of 1970 the hardhat image was sufficiently entrenched in the national imagination to provoke *Psychology Today* to conduct an inquiry into "Why Hard Hats Hate Hairs." Ultimate recognition for the movement came a few months later when CBS television introduced Archie Bunker and "All in the Family" to the television audience.

Had working-class attitudes about the war changed significantly since 1968? The answer was, "not at all," according to a major inquiry entitled "Dove Sentiment Among Blue Collar Workers" published by *Dissent* in the summer of 1970. "Manual workers expressed stronger support for both immediate withdrawal and/or gradual withdrawal from Vietnam than persons in white-collar or professional business occupations," concluded the article. Alongside data gleaned from Gallup polls, the article pointed to the results of several referendums on the war held in numerous cities. "Vote against the war in nearly all referendums was concentrated in working-class rather than in upper middle class segments of the communities."

Why then the hardhat phenomenon? Just as student activists represented only a fraction of all youth, so too did demonstrating prowar hard hats represent only a minority of their class. Particularly in New York the demonstrators came from among the most privileged and well-paid unions: skilled construction workers and longshoremen. In addition, local grievances by the demonstrators against Mayor Lindsay may have provoked more marchers than support of the war—the rally's focal point was city hall.

But the movement was too large to be explained away by local peculiarities. While working-class opposition to the war continued to exist and union officials became increasingly active in that movement, their opposition remained pragmatic rather than ideological. As Harry Evans, an official of the United Auto Workers, explained:

The majority of working men want us to get the hell out of Vietnam. . . . Some think there has been just too much killing and they want it stopped. . . . Others have kids that will be eligible for the draft pretty soon.

The one line blue-collar workers would not cross was the one that would put them on the side of the demonstrators, on the side of all those who had rejected the tradi-

tional American values. As Father Andrew Greeley of the National Opinion Research Center in Chicago explained:

In the eyes of the white ethnic, "peace" has been identified as a "radical" cause. The ethnics want no part of contemporary radicalism, especially as it is advocated by long-haired college students. . . . If the white ethnic is told in effect that to support peace he must also support the Black Panthers, women's liberation, widespread use of drugs, free love, campus radicals, Dr. Spock, long hair, and picketing clergymen, he may find it very difficult to put himself on the side of peace.

No one better understood this fact than Vice President Spiro Agnew. During the 1970 Congressional campaigns both Agnew and the president did their best to associate all who opposed their policies in Vietnam with those who rejected traditional values. A new term that was to be the *leitmotif* of the Republican campaign was born: "radical-liberal." A memorandum prepared by Jeb Magruder and H. R. Haldeman, two White House assistants, laid out the plan for the campaign:

The Democrats should be portrayed as being on the fringes: radical-liberals who bus children, excuse disorders, tolerate crime, apologize for our wealth, and undercut the President's foreign policy.

The order of the invective was important, for opposition to the president's foreign policy, which was widespread among blue-collar workers, would then become associated with the most intolerable—and often inaccurate—charges on social questions. Both Agnew and Nixon performed according to script. In September Agnew asked, "Will we be intimidated and blackmailed into following the path dictated by a disruptive, radical, and militant minority—the pampered prodigies of the radical liberals in the United States Senate?" And the following week, Nixon attacked "the passive acquiescence or even fawning approval of violence that in some fashionable circles has become the mark of being 'with it.'"

For all this, the administration gained very little in the 1970 elections. The Republicans gained three seats in the Senate but still trailed the Democrats 55 to 45. More important, of the fourteen key races considered to be tests between hawks and doves, antiwar candidates won nine. In the House, Democrats picked up nine seats, far fewer than the twenty or so usually lost by the White House in an off-year election. However, Nixon's failure to bring a Republican majority into the House when elected in 1968 meant that the Democrats had fewer lost seats to recover.

Most observers, however, believed that Vietnam played only a small role in the results. Political pollster John Kraft reported, "People just didn't feel this was a war that either party had the ability to solve faster or better than the other." The answers to two questions Kraft asked his interviewees seemed to bear out his hypothesis. When asked, "How do you feel about [New York] Senator [Charles]

Goodell's proposal to pull everyone out of Vietnam right away, by the end of 1970?" he got a three-to-one approval. Then when asked how well they thought the president was doing in withdrawing troops from Vietnam, Kraft found that the president also received a three-to-one approval rating. Kraft concluded, "There's a distinct difference between what Goodell was proposing and what Nixon was doing."

Perhaps the best explanation for this discrepancy was that the politics of polarization were working. The positive response to the Goodell plan suggested that Americans at the end of 1970 were more dovish than ever before, more desirous of ending the war than one or two years earlier. But when asked to show their patriotism, the American people would support the presidency, thereby giving Richard Nixon both public support and time. The crucial question was how long he could retain that support and how much time he had left. Pollster Kraft warned that Nixon's reelection would depend on ending the war by 1972. "There are ample signs," his polling results told him, "that it will hurt him if he doesn't. . . . Getting out slowly may not be enough."

Media: the great scare

In order for the politics of polarization to succeed, the White House required cooperation from an unlikely source, the national news media. Not only would the administration's message have to be carried through national news outlets, especially television, but it was equally important that the media not contradict the charges flowing from the executive or expose the strategy itself. In the fall of 1969 the White House undertook a campaign to intimidate or at least neutralize the press.

It began in Des Moines, Iowa, on November 13, when Vice President Agnew attacked the "small and unelected" elite of the media who have the power to "distort our national search for internal peace and stability." Agnew went on to criticize in particular the practice of network anchormen and invited guests to analyze a presidential speech immediately at its conclusion, a practice he called "instant analysis." Agnew, unlike most members of the public, knew well that it was hardly "instant analysis." Presidential statements were routinely given to the media hours in advance, in part to prepare postspeech commentators. Despite the insistence on the part of all three networks that Agnew's speech would not affect their news practices, "instant analysis" immediately disappeared from CBS. The president could now deliver his message without immediate elaboration or criticism from CBS television commentators.

Ironically the Agnew speech—and the White House readily admitted that it had been written by presidential speech writer Patrick Buchanan—came at a time when the major networks had already begun to exercise self-restraint. Following the public-relations debacle at the Chicago convention and the election of Richard Nixon, network executives sent out a series of memorandums that drastically changed the type of coverage Americans saw in 1969, both of the war in Vietnam and of domestic politics.

Agnew had charged that "one minute of Eldridge Cleaver is worth ten minutes of Roy Wilkins," executive director of the NAACP. But at that very moment it was impossible for Cleaver to get even one minute of air time. In early 1969, the executive producer of NBC's "Nightly News" "banned" him and other radical black figures, Stokely Carmichael and H. Rap Brown, from the air. In addition, the producer prohibited the use of any film that called attention to impending demonstrations.

More important were the changes demanded of reporters stationed in Vietnam. In March 1969 Av Westin, executive producer of ABC "Evening News," wrote to all correspondents, "I have asked our Vietnam staff to alter the focus of the coverage from combat pieces to interpretive ones, pegged to the eventual pullout of the American forces." And Westin told the Saigon bureau itself to "shift our focus . . . to themes and stories under the general heading: We Are On Our Way Out of Vietnam."

Reuven Frank, executive producer of NBC's "Nightly News," made virtually the same decision, telling his staff in late 1968 that the "story" to be covered was the negotiations, not the fighting. In a two-month period following Frank's directive, NBC showed filmed footage of combat only three times, compared with an average of three or four times per week the preceding year.

Television networks were not the only national news media to adjust their Vietnam coverage. From the inauguration until the bloody battle of Hamburger Hill in May 1969, neither *Time* nor *Newsweek* reported a single major engagement involving American troops, ignoring in the process the vicious fighting in and near the A Shau Valley during the first three months of the year.

Thus, even before Agnew spoke the national networks and national news weeklies had already taken steps that, deliberate or coincidental, went far to appease the new administration. But it was not far enough. For many months following Agnew's Des Moines speech, network executives were bombarded with a host of White House-inspired complaints. The FCC threatened investigations into news-gathering practices; heads of local network affiliates—most of them Republicans—threatened to drop network programs; and, in speeches, Agnew continued his attacks on the media. Later there were reports of midnight calls from White House assistant Charles Colson to network executives complaining about particular stories.

Of course, the Nixon White House could not muzzle all of the media all of the time. There were few stories that so angered the White House as one run by *Life* magazine in its June 27, 1969, edition. It was so infuriating because it contained not a single word and was therefore invulnerable to attack. The story consisted simply of 242 pictures: passport photos, high-school yearbook pictures, small family snapshots. Each picture showed the face of a young American serviceman who had died in Vietnam during one week of fighting.

If there was a turning point in Nixon's battle with the media, it took place in the early summer of 1971. On Sunday, June 13, 1971, the *New York Times* published a host of documents together with a study bearing the innocuous-sounding title of "U.S.-Vietnam Relations, 1945–1968." They soon became known as "The Pentagon Papers."

The Pentagon Papers had been prepared by the Department of Defense in 1967 and 1968 at the behest of Robert McNamara. McNamara's goal was to determine how the United States had become so deeply committed to South Vietnam. The study began with the earliest policy decisions by the Truman administration to support the French return to Indochina after World War II and continued through the Johnson years. Among the contributors to the study was a young civilian employee of the Pentagon with extensive field experience in South Vietnam, Daniel Ellsberg.

In March 1968 Ellsberg arranged to get a copy of the secret study into the hands of Neil Sheehan, who had covered the Vietnam War for UPI and then returned home to become the *New York Times*'s resident Vietnam expert. Sheehan immediately recognized the importance of the study and stressed to the editors of the *Times* that the value of the story would be conveyed only by printing a wealth of documents. Sheehan and a large crew of editors and writers then secretly began the preparation of a multipart series reprinting and analyzing the papers.

Since the documents were classified, the *Times* sent the papers to its legal counsel, Louis Loeb, a distinguished seventy-two-year-old corporate lawyer. Loeb was appalled. He argued that printing the documents would not only be illegal, but, because of the *Times*'s unusual fiscal structure, a protracted legal case could ruin the paper financially. Other attorneys for the *Times* disagreed, and on Saturday, June 12, 1971, executive editor A. M. Rosenthal secured the approval for publication from Arthur Ochs Sulzberger, the *Times*'s publisher. To protect him from the inevitable furor—and to insure that he did not change his

mind—Rosenthal persuaded Sulzberger to spend the weekend on Long Island. The Sunday *Times* carried the first installment of the Pentagon Papers story, beginning on page one and continuing for three more full pages.

Sunday is usually a "weak" news day, and TV network anchors traditionally have difficulty filling the half-hour of weekend news. Yet on Sunday, June 13, only NBC, among the three networks, found the story of the Pentagon Papers sufficiently compelling to be worthy of mention. NBC may have been an exception only because David Brinkley had sensed their importance when reading his Sunday *Times.* It is doubtful whether the Pentagon Papers would ever have fallen into oblivion, but the Nixon administration insured that they would not when it took the *Times* to court and moved for an injunction against further publication of the classified documents.

The White House would lose twice in its battle to prevent publication of the Pentagon Papers. On Tuesday, June 15, the U.S. government went into the district court in New York City where Judge Murray I. Gurfein, a Nixon appointee, issued a temporary injunction that forbade the

Times from further publication of the papers. The *Times* obliged. Three days later, however, the U.S. Court of Appeals overruled Gurfein in principle but permitted the injunction to remain in force until the Supreme Court heard the case. Just eight days later, on June 26, the Supreme Court heard oral arguments from the two sides. On June 30 the Court announced its landmark decision, ruling, by a 7 to 2 majority, to uphold the appeals court decision in favor of the *Times.* The Court held, in effect, that the government was free to file criminal charges against anyone involved in the theft or possession of classified documents, but it could not engage in prior restraint of the press.

The administration lost again when other newspapers refused to be intimidated by the government's action against the *Times* and began publication of the Pentagon Papers themselves. The government was thus forced to bring suits against the *Boston Globe,* the *St. Louis Post-Dispatch,* and the *Washington Post.* These government legal moves became moot after the Supreme Court decision.

The publication of the Pentagon Papers may have been the final blow to public support of the war effort. The story

Dramatic stories by the nation's press kept Americans from forgetting the continuing fighting in Vietnam. Left. Life magazine's article "One Week's Dead," *from the June 27, 1969, issue, reminds visitors to a Big Sur, California, folk music festival of the war's human cost. Above. Two years later, on June 30, 1971, pressmen from the New York Times applaud upon learning that the Supreme Court will permit the* Times *to resume publication of The Pentagon Papers.*

they told of government complicity in questionable practices in Vietnam, such as supporting the South Vietnamese generals who assassinated Ngo Dinh Diem in 1963, had often been suspected but were now confirmed. They also revealed that Lyndon Johnson's escalation of the war had been planned even while he was telling the American people that there would be "no wider war." But, as many of Nixon's advisers had suggested to the president, the revelations did little to damage his political standing since they dealt with events before his election. By the summer of 1971 troop withdrawals from Vietnam had passed the 50 percent mark. The politics of polarization continued to work, even to intensify. It was apparent wherever parents and children glared across the "generation gap."

When Vice President Agnew defended the administration against charges that Richard Nixon was deliberately dividing American society he called the administration's policy one of "positive polarization." The concept, however, was a contradiction in terms, for polarization requires a "negative" pole as well as a positive one. And there was no doubt that the negative pole of this strategy was youth in general, radical students in particular.

Appropriately, this new status of the student first became apparent in Berkeley, California. By the late 1960s the Berkeley "student body" had become an amorphous group. The media was forever trying to distinguish between "real" students, graduates, former students, and just plain hippies who hung out near the campus. In reality only a legalistic distinction could be made. Enrolled students might be found hanging out on Telegraph Avenue, smoking marijuana with high-school dropouts, while unregistered hippies often packed the lecture halls when popular professors taught. The new so-called "counterculture" blended intellectual pursuits with free use of drugs and a commitment to political change.

The age of Aquarius

Berkeley became "liberated territory." Youthful dissidents, often accused of criticizing without offering any replacements, had in Berkeley built an impressive array of "counterinstitutions." These included everything from a "free university" to cooperative ventures in supermarkets, automobile garages, and clothing stores, where prices were cheap and profits were distributed among the members. It

A common sight in the late 1960s. Two hippies "lay back" outside a store in San Francisco.

was hardly unexpected then when in mid-April 1969, this amalgam of youth decided to build a "People's Park."

Claiming squatter's rights to a vacant three-acre mudfield, Berkeley's young covered the mud with sod, planted a three-tree apple orchard, laid a brick walkway, and sowed a "revolutionary cornfield." Others rented welding equipment and built swings and a sandbox for children. A fishpond was dug. At night bonfires blazed in a central pit while volunteers ladled free soup to the needy. It was blessed by a local countercultural clergyman, and architectural critic Alan Temko hailed it as "the most significant innovation in recreational design since the great public parks of the nineteenth and early twentieth centuries."

The park belonged to the people, or so the street people thought. But the university owned the land, which it had bought in 1967 but had never developed. UC Berkeley Chancellor Roger Heyns announced the bad news: "We will have to put up a fence to reestablish the conveniently forgotten fact that the field is indeed the university's."

In mid-May university officials ordered that "No Trespassing" signs be posted. When a crowd of students and "street people" moved to retake the lot, the police moved in. For two-and-a-half hours a battle raged, one that a reporter described as "guerilla warfare through Telegraph Avenue." Thirty-two persons were injured, and one student was rushed to the hospital in critical condition. The next day he died from a number eight bird shot wound, inflicted when police opened fire into the crowd.

The battle over People's Park differed from the usual confrontation over university rules or regulations. It was not an attack on the establishment or a demonstration against the war or racism or injustice. Rather it represented the "defense" of a new lifestyle, an assertion by young people of a right to live beyond the morality, conventions, and even property laws of America. The response of increasing numbers of young people—both college students and nonstudents alike—to polarization was simply to "drop out" of society.

The origins of the resulting counterculture went well back into American history, drawing inspiration from Henry David Thoreau, among others. More immediate precursors included the "beats" of the 1950s and the "flower children" of the mid-1960s. But what emerged in 1969 and for a few years thereafter changed what had

A "head shop" serves the countercultural lifestyle of late 1960s youth in San Francisco.

People's Park

People's Park in Berkeley, California, swarms with peaceful activity in early May 1969 (center), but one week later National Guardsmen clash with students near the park (inset left) in order to reclaim the land for the University of California.

Above. The guard forces students into a parking lot where 400 were arrested.

After being evicted from the park, youths prepare a new People's Park "annex" northwest of the original site.

165

been an elite personal philosophy of a small number of upper-middle-class youths into an amorphous movement that spanned much of an entire generation.

At first this counterculture was concentrated in a few "youth ghettos": New York's Greenwich Village, Harvard Square in Cambridge, Massachusetts, as well as Berkeley, California. But the place that became the most important symbol of the generation gap was the 600-acre dairy farm of one Max Yasgur in Bethel, New York. On Yasgur's farm, during the weekend of August 15, 1969, nearly half a million young people joined together at the "Woodstock Music and Art Fair, An Aquarian Exposition."

The Woodstock festival was planned by John Roberts, a twenty-four-year-old businessman. Roberts expected the festival to attract up to 200,000 for the weekend, with half of them present at any given time. Soon after the festival's opening on Friday evening it became apparent that he had vastly underestimated the size of the audience. Three hundred thousand patrons flooded the farm that evening, wreaking havoc on the ticket-selling system. Late that day the festival promoters, resigned to their losses—estimated at $500,000—declared the festival free to all comers.

As the program began a festival official looked out over the sea of bodies assembled shoulder to shoulder across the thirty-five acre alfalfa field. "There are a hell of a lot of us here," he announced. "If we are going to make it, you had better remember that the guy next to you is your brother." The music began.

Remarkable throughout the weekend was the good behavior of the crowd. There were no major crimes, but 400 people were treated for drug or alcohol overdoses. On Saturday, the *New York Times* reported:

The police and the festival's promoters both expressed amazement that despite the size of the crowd—the largest gathering of its kind ever held—there had been neither violence nor any serious incident. As a state police lieutenant put it, "There hasn't been anybody yelling pig at the cops and when they ask directions they are polite and none of them has really given us any trouble yet."

Life magazine noted that what had become New York State's "third largest city" that weekend experienced "not so much as a fist fight."

As much as the music, perhaps more so, drugs dominated Woodstock. Explained one nineteen-year-old on Sunday, "There was so much grass being smoked last night that you could get stoned just sitting there and breathing." The *New York Times* felt compelled to translate for its readers:

In the argot of the drug scene . . . "grass" is marijuana and getting "stoned" is getting high on it.

Although participants estimated that 99 percent of their peers were smoking pot at Woodstock, no one was arrested for the offense. Explained one state patrolman, "If

we did [make arrests for pot], there isn't enough space in Sullivan or the next three counties to put them in."

If the promoters of the festival were surprised at what they had wrought, the national media seemed thoroughly befuddled by the event. The *New York Times* editorialized at the festival's conclusion, "The dreams of marijuana and rock music. . .had little more sanity than the impulses that drive lemmings to march to the sea. They ended in a nightmare of mud and stagnation."

But one day later, the *Times's* editors thought better of their assessment, now telling its readers that "the rock festival begins to take on the quality of a social phenomenon. . . . And in spite of the prevalence of drugs it was essentially a phenomenon of innocence." The *Times* recognized that it was more than drugs and music that attracted the hordes of young:

They came, it seems, to enjoy their own society, free to exult in a lifestyle that is its own declaration of independence.

Said one young participant, "Just being here with

people like me makes it all worthwhile. I guess it will reinforce my lifestyle, my beliefs, from the attacks of my parents and their generation."

Indeed, Woodstock dramatized the link between the youthful lifestyle and youthful politics: generational, moral, and antiwar. *Time* magazine reminded its readers:

The same kind of people who basked in the spirit of Bethel also stormed the deans' offices at Harvard and Columbia and shed tears or blood at the Chicago convention last summer—all in the name of the new morality.

In this regard, the counterculture of the late 1960s differed markedly from the "flower children" of a few years previously. The flower children had deliberately rejected politics. They were "other worldly" and wanted to "transcend" the ugliness of contemporary society in favor of a new consciousness. But the new counterculture deliberately entwined politics and lifestyle. A scientific survey conducted by Daniel Yankelovich in 1969 confirmed the opinion of *Time*'s editors:

A "new dawn." A young couple embraces as the morning fog lifts over the Woodstock music festival.

New lifestyles and radical politics appear together: granny glasses, crunchy granola, commune-living, pot smoking, and long hair seem inseparable from radical politics, sit-ins, student strikes, protest marches, draft card burnings.

A revolutionary youth movement

Bewilderment about Woodstock was not confined to a few editors. By early June 1969, almost three-quarters of the population believed that there was a "major generation gap" in the country, according to a Gallup poll. Young people were more than twice as likely to believe that marijuana should be legalized; those under thirty more than four times as likely to have tried it. More than 80 percent of all students thought that they should have a greater say in the running of their colleges; 75 percent of those over thirty disagreed. Over 60 percent of all students agreed with the goals of demonstrators; almost 95 percent of the country thought student demonstrators should receive harsher punishments.

In the next four years this generation gap would only widen. More significant, what began in 1969 as largely a student-oriented youth culture spread rapidly among nonstudent youth in the early 1970s. Daniel Yankelovich wrote in early 1973:

Noncollege youth today is just about where the college population was in 1969. Virtually every aspect of the New Values have deeply penetrated noncollege youth. Moral norms have changed dramatically.

Survey data showed that there were still significant differences between college and noncollege youth. Students tended to have a more consistent response to questions testing their adherence to what Yankelovich termed the "New Values." Noncollege youth in some cases gave more radical responses, in other cases more conservative ones. One-quarter of all nonstudents believed that "radical change is needed" or the "whole system should be replaced," compared to one-fifth of college students. On the other hand, the noncollege group was more likely to believe that the "American way of life is superior," by 19 percent to 12 percent. Noncollege youth was also less willing to accept society's prohibition against the use of marijuana, although a majority of both groups opposed anti-marijuana laws.

More important than these areas of disagreement was the remarkable degree of agreement between the two sides of the generation found in the 1973 survey. One-third of each group believed that America "had no right to be" in Vietnam, a statement that revealed an unqualified moral indictment of the war by this segment of youth. Only about one-tenth of both college and noncollege youth believed that America's actions in Vietnam were "honorable." Virtually no one believed that America was winning the war. Thirty-five percent of each group believed that "we are a sick society," and there was virtual unanimity that "business is too concerned with profits"; over 90 percent of those questioned in both groups agreed with that statement.

The spread of countercultural values throughout the baby-boom generation had important implications for radical student politics and in many ways precipitated an ideological split in the Students for a Democratic Society. When SDS leaders met for the organization's annual summer convention in 1969, two distinct factions emerged, split over the significance of the counterculture. One faction, the Worker–Student Alliance, remained orthodox Marxist, although WSA did remain true to the spirit of the New Left by condemning the Soviet Union. The other faction was called the Revolutionary Youth Movement, or RYM.

Within days after this initial split, RYM split into two factions. One, led by Mark Rudd of Columbia, became

known as the Weathermen, a name derived from a line in a song by Bob Dylan: "You don't need a weatherman to know which way the wind blows." Their goal was to attract noncollege youth to the "movement" by displaying their "toughness" at youth hangouts. They were wholly unsuccessful in their efforts, and their frustration, in part, led to a series of violent, even terrorist actions after 1970.

The other faction in RYM, which went by the simple name of RYM-II, was left to pick up most of the pieces. Described by *Time* magazine as a mixture of "the Beatles and Marcuse" (after the German-born, leftist philosopher, Herbert Marcuse), RYM-II demanded little in the way of ideological discipline and looked with approval on youthful lifestyles. The three-way split in SDS had left the national office in complete disarray, further reinforcing the antipathy of SDSers to any central control. RYM-II local chapters were thus left "to do their own thing."

The combination of a loosely organized group of radicals and a widely diffused counterculture brought the student movement to its greatest influence by 1970. By that time 37 percent of all students considered themselves "far-left" politically according to a special Gallup survey of college students. College unrest had first been identified as one of the "most important problems facing this country," according to a Gallup survey of January 1969, when it ranked fifth. By the summer of 1969 "youth protests and college demonstrators" ranked second only to the war in Vietnam as the most frequently mentioned problem facing America. And one year later "campus unrest" replaced Vietnam as the nation's most serious problem according to Gallup. It was no secret as to what had caused the dramatic change: four students shot dead in Ohio.

Kent State

There were few universities in America that could lay better claim to the title of "Baby Boom" University than Kent State University in Ohio. At the end of World War II Kent State Teachers College, as it was then known, had an enrollment of only 1,279 students. Twenty-five years later the student body had mushroomed to over 21,000, making Kent State University the twenty-fourth largest institution of higher education in America.

It was not just the growth of Kent State that characterized the institution. It was also the university's clientele. More than 90 percent of the student body was made up of Ohio natives. Most students came from Cleveland (thirty-five miles to the north), from Akron (eleven miles to the west), and from the steel towns of Lorain and Youngstown, and not from the well-to-do families in these towns. Half of the students reported that their father's income was less than $10,000 per year. Less than half received primary financial support from their parents. Most students funded their education by working, 31 percent of them full time. Less than 10 percent ranked their parents as liberal.

A False Millennium

On September 26, 1970, long excerpts of a book by an obscure Yale law professor appeared in the usually sophisticated *New Yorker* and created a sensation. Copies of the issue became unobtainable, and the book instantly hit the best-seller lists, selling 20,000 copies per week. *The Greening of America* by Charles A. Reich had, in the words of one reviewer, touched a national nerve center.

Reich had graduated from Yale Law School with one of the highest averages in the school's history, served as clerk to a Supreme Court judge, and worked for a prestigious Washington law firm. But, after teaching Yale undergraduates for the first time, he had traded in his three-piece suits for bell-bottom pants. The many manifestations of the youthful counterculture, he decided, meant something radical for America. "There is a revolution coming," Reich wrote:

This is a revolution of the new generation. Their protest and rebellion, their culture, clothes, music, drugs, ways of thought, and liberated lifestyle are not a passing fad or a form of dissent and refusal, nor are they in any sense irrational. The whole emerging pattern, from ideals to campus demonstrations to beads and bell bottoms to the Woodstock Festival, make sense and is part of a consistent philosophy. It is both necessary and inevitable, and in time will include not only youth, but all people in America.

At the heart of his book Reich posited a radical change of consciousness, which he defined as one's "whole perception of reality." Consciousness III, as he called it, was replacing two other stages of consciousness that had preceded it. Consciousness I was the mindset of frontier, preindustrial America, an ethic of individual freedom and prosperity through hard work that, according to Reich, lived on in many farmers, small-town businessmen, and blue-collar workers.

Consciousness I, however, was based on an unreal perception of society, for the free enterprise system had given way to the postindustrial "Corporate State," which emerged during the Great Depression to alleviate the harshness of life in industrial America. He labeled the world view of this new organizational society Consciousness II and offered a scathing indictment of what it had wrought in the name of "the public interest": war, civil strife, poverty, powerlessness, and runaway technology.

The villain in Reich's book—the Corporate State—depended on a consciousness that accepted it; a change in consciousness could thus cause the entire structure to tumble. Reich claimed this transition to Consciousness III came with the Vietnam War. Forced to fight or to accept what seemed an unjust war, the youth of America, and more slowly their parents, were coming to question the tenets that held the Corporate State together.

At this juncture in his book critical analysis gave way to a paean to the new lifestyle of youth. Their faded jeans brought out the individuality of different body shapes and permitted a new freedom of movement; their rock music expressed a new appreciation of nature, sensuality, and feeling; their use of drugs signified a liberation of the mind and extension of self-knowledge. He even eulogized their term "oh, wow!" as the "ultimate sign of reverence, vulnerability, and innocence."

The new lifestyle was but an outward manifestation of the new consciousness, which heralded a "greening" of the concrete pavements of corporate America. Consciousness III was going to transform institutions from within, as businessmen and FBI agents began to wear comfortable clothes, listen to rock music, take drugs, join communes, love people, and open themselves to "dread, awe, wonder, mystery, accidents, failure, helplessness, magic." A revolution of consciousness, he argued, must precede a revolution in the structure of society and not the reverse. His advice to political activists: "Forget it—drop out, do nothing, achieve Consciousness III."

The media lavished attention on Reich's utopian manifesto. The *New York Times* printed three articles about the book by Reich himself, four by noted scholars and authors, one long news story, and two reviews. Much of the response was laudatory. John Kenneth Galbraith claimed Reich had put to paper just what he had wanted to say. Some was critical. Stewart Alsop of *Newsweek* called it "a bag of scary mush." But all who reviewed it treated *The Greening of America* as an important book.

In a short time, however, Reich's immensely popular vision seemed almost ludicrous. It became obvious that no revolution had come to pass as young people shed their comfortable clothes and joined the work force, communes faded from the scene, and the majority of Americans remained firmly entrenched in Consciousness II. In March of 1971 left-wing journalist Andrew Kopkind was already asserting that Reich was having second thoughts about his book. "For it's clear to all," wrote Kopkind, "that revolution is a longer and harder road than any of us wanted to think, and that hippies aren't going to man the FBI."

How could such an ephemeral book have gained so much influence over American thinking? At least part of the answer lay in its timeliness: A decade earlier, or as little as a year later, the book would probably have been laughed out of a publisher's office. But Reich composed his manuscript just as the hopes and dreams of the "Camelot years" had been replaced by war and civil disorder, and many Americans felt the need for a new vision of the future. They wanted to believe Reich's benign and hope-filled interpretation of what the sometimes frightening new counterculture meant. "Reich brings both faith and hope to a group of people who in 1970 had precious little of either," wrote a book reviewer in the Catholic journal *America*.

Reich's prophecy, however, was but a sand castle built on shifting sands. He based his conclusions solely on the epiphenomena of change. Clothes, music, and drugs could not a revolution make. Dropping out, loving people could do little to challenge the social ills that Reich documented. His was a sentimental vision, ignoring the dark side of the counterculture. The violence of the Altamont, California, rock concert, the misery of drug addiction, the terror and isolation experienced by many rootless young people—all this and more were omitted from his depiction of the new culture. Reich was indulging in wishful thinking, and for a short time many Americans were wishing along with him.

169

Kent State was, in short, a working-class university. It boasted a reputation as Ohio's finest "party school," in the campus lingo of the day. Many young Ohioans, recently graduated from high school, faced a simple choice: either VCU (Vietcong U.) or KSU. Kent's burgeoning enrollments showed how many had made their choice.

Not surprisingly, Kent State had little tradition of campus radicalism. In April 1969, the SDS members confronted the university with a list of demands to end university "complicity" with the war. Their central demand was the abolition of ROTC. The demonstration ended with a melee after which SDS was ordered off the campus and four SDSers received six-month jail terms.

But the lack of activism did not mean that Kent students were apolitical. Nearly half believed that troops should be withdrawn from Indochina immediately and that "the power of the president of the United States should be severely restricted and the power given to the people." James Michener, the novelist who wrote an intensive study of the events at Kent State, reported that even the fraternity members were "bitterly opposed to many government policies." One fraternity student explained that his feelings toward SDS changed from opposition to "tacit support" in reaction to the unfair treatment he believed the group had received in the April 1969 demonstration.

But more important than their political beliefs was the domination of the campus by a countercultural lifestyle. By the spring of 1970 over 80 percent of the student body had smoked marijuana. There was little antagonism between "straight" students and those who practiced "the new lifestyle." In many ways the popularity of the counterculture merely reflected a continuation of the campus's reputation as a good party school. But there was a crucial difference: Marijuana was illegal and long hair, even if it could not be legally prohibited, was a red flag to the conservative authorities of rural Portage County, Ohio. Wherever student parties turned rowdy there was bound to be conflict between party-goers and police—a fact of life that many of Kent's working-class students had learned in high school. But in the spring of 1970 the visible badges of the counterculture, coupled with a national mood of polarization, built the tensions into a major political tragedy.

As at many campuses across the country, the announcement by President Nixon late Thursday night, April 30, that American and South Vietnamese troops had invaded Cambodian territory provoked an immediate response from political activists at Kent State. At noon on Friday about 500 students attended an antiwar rally and called for the abolition of ROTC on the campus.

By 1970 ROTC had become the most visible sign of university "complicity" in the war. Moderate students and faculty were often disturbed by the requirement that ROTC students receive academic credit despite the fact that the university had no control over the appointment of professors or the content of classes. More radical students believed that banning ROTC would cause a severe manpower shortage for the armed forces and was thus one of the few ways in which they could directly hinder the war effort. The composition of America's officer corps seemed to justify their analysis. A full 50 percent of all army officers were ROTC graduates. Thirty-five percent of the air force's officers and 20 percent of the navy's also came from ROTC programs. Particularly in the aftermath of 1968's bloody Communist offensives, qualified NCOs and junior officers were at a premium in the armed forces.

The anti-ROTC movement was among the most successful launched by antiwar activists. Particularly at "elite" institutions like Yale, Harvard, and Stanford, the argument of moderates, that ROTC violated the norms of academic standards, proved persuasive. At those campuses and several others, ROTC was downgraded to the status of "extra-curricular activity." Since this was repugnant to the armed forces, the programs were disbanded.

At the vast majority of college campuses ROTC was not abolished, but enrollments plunged by more than two-thirds. The army ROTC program, by far the largest, fell from over 165,000 cadets before 1965 to only 50,234 in 1971–72. The much smaller air force program experienced a falloff from 80,000 in 1965 to 23,000 in 1972.

During the month of April Kent State students were aware that the normally conservative campus of Ohio State University at Columbus had been wracked by violent confrontations over the ROTC issue. The announcement of the invasion of Cambodia gave KSU students an opportunity to reopen the issue on their campus.

The noon rally on the Kent State campus on Friday, May 1, concluded peacefully, with a call for another rally the following morning. By midafternoon half of the student body, as it normally did, began an exodus from Kent to make the short trek to their hometowns in Cleveland, Akron, and elsewhere in northern Ohio. The evening of May 1 was one of the first warm spring nights of the year. The students remaining on campus flocked to the string of bars along Water Street, bordering the campus.

The Friday evening crowd was large and boisterous. Emotions ran high as a result of the Cambodian announcement. Virulent antiwar slogans were spray-painted in and around bars. Students blocked the streets to inquire of passing motorists their opinion on Cambodia. Some built a bonfire.

The crowd grew angry when a passing motorist refused to stop and nearly hit a student. Around 11:30 P.M. someone threw a bottle at a passing police car. City officials now moved in. Mayor Leroy Satrom closed the bars and announced a 1:00 A.M. curfew. By the early morning fifteen students had been arrested.

Friday night's events were a curious mixture of springtime high spirits and radical politics. Five years earlier it might have ended in a panty raid. But it was 1970, not 1965, and the students of Kent State were politicized. More

Fire destroys the Kent State ROTC building on May 2, 1970.

than 70 percent of the students involved later reported that Cambodia specifically and national policies in general were "very responsible" for the Friday night disturbance.

On Saturday local and state officials began to take control of the situation away from the university. Governor James Rhodes approved sending the National Guard to Kent, and a contingent stationed ten miles away was placed on standby. Mayor Satrom also set an 8:00 P.M. curfew for the town and banned the sale of liquor. A campus curfew was set for 1:00 A.M.

The university attempted to keep matters in control on Saturday night by providing live bands in campus dormitories. Early in the evening a crowd began to form on the campus commons. "They're trying to keep the kids penned up in the dorms," shouted one young man. "Let's go." The crowd moved past the dorms, picking up more students as it went along. Nearly 1,000 students approached the ROTC building, while some chanted, "One, two, three, four. We don't want your fucking war." Rocks and ignited flares struck the building; it began to burn. When firemen arrived, demonstrators slashed the hoses and threw rocks. The firemen retreated and the building continued to burn.

Finally campus police arrived in riot gear and dispersed the crowd with tear gas. Informed of the situation,

Mayor Satrom called in the National Guard. A later survey showed that 82 percent of the student body felt that the burning of the ROTC building was either "not at all justified" or "minimally justified." Most also believed that the burning was a means of protesting both ROTC's presence on campus as well as the Cambodian invasion.

What then was the situation on campus on Saturday night? Kent State students had shown themselves nearly unified in their condemnation of the new incursion into Cambodia. They would come together to protect and defend their youthful lifestyle. But they did not support violent or radical political action. Events on the next day were to change all of that.

On Sunday morning Governor Rhodes announced a "state of emergency," banning outdoor demonstrations, on or off campus. Sunday afternoon passed uneventfully. An easy camaraderie developed between the students and National Guardsmen now stationed on campus. Students and guardsmen did not "stare across the gulf of classes," as Norman Mailer described the 1967 marchers on the Pentagon. They were of the same class. Photographs taken that afternoon showed cigarette-smoking guardsmen smiling as they stood alongside a long hair. Another captured a guardsman flashing a peace sign. When one student flashed a peace sign, a guardsman opened his tunic and exposed the peace symbol printed on his T-shirt.

By evening the mood turned somber. The guard placed in effect a new 9:00 P.M. curfew. The students now moved off campus to Main Street. Their demand: to meet with Mayor Satrom and university President Bob White and negotiate the end of the curfews and the removal of guardsmen from campus. White refused to meet with students and Satrom did not show up as promised.

It was, according to James Michener, "the watershed of the weekend." There was no friskiness left in the students. They were angry. They felt betrayed that Mayor Satrom's earlier promise of negotiation had been broken. Some in the crowd threw rocks at guardsmen and police. They were herded back into campus by tear gas as helicopters swirled overhead. Hysteria took over; rumors circulated that students had been bayoneted. Many were forced to bed down for the night in the nearest dormitory. Plans were made for a noon rally for the next day, May 4.

On Monday morning returning weekend commuters were met by the National Guard on campus. Bomb threats canceled some classes, but most were held as usual. Scrawled across many blackboards was announcement of the noon rally on the campus. The purpose of the demonstration was no longer to protest national policy but to reclaim the campus from the guard. Over two-thirds of the student body was aware of the "state of emergency" that banned the rally, but less than one-third agreed "that peaceful gatherings should have been prohibited."

At noon over 40 percent of the student body assembled near the commons. Many more students passed by on their way to and from classes. One student explained why she stopped:

I just couldn't believe the Guards were on campus. It was mostly, just outrage and disgust and fear, and all sorts of crazy things. I just couldn't believe that my campus had been taken over by the Guards.

A commission formed later and headed by former Pennsylvania Governor William Scranton concluded that "even students who described themselves as 'straight or conservative' attended the rally to protest the presence of the National Guard."

As the students began to assemble, guard officers roamed the area in jeeps, ordering students to "evacuate." "You have no right to assemble," they shouted. But students responded, "Pigs off campus!" A detachment of guardsmen approached the students only to be repulsed with hurled rocks. The guard answered with tear gas.

As the students began to disperse to avoid the gas, one detachment of guardsmen pursued a group of students but soon found itself approaching a fence. The guard retreated, followed by rock-throwing students and cheering onlookers. Some of the guardsmen knelt and pointed their rifles, then rose, turned around, and walked farther up the

hill. Abruptly, they turned and fired. A single shot was followed by a thirteen-second fusillade. Nine students were injured. Four others were killed.

Two of the dead, Jeffrey Miller and Allison Krause, had actively participated in the rally. A third, William Schroeder, an ROTC cadet, had spent the weekend in a moral struggle over his increasing misgivings about the war. He had also attended the rally, but a photograph shows him leaving the area just as the bullet struck him. The fourth victim, Sandy Scheuer, was merely passing by on her way to class.

Strike! Strike!

Even before the shots had been fired at Kent State University, the president's announcement of the invasion of Cambodia had spurred the beginnings of a nationwide student strike. By Sunday May 3 three different "National Student Strike Centers" had been established in Boston, New York, and Philadelphia. At this point organized student protest was largely limited to the East Coast, but those colleges had already agreed upon the grievances that would form the basis for a national strike:

- An immediate end to the war in Indochina.
- An immediate end to all university complicity in the war effort.
- An end to political repression.

The first two demands neatly summed up five years of antiwar protest by college students. The third, a reflection of the student alliance with black activists, was inspired by a Black Panther rally taking place that same weekend in New Haven, Connecticut, home of Yale University.

The National Student Strike was thus the response of those who had been the victims of Nixon's politics of polarization. The events at Kent State transformed what had begun as a largely regional effort into a national movement.

The Carnegie Commission on Higher Education later surveyed the results of the upheaval, calling it "by all odds . . . the most massive expression ever of American college student discontent." Nearly 60 percent of all institutions of higher education in America, including two-year colleges, reported that post-Cambodian demonstrations had a "significant impact" on campus operations. Over one-third of the nation's students boycotted classes. The protests were no longer confined to the elite private and public institutions that had for so long captured the nation's headlines. Even a majority of religiously affiliated institutions felt the effects.

Nowhere were the results more tragic than at Jackson State College, a predominantly black institution in Mississippi. There on May 7, a peaceful rally to protest the invasion of Cambodia had resulted in a one-day student strike and a week of minor campus disorders. On May 13 the disorders turned violent, as protesters began stoning passing cars. When police and state patrolmen responded with a roadblock and a curfew, the students escalated their tactics, setting trash bins on fire and vandalizing campus security vehicles.

The following day, May 14, began with more rock throwing. A highway patrolman fired at a dorm window in response, and the National Guard moved in. Coordination between the guard, highway patrol, and city police was poor. All three groups moved toward Alexander Hall, a dormitory, where a large group of students was gathered. The sound of breaking glass was heard, followed by a single shot. Then all hell broke loose. In twenty-eight seconds, officers fired more than 400 buckshot shells at the dormitory. One student and a local youth were killed.

At most universities the events of May were far from tragic. Almost a quarter of all college presidents reported that the disturbances caused by the Cambodian incursion "had led to greater unity between faculty and students." The Carnegie Commission concluded, "People got a feel for what education could be like." Perhaps most significantly, presidents of small secular colleges and Protestant

and Catholic institutions were the most likely to accent the positive. Many of them reported to the Carnegie Commission that the "spirit of May" was like a "breeze of fresh air" enlivening their institutions.

For better or worse, many university administrators made preparation for a renewal of protest when campuses reopened in the fall of 1970. At the University of Illinois, the gravel in walkways was replaced with far less lethal wood chips. At Princeton, the administration prepared an emergency plan to expel the entire student body and close the university for a year if the campuswide strike was renewed. Students would then have to reapply for admission with a promise of good behavior.

But all of the planning proved unnecessary. *Newsweek* announced it in a headline: "Cease fire on Campus." *Time* magazine attributed the "profound hibernation of the radical movement" to the feelings expressed by a Texas radical who explained, "Why try at all if all you are going to do is maybe get busted and bring on the far right?" A leader of Dartmouth's Cambodia protest added, "Students

Students gather around the body of fellow student Jeffrey Miller, one of four killed by National Guard bullets on May 4, 1970.

The Berrigan Brothers

In suburban Catonsville, Maryland, on May 17, 1968, seven men and two women quietly entered Local Draft Board 33. They walked directly to the file cabinets, grabbed handfuls of draft files, and stuffed them into the wire trash baskets they carried. Firmly pushing aside the office workers, the raiders rushed to the parking lot where they incinerated the heap with homemade "napalm." Waiting for the police to arrest them, they held hands and recited the Lord's Prayer.

At the fore stood the Berrigan brothers, Daniel and Philip, both Catholic priests. Among their accomplices were four present or former members of Roman Catholic religious orders. As the draft records went up in flames, previously alerted members of the press read a statement prepared by the raiders:

We are Catholic Christians who take our faith seriously. We use napalm because it has burned our people to death in Vietnam. . . . We believe some property has no right to exist.

Extensive media coverage brought nationwide attention to this brazen episode in the activist histories of the Berrigan brothers. Daniel, forty-seven, a Jesuit priest and award-winning poet, raised the ire of the Catholic Church with his unconventional masses and civil rights activism. He joined the Catholic Worker Movement, which was established in the 1930s to aid New York's destitute. He marched in Selma in 1965. As the sixties wore on, this activist-poet-priest, a "hippie priest" who preferred turtleneck jerseys to traditional cleric's garb, focused his attention on the Vietnam War.

Philip Berrigan, forty-four, a priest with the Josephite order, began his activism among impoverished blacks in New Orleans and Newburgh, New York. A popular lecturer by the midsixties, he in-

creasingly spoke of a choice between applying American resources to a foreign war and curing domestic ills.

As the antiwar campaign of the Catholic left escalated, the Berrigans stood close to the action. They founded the nation's first Catholic antiwar organization. In October 1965 they publicly commended Catholic Worker David Miller for burning his draft card. The church expressed its disapproval by transferring the Berrigans from city to city in an attempt to cool their activism. In 1965 Daniel

Philip Berrigan pours blood on draft files at Baltimore's Selective Service Headquarters on October 27, 1967.

was sent to South America, but after a public outcry, church authorities relented and Daniel returned to the U.S. In October 1967 he was jailed briefly for his participation in the March on the Pentagon.

Meanwhile, Philip and three others moved from dissent to resistance in a dramatic protest. On October 27, 1967, the "Baltimore Four" entered the city's Selective Service headquarters and poured blood into draft files. While awaiting trial for the deed, Philip enlisted Daniel, who had just traveled to Hanoi, for the next action—"napalming" draft files in Catonsville.

After Catonsville, imitative raids occurred in Silver Spring, Maryland; Providence, Rhode Island; Chicago; and New York—all led by members of the Catholic

left. On September 24, 1968, the "Milwaukee Fourteen," including five Catholic priests and one Protestant minister, incinerated more than 10,000 1-A draft files.

The Catonsville Nine came to trial in October 1968. Outside the courthouse, antiwar demonstrators carried a black coffin representing the dead in Vietnam. Inside, the defense conceded all charges at the outset, then implored the jury to consider the larger moral issues. Actions, not opinions, were on trial, argued the prosecutor. But for many, the motivations of the Berrigan brothers were compelling. In an unusual exchange with the defendants while awaiting the jury's verdict, the judge expressed eloquently the dilemma the Berrigans presented to many Americans:

I agree with you completely, as a person. We can never accomplish, or give a better life to people, if we are going to keep on giving so much money to war. It is very unfortunate but the issue of war cannot be presented as clearly as you would like. The basic principle of the law is that we do things in an orderly fashion. People cannot take the law into their own hands.

Priests breaking the law in moral protest of government policy crystallized the quandary for some Catholics between loyalty to their church (and country) and moral objection to the escalating war. Traditionally, the Catholic Church was not pacifistic. Because Catholic doctrine allowed for "just wars," members of the church were virtually excluded from obtaining conscientious objector status. The church was also staunchly anti-Communist. During the early 1950s, many prominent Catholics had affirmed their patriotism by supporting Senator Joseph McCarthy's campaign against "subversion." As Daniel Berrigan explained, "American Catholics had never before, in the history of American wars, been found wanting," a position that continued into the 1960s and was personified by New York's Francis Cardinal Spellman. During a Christmas visit to Vietnam in 1966, Spellman lauded the "war for civilization." One month earlier, the American Catholic bishops concluded, "it is reasonable to argue that our presence in Vietnam is justified."

Not all Catholics agreed. The Catholic Worker Movement, which had activated the Catholic left, became during the 1950s the "center of a unique brand of anarchist pacifism," according to an historian. In the 1963 "Peace on Earth" encyclical of Pope John XXIII, some Catholics perceived a call to civil disobedience:

If civil authorities legislate or allow anything that is contrary to [moral order] and therefore to the will of God, neither the laws made nor the authorizations granted can be binding on the conscience of the citizens.

The apparently foolhardy actions of the radical priests annoyed and bewildered many. The liberal Catholic journal *Commonweal* agreed that the civil disobedience appeared "impractical" yet

raided draft boards were acting as responsible Christians, 69 percent said "No."

Nevertheless, the Berrigans placed antiwar protest in the context of Christian theology. In addition, wire service photos of gray-haired Philip Berrigan—collared and stately—pouring blood on draft files undeniably presented a different image of war resistance than long-haired, unruly youth.

"Those damn college students think they're the only ones who want this world to be a better place," said a policeman.

weeks. Daniel, during his four months underground, became the first priest to appear on the FBI's most wanted list. The FBI apprehended him in August 1970. After a year and a half in prison, he was paroled because of ill health.

While Philip was in prison, he was charged with conspiring to kidnap Henry Kissinger and to blow up tunnels beneath Washington, D.C. The case ended with a hung jury. Following his parole in December 1972, Philip and codefendant Sister Elizabeth McAlister announced that

Daniel Berrigan (third from right), Philip Berrigan (center), and other members of the Catonsville Nine watch the conflagration of draft files, May 17, 1968.

conceded, "The world would be better off with more rather than fewer Berrigans, and it will profit from their witness."

The Berrigans hoped to inspire others. "We are teachers of the people who have come on a new vision of things," Daniel wrote. One Catholic priest responded, "I have lived fifty-seven years, thirty-nine as a Jesuit, twenty-seven as a priest. After all these years of caution, a little of the Berrigan courage has finally rubbed off on me." In the Berrigans, a young seminarian found "another image of a priest that I would like to be."

But most people rejected the unorthodox—and illegal—actions of the maverick priests. When Catholics were asked in 1971 if they thought that Catholics who

He doubted that the Berrigans accomplished anything, yet their civil disobedience made him wonder, "How far can you go if you think something is wrong and no one is doing anything about it in City Hall or the State House or down there in Washington, D.C.?"

The Berrigans showed how far they would go: They took deliberate actions that led them to jail. For destroying draft files at Catonsville, Daniel was sentenced in April 1970 to three years in jail to be served concurrently with his six-year sentence for the Baltimore action. After sentencing, both brothers disappeared "underground," occasionally surfacing unexpectedly to speak at churches or antiwar rallies. Philip was jailed within

they would marry, without seeking dispensation from their vows.

The deeds of the Berrigan brothers, although condemned by many, jostled America's conscience. By 1971, nearly a third of all American Catholics thought the church should take a stand against the war in Vietnam. In the name of Christian morality, these maverick priests chose to surrender their physical freedom to give expression to their consciences.

A decade later the civil disobedience of the Berrigan brothers continued in the antinuclear movement. Philip, his wife, and children joined a "resistance community" in Baltimore. Daniel remained a member of a New York Jesuit community.

have seen that politics doesn't work, demonstrations don't work, and violence doesn't work."

Most students seemed to agree with the Dartmouth student, but a tiny minority of radical activists turned to a romantic, nihilistic orgy of violence. Of all the expressions of student discontent during the decade, this was surely the sorriest and most inexcusable.

The turn to violence began with Mark Rudd's Weatherman faction of SDS. Defying the otherwise unanimous support for the October 15, 1969, Moratorium by the rest of the antiwar movement, the Weathermen scheduled "Four Days of Rage" in Chicago for mid-October. Their cause was to protest the trial of the "Chicago Eight," eight men charged with conspiracy to riot during the 1968 Democratic Convention. The Weathermen predicted that "10,000 revolutionaries" would support their cause; only 600 appeared. After vandalizing downtown Chicago and provoking violent confrontations with the police, 300 Weathermen were arrested. Total bail exceeded $2.6 million. The leadership of the Weathermen, 12 of whom were later indicted for conspiracy to riot, dropped out of sight, beginning long odysseys in the "underground."

The "Weather underground" planned a series of bombings as part of its "National War Council." The first bomb destroyed the home of a judge presiding over the case of militant black radicals. A second bombing was planned for an army dance at Fort Dix, New Jersey. On March 6, 1970, three Weatherleaders were in the basement of a Greenwich Village town house preparing the bomb. Two others were resting upstairs. Suddenly the town house exploded, leaving the dismembered bodies of the three in the basement among the ruins. The two women upstairs, Cathy Wilkerson and Kathy Boudin, escaped unharmed.

Weather bombings continued. In early June an explosion shook the headquarters of the New York City police department. The Weathermen claimed credit for the bombing of a ladies' room in the U.S. Senate on March 1, 1971. On May 1, 1972, they hit a bathroom in the Pentagon.

Although their actual bombings remained few in number and they were disavowed by virtually all of the remainder of the New Left, the Weathermen may have inspired one of the most vicious epidemics of bombing in American history. The Treasury Department estimated that there were 5,000 bombings across the country between January 1969 and April 1970. Miraculously, none injured an innocent person until August 24, 1970. At 3:42 that morning a bomb destroyed Sterling Hall on the campus of the University of Wisconsin, home of the U.S. Army's Math-

SDS/Weathermen rampage through downtown Chicago on October 11, 1969, during the Days of Rage.

ematics Research Center, known on campus as Army Math. The explosion caused damage in excess of $6 million, destroyed the life work of five professors and the doctoral papers of two dozen graduate students, and injured three individuals. And it killed Robert Fussnach, a thirty-three-year-old postdoctoral researcher. Although terrorist bombings would continue to haunt the nation for another two years, their frequency dramatically declined after the bombing of Army Math.

The cease-fire did not, however, mean reconciliation. In February 1971, Gallup found that 44 percent of students believed that "violence is sometimes justified to bring about change in American society," as compared to 14 percent of the general public. Although campuses had been relatively quiet since May 1970, the Carnegie Commission found in late 1971 "a seemingly dramatic spread of oppositional values since the Cambodian invasion." The commission pessimistically concluded, "We find large elements of the 'counterculture' or 'adversary culture' on the campuses polarized in opposition to the state and its supporters in 'loyal' America, seemingly waiting for some provocation that will ignite the conflict anew."

No new conflict developed. Even the American-supported invasion of Laos by South Vietnamese troops did not heat up the campuses again. Working-class American boys were still being sent to Vietnam, and still being killed, but America's campuses were quiet again. Student opposition had been unable to force an end to the war. Still, other Americans were being moved to protest in even greater numbers.

The vocal majority

In the spring of 1971, Washington again braced for what had become the perennial blossoming of antiwar protests. But the people who were journeying to the capital that spring bore little resemblance to the youthful brigades of previous years. To be sure, the coalition, which organized the 1971 March on Washington, included such familiar names as the Student Mobilization Committee and the Black Third World Task Force, in addition to such newly formed movements as Women's Liberation and Gay Liberation. But most important was the involvement of organized labor unions in planning the march and in bringing their members to Washington.

John Williams, president of Los Angeles Teamster Local 208, was a member of the demonstration's planning steering committee. The rally itself was led by, among others, Abe Feinglass of the Meatcutters union and David Livingston of the Distributive Workers. For the April 24 rally New York unions chartered a special train. Hospital workers made the trip in a caravan of twenty-five buses. Cincinnati unions chartered thirteen buses to bring their members to Washington.

The 1971 March on Washington proved to be the largest of the war. Estimates of the crowd size ranged up to 750,000 which, if correct, would have made it the largest demonstration in the history of the country. In addition, another 200,000 to 300,000 demonstrators attended a companion rally in San Francisco.

Support for the rally came from local union leaders and rank-and-file members, not organized labor's national leadership. The AFL-CIO, led by crusty old George Meany, had, in fact, strongly supported President Nixon's Vietnam policies. When at a meeting of the San Francisco Central Labor Council one member suggested that Meany's approval be sought before the council endorsed the rally, a shout filled the hall: "To hell with Meany!" "You want to evade the most crucial issue facing the nation," declared Ann Draper of the Amalgamated Clothing Workers. "Quit being copouts," yelled Mike Schneider of the Electrical Workers. "A lot of us didn't speak out earlier and a lot of kids are dead because of it."

The speakers at the rally itself reflected the new faces in the country's antiwar constituency. Debby Bustin, national coordinator for the Student Mobilization Committee, recalled being preempted over and over again as older speakers stood up to condemn the war and urge America's withdrawal. "No one under the age of thirty-five or forty had spoken by three o'clock after the first three hours of the rally," Bustin remembered.

No longer could it be charged that the antiwar protesters included only a youthful and, in Vice President Agnew's words, an "effete corps of impudent snobs." Max Frankel, then Washington bureau chief of the *New York Times*, commented:

The effect of any single outpouring like today's cannot be measured, but the cumulative effect of the popular protest here over the years is abundantly clear. The marching minority now feels itself becoming a national majority.

The antiwar message of the marchers was perhaps most graphically conveyed by the homemade banner carried by a middle-aged mother and her two young daughters. "The Majority is Not Silent," it announced. "The Government is Deaf."

There were other new and important faces as well in the crowd on that April 24, the sons of the union rank and file that had swelled the throngs of marchers that Saturday afternoon. They were veterans of the war in Vietnam. Organized as the Vietnam Veterans Against the War, their presence in the Saturday march was the culmination of a week of protest that had moved the nation as no previous Vietnam antiwar demonstration had.

The VVAW had grown slowly from inauspicious beginnings in 1967. As late as April 1970 it could claim a membership of only 600 veterans. A major breakthrough occurred in early 1971 when 150 veterans gathered in Detroit to conduct a sort of war crimes "trial" for violent acts and atrocities that the veterans had witnessed or committed while in Vietnam. The VVAW called the hearings "The Winter Soldier Investigation," thereby identifying themselves with the patriots who had weathered the winter of 1777–78 in Valley Forge. During that year Thomas Paine had written his immortal words, "The summer soldier and the sunshine patriot will, in this crisis, shrink from the service of his country." The goal of the VVAW was to speak with the force of a collective voice "to tell Americans what their country was really doing in Vietnam."

During the hearings, which were organized on a service-by-service, unit-by-unit basis to show a pattern of behavior by the American military, veterans exposed details, frequently gruesome, of violations of the rules of warfare that they had seen or participated in while in Vietnam. The Pentagon later asked the men to provide sworn testimony. The veterans refused to cooperate, arguing that they would not implicate their wartime buddies in events that resulted not from the acts of grunt soldiers, but from the strategy of government leaders. Although this position was entirely consistent with the beliefs of the VVAW, the administration attempted to use this lack of cooperation to discredit the testimony, and the government made little effort to accumulate evidence of the alleged misdeeds.

The government was somewhat more successful in its investigation of the hearing's participants. In at least two cases a careful check of Pentagon records revealed that the witness could not have been in the place described at the given time. The result was devastating for the Vietnam Veterans Against the War, causing the organization to lose much credibility in the public eye. To avoid a repetition of such mistakes, the VVAW insisted that any witness in future forums make available a copy of his military service records before testifying.

The response both of the public and the government to the Winter Soldier Investigation disappointed many veterans against the war. "It was difficult for these men to swallow the public's indifference," explained one VVAW spokesman. But instead of giving up, the members embarked on an even more dramatic demonstration of their opposition to the war. They called it Operation Dewey Canyon III.

Operation Dewey Canyon I was the code name for the 1969 marine operation that included a five-day incursion into Laos. Dewey Canyon II was the American name for the first seven days of the South Vietnamese invasion of Laos in February 1971. Dewey Canyon III began on April 19, 1971, when 1,100 veterans staged a five-day "invasion" of Washington, D.C., "a limited incursion into the country of Congress."

Thanks to the publicity generated by the Winter Soldier hearings and advertising space donated by *Playboy* magazine, VVAW membership had leaped to 12,000 by the spring of 1971. Fifteen hundred men still serving in Vietnam had also joined their ranks. But the size of the organization was of relatively little importance. As one

journalist suggested, the VVAW carried "a moral and symbolic freight . . . which far exceeded its contribution in numbers."

Fervent opposition to a war while it was still going on and expressed by the men who had fought in it provided the nation, and its policymakers, with a unique and compelling argument for American withdrawal from Vietnam. Men wearing the uniforms in which they had fought for America in Vietnam now also displayed long hair. The countercultural aspects of their protest were not lost on the media. One report described

a motley assortment of college students, high school dropouts, young men from the cities and the farms. With their long hair, beads, peace medallions and the whiff of pot that hovered over their encampment on the Mall they could easily have passed for veterans of previous springtime demonstrations. But they were something else in their dusty, baggy jungle fatigues and Army boots—and in the horror stories they swapped about "Nam."

Like so many demonstrators before them, the troops of Dewey Canyon III had to fight the opposition of the Nixon administration. Their attempt to march into Arlington National Cemetery was at first repulsed by officials, but on a second try the vets entered in single file, somberly paying tribute to fallen companions.

Then the Justice Department attempted to outlaw the veterans' encampment on the Mall near the Capitol. The Justice Department gained an injunction against the encampment from a Washington district court, and the VVAW's appeal made its way speedily to the Supreme Court, which ruled that the vets could remain on the Mall but not sleep there. The soldiers decided to defy the ruling and sleep in their encampment. That evening the *Washington Star* headline read, "Vets Overrule Supreme Court." There were no arrests; the police were not eager to battle a group of veterans, many of them disabled. The following day the Washington district court publicly rebuked the Justice Department for requesting but not enforcing the injunction and angrily dissolved it.

The controversy over the Mall was only a side show. Vets performed guerrilla theater reenactments of Vietnam battles on the steps of the Capitol, outside the Justice Department, and in the halls of Congress. Others wandered through the halls of the Capitol urging lawmakers to cut off funds for the war. They also demonstrated at the Supreme Court, demanding "an immediate ruling on the constitutionality of the war."

The most moving protest, however, came on Friday, April 23, the final day of Dewey Canyon III. Marching to the steps of the Capitol, veterans came up against a barrier erected to stop them. They halted and one by one hurled medals they had won in Vietnam over the barrier onto the steps of the Capitol Building. One vet explained that returning his medals was "the final act of contempt for the way the executive branch is forcing us to wage war." Many of the veterans embraced each other and broke into tears. One remembered, "It was like two hours before I could stop crying." Another explained:

My parents told me that if I really did come down here and turned in my medals, that they never wanted anything more to do with me. ... [My wife] said she would divorce me if I came down here because she wanted my medals for our son to see when he grew up.

Coming home

The obvious presence of so many veterans at the antiwar demonstration in April did more than bring attention to the continuing war in Vietnam. It also signaled to many Americans the emergence of a new problem that would continue to exist long after the final shot had been fired in Saigon. The veterans of this war were different from those of any other. The need of many of them for help was to become a constant reminder of the unpopular war.

Vietnam veterans differed from their counterparts of World War II in the most basic and material way. Whereas those earlier vets returned to an America of emerging prosperity and seemingly unlimited opportunity, the veterans of the 1970s had to "find themselves" in a country plunging into recession and restricted chances. In many ways the two or three years the men lost in military service created a gap between them and their nonveteran peers that many would never overcome.

Ironically, the gradual disengagement of America from Vietnam contributed mightily to the economic downturn. As Pentagon procurement diminished, more than 230,000 jobs were lost in the aircraft and helicopter industries alone, while the decline of troop strength in Vietnam put more veterans than ever before into the job market.

These Vietnam-related changes in the economy were augmented by a longer-term trend that the war had partially disguised in the 1960s and 1970s: Blue-collar employment was declining while white-collar employment was rising.

Most Vietnam veterans came from blue-collar families, and many envisioned futures in the factories where their fathers worked. Had they not gone to Vietnam they would certainly have been able to find employment in the overheated economy of the late 1960s. But returning to the U.S. just a few years later they found no work. Whereas unemployment among veterans was proportionately less than that of the general population in 1968, the situation had been reversed by the end of 1969 and continued to grow worse. By the end of 1971, 8.8 percent of all veterans were unemployed, compared to 5.3 percent of the population.

The obvious solution to the problem was to provide college educations so that veterans could find employment in the growing white-collar sector of the economy. But here, too, veterans faced problems. In the late 1960s virtually anyone with a college degree could find secure employment, but by the early 1970s the boom in higher education had produced a glut of the highly educated for whom there were no jobs. Between 1965 and 1970 the number of bachelor's degrees awarded in the U.S. increased by over 50 percent and passed the half-million mark per year in 1971. The time had come when a college degree was no guarantee of employment.

Whatever its value, gaining a degree was no easy task for veterans. Veterans benefits were parsimonious, especially in comparison with those given to World War II veterans. In addition, veterans faced a host of problems of which their nonveteran peers were normally free. Starting college at the age of twenty-two rather than eighteen, and already having "seen the world," they were less likely to want to live with their parents and obey family rules, or parietal ones at college. They were less likely to be offered, or willing to accept, financial assistance from their parents. They were more anxious to get married and raise a family, taking on responsibilities that seldom confronted the usual undergraduate.

If they got into college, veterans were much more likely to work, and work full-time, than other undergraduates. A Veterans' Administration study completed in 1981 showed that nearly 50 percent of all veterans worked full-time while engaged in full-time college study, compared to less than one-quarter of nonveterans. Overall, less than 20 percent of all veterans were able to work less than half-time while enrolled in college. The effects of such outside work on veterans were the same as those experienced by nonveterans: higher dropout rates and a lengthening of the educational process for the very men who were trying to make up for "lost time." When they dropped out they found themselves where they had begun: searching for employment in a shrinking blue-collar sector.

High unemployment was only the most visible problem confronting Vietnam veterans in the early 1970s. Many of them wrestled with deeper psychological problems of adjustment. These problems—more a legacy of the war than a part of the story of the war itself—were for many years not officially acknowledged as Vietnam-related, not until the publication of the VA study in 1981. The study determined that Vietnam veterans faced economic and psychological problems in excess of those felt by their nonveteran peers. In addition, a sophisticated statistical analysis disproved a theory advanced by some critical of the veterans' complaints, that the problems of veterans were attributable to their premilitary experiences. The study acknowledged that veterans were more likely to come from the same disadvantaged backgrounds that spawn psychological problems and antisocial behavior in the general population but also showed that these factors were insufficient to explain fully the extent of the veterans' mental problems.

The veterans study also officially acknowledged the existence of the potential for "post-traumatic stress disorder"

Dewey Canyon III

In April 1971, 1,100 veterans staged a five-day antiwar protest in Washington, D.C. They named it "Operation Dewey Canyon III ... a limited incursion into the country of Congress." Vietnam Veterans Against the War came to the capital to express their outrage at government policy and their concern about their own role in the war. They were joined by Gold Star Mothers and Wives and by a scattering of veterans from earlier wars. Two hundred attended Senate Foreign Relations Committee hearings on proposals to end the war. After days of marching, rallying, lobbying, and performing guerrilla theater, many veterans issued a very personal challenge to the government: They returned medals won in Vietnam by hurling them onto the steps of the Capitol.

Members of Vietnam Veterans Against the War converge on the Supreme Court building on April 22, 1971, to demand that the nation's highest court rule on the legality of the continuing war in Southeast Asia.

Three veterans explain their antiwar position to Representative Albert Quie, a Republican from Minnesota, April 20.

Above. Guerrilla theater on the steps of the Capitol reenacts combat in Vietnam.

Rusty Sachs, who served in Vietnam with the 1st Marine Division, hurls his Bronze Star onto the Capitol steps on the last day of Operation Dewey Canyon III, April 23, 1971.

among an estimated two-thirds of the veterans population, especially among those who had participated in "heavy combat." Drawing upon a wealth of psychological literature that described the same syndrome among survivors of natural disasters, the American Psychiatric Association recognized PTSD as a *bona fide* psychological malady.

1972: the final referendum

As the United States headed into the presidential election year of 1972 the problems of veterans, however, were largely ignored by the public. Indeed, even the Vietnam War had become a secondary concern. At the end of 1971 the Gallup organization announced that for the first time since 1964, Vietnam had not been identified in its survey as the most important problem facing America in the coming year. Indeed, a survey conducted in late November revealed that concern for the economy was listed as the most pressing problem by an almost three-to-one margin over Vietnam.

When George McGovern locked up the Democratic nomination for president with his victory in the California primary in early June 1972, it appeared that Vietnam policy would again move to the forefront and become the most important issue of the election. The 1972 election seemed to be shaping up as a clear referendum. For the first time the American public had a choice between two candidates with clearly opposed positions on the war.

Gallup polls conducted at the end of 1971 and in early 1972 seemed to offer the McGovern campaign its best hope. By a 61 percent to 39 percent margin Americans believed that the "U.S. should withdraw all troops from Vietnam by the end of next year [1972]." This was precisely McGovern's position, while President Nixon insisted that troops should remain in Vietnam until a peace settlement was negotiated.

But the public's apparent agreement with McGovern did him little good. The same polls showed that Americans would overwhelmingly reelect Richard Nixon. On other issues the American public expressed much greater confidence in Nixon than in McGovern. They thought that Nixon was better able to deal with the nation's economic problems by a 47 to 31 percent margin and with the problem of crime and lawlessness by 50 to 26 percent.

There were other positive factors contributing to the Nixon landslide. No opponent could compete with the president's highly visible summit meetings in the People's Republic of China and the Soviet Union. The success of these meetings, perhaps more than his handling of the Vietnam War, secured for the incumbent a confidence in his ability to handle foreign affairs.

In the campaign of 1972, as in most presidential contests, there were "negative" tactics as well. For the Nixon-Agnew ticket, this meant the politics of polarization. When Vice President Agnew characterized McGovern as the candidate of "amnesty, abortion, and acid," he did more than create a catchy slogan. He was also able to identify McGovern with the ideological opponents of the war and drive a wedge between his candidacy and the war's "pragmatic" opponents. The result was that a crucial component of the Democratic party's coalition, the urban, white ethnic voter, was prepared to desert the party. Father Andrew Greeley's prediction of how these working-class voters would react proved to be one of the most astute descriptions of the fate of the McGovern candidacy.

By the fall of 1972 peace did seem so near, almost—as Henry Kissinger promised in the heat of the campaign—"at hand," that many Americans believed they could select the next president on the basis of issues other than Vietnam. The war in Vietnam, however, was not over. America was still to witness a final dramatic escalation of the war, the capture of an additional 131 prisoners of war in 1972 (the largest number in any year since 1967), and complicated negotiations with the nation's allies in Saigon and enemies in Hanoi whose vicissitudes seemed to befuddle much of the public. The divisions within the nation were destined to continue even after the return of the American prisoners of war.

Long after the guns in Vietnam fell silent in the spring of 1975, the debate over the war and its conduct continued to rage in America. Subsequent events in Southeast Asia only added fuel to the fires. Did these events justify America's involvement in the war, or had that involvement somehow helped to shape the nature of the regimes that later took control of South Vietnam and Cambodia? Equally important was the debate over the "lessons of Vietnam." To George Santayana's dictum that "those who cannot remember the past are condemned to repeat it," Arthur Schlesinger, Jr., referring to Vietnam, added, "and those who remember the past are condemned to misread it." As America struggled to meet foreign policy challenges in the Near East, the Persian Gulf, and Central America, "the lessons of Vietnam" were applied from every ideological angle and political perspective.

Perhaps none of this should have been surprising. The national divisions of the Civil War persisted in every presidential election for a century afterward—until Vietnam. The Great Depression haunted America's political process for thirty years, again until Vietnam. The past is not easily forgotten. Perhaps the truest measure of how the nation learns the "lessons of Vietnam" will not be how well it remembers that experience, but how wisely.

Coming home. Norristown, Pennsylvania, 1971.

Bibliography

I. Books and Articles

Acheson, Dean. *Present at the Creation*. Norton, 1969.

Aliano, Richard A. *American Defense Policy from Eisenhower to Kennedy: The Politics of Changing Military Requirements, 1957-1961*. Ohio Univ. Pr., 1975.

American Friends Service Committee. *Peace in Vietnam*. Hill & Wang, 1966.

Arlen, Michael J. *The Living Room War*. Viking Pr., 1969.

Astrachan, Sam. "The New Lost Generation." *The New Republic*, February 4, 1957.

Avorn, Jerry L. et al. *Up Against the Ivy Wall*. Atheneum, 1970.

Babbidge, Homer D., and Robert M. Rosenzweig. *The Federal Interest in Higher Education*. McGraw-Hill, 1962.

Barnet, Richard J. "Annals of Diplomacy (U.S.-German Relations)." *New Yorker*, October 10 & October 17, 1983.

Barzun, Jacques. *The American University*. Harper & Row, 1968.

Baskir, Lawrence M., and William A. Strauss. *Chance and Circumstance: The Draft, the War and the Vietnam Generation*. Knopf, 1978.

Bell, Daniel, and Irving Kristol, eds. *Confrontation: The Student Rebellion and Universities*. Basic Bks., 1968.

Bernardo, C. Joseph, and Eugene Bacon. *American Military Policy: Its Development Since 1775*. 2d edition. The Stackpole Co., 1961.

Bernstein, Peter. "Vietnam and the Gold Drain." *The Nation*, April 1, 1968.

Berrigan, Daniel. *The Dark Night of Resistance*. Doubleday, 1971.

———. *No Bars to Manhood*. Doubleday, 1970.

———. "From the Catonsville Nine: Greetings." *Commonweal* 22(September 27, 1968): 646.

———. "My Brother, the Witness." *Commonweal* 6(April 26, 1968): 180-82.

Borklund, C. W. *The Department of Defense*. Praeger, 1968.

Braestrup, Peter. *Big Story: How the American Press and Television Reported and Interpreted the Crisis of Tet 1968 in Vietnam and Washington*. Westview Pr., 1977.

Cantril, Albert H. "The American People, Vietnam, and the Presidency." Paper presented at the American Political Science Association Meeting, September 1970.

Casey, William Van Etten, SJ, and Philip Nobile, eds. *The Berrigans*. Praeger, 1971.

Clarke, Douglas. *The Missing Man: Politics and the MIA*. National Defense Univ., 1979.

Cohen, Mitchell, and Dennis Hale, eds. *The New Student Left: An Anthology*. Beacon Pr., 1966.

Cohen, Nathan, ed. *The LA Riots*. Praeger, 1970.

Collier, Peter, and David Horowitz. "Doing It. The Inside Story of the Rise and Fall of the Weather Underground." *Rolling Stone*, September 30, 1982.

Compton, James V., ed. *America and the Origins of the Cold War*. Houghton Mifflin, 1972.

Cook, Fred J. "Hard-Hats: The Rampaging Patriots." *The Nation*, June 15, 1970, 712-19.

Curtis, Richard. *The Berrigan Brothers. The Story of Daniel and Philip Berrigan*. Hawthorn Bks., 1974.

Dalfiume, Richard M. *Desegregation of the U.S. Armed Forces: Fighting on Two Fronts, 1939-1953*. Univ. of Missouri Pr., 1969.

Davenport, R. W., and the editors of *Fortune*. *U.S.A., the Permanent Revolution*. Prentice-Hall, 1951.

Davis, James W., and Kenneth M. Dolbeare. *Little Groups of Neighbors: The Selective Service System*. Markham Publishing Co., 1968.

Deedy, John. "News and Views." *Commonweal* 12(June 7, 1968).

Deighton, Lee C., editor-in-chief. *The Encyclopedia of Education*. Macmillan, 1971.

Diamond, Edwin. "Chicago Press: Rebellion and Retrenchment." *Columbia Journalism Review* (Fall 1968): 10-17.

"The Direction of the March." *Negro History Bulletin* 27, no. 3 (December 1963): 63.

Divine, Robert A. *Eisenhower and the Cold War*. Oxford Univ. Pr., 1981.

Donovan, James A. *Militarism, USA*. Scribner's, 1970.

Douglas, Jack D. *Youth in Turmoil: America's Changing Youth Cultures and Student Protest Movements*. National Institute of Mental Health, 1970.

"Draft-Agers' Odds for Survival." *U.S. News and World Report*, July 11, 1951.

Economic Impact of the Vietnam War. Center for Strategic Studies, 1967.

Ehrmann, Peter N. "Buzzy the Bomber." *National Review*, October 1, 1976.

Epstein, Edward Jay. *News From Nowhere: Television and the News*. Random, 1974.

Faber, Harold, ed. *The Road to the White House: The Story of the 1964 Election by the Staff of the New York Times*. McGraw-Hill, 1965.

Falk, Charles J. *The Development and Organization of Education in California*. Harcourt, Brace & World, 1969.

Fallows, James. "What Did You Do in the Class War, Daddy?" *Washington Monthly*, October 1975.

Fogelson, Robert M., ed. *Mass Violence in America. The Los Angeles Riots*. Arno Pr., 1969.

Foner, Jack D. *Blacks and the Military in American History*. Praeger, 1974.

Foster, Julian, and Durward Long. *Protest! Student Activism in America*. Morrow, 1970.

Fontaine, Andre. *History of the Cold War from the October Revolution to the Korean War, 1917-1950*. Translated by D.D. Paige. Vintage Bks., 1970.

Friendly, Fred. "TV at the Turning Point." *Columbia Journalism Review* (Winter 1970-71).

Gabriel, Richard A., and Paul L. Savage. *Crisis in Command: Mismanagement in the Army*. Hill & Wang, 1978.

Gaddis, John L. *The United States and the Origins of the Cold War, 1941-1947*. Columbia Univ. Pr., 1972.

Galbraith, John Kenneth. *The Affluent Society*. Houghton Mifflin, 1958.

Gallup, George H. *The Gallup Poll: Public Opinion, 1935-1971*. Random, 1972.

Gallup Organization. *Gallup Opinion Index*. Gallup, June 1965-January 1981.

"The GI Antiwar Movement: Little Action and Money . . . and Few GIs." *Armed Forces Journal*, September 7, 1970.

Gilbert, James. "The Teach-In: Protest or Cooptation?" *Studies on the Left* 5, no. 3 (Summer 1965): 73-81.

Gitlin, Todd. *The Whole World is Watching*. Univ. of California Pr., 1980.

Glass, Andrew J. "Draftees Shoulder Burden of Fighting and Dying in Vietnam." *CPR National Journal*, August 15, 1970.

Goldberg, Art. "Vietnam Vets: The Anti-War Army." *Ramparts*, July 1971, 11-17.

Goldman, Eric. *The Crucial Decade: America, 1945-1955*. Knopf, 1956.

Good, Paul. "A White Look at Black Power." *The Nation*, August 8, 1966, 112-17.

Gravel, Mike, ed. *The Pentagon Papers*. Beacon Pr., 1971.

Greeley, Andrew M. "The Redeeming of America According to Charles Reich." *America*, January 9, 1971.

Greenstein, Fred I. *The Hidden-Hand Presidency: Eisenhower as Leader*. Basic Bks., 1982.

Guthrie, E.R. *The State University: Its Function and Its Future*. Univ. of Washington, 1959.

Hahn, Harlan. "Dove Sentiment Among Blue Collar Workers." *Dissent* (May-June 1970): 202-5.

Halberstam, David. *The Best and the Brightest*. Random, 1972.

———. "How the Economy Went Haywire." *The Atlantic Monthly*, September 1972.

———. *The Making of a Quagmire*. Random, 1964.

———. *The Powers That Be*. Knopf, 1979.

———. *The Unfinished Odyssey of Robert Kennedy*. Random, 1968.

Halstead, Fred. *Out Now! A Participant's Account of the American Movement Against the War*. Monad Pr., 1978.

Hauser, William L. *America's Army in Crisis*. Johns Hopkins Univ. Pr., 1973.

Hays, Col. Samuel H. *Defense Manpower: The Management of Military Conscription*. Industrial College of the Armed Forces, 1968.

Head, Richard G., and Ervin J. Rokke, eds. *American Defense Policy*. 3d edition. Johns Hopkins Univ. Pr., 1973.

Heinl, Col. Robert, Jr. "The Collapse of the Armed Forces." *Armed Forces Journal*, June 7, 1971.

Helmer, John. *Bringing the War Home*. Free Pr., 1974.

Hensley, Thomas R., and Jerry M. Lewis. *Kent State and May 4th. A Social Science Perspective*. Kendall/Hunt Publishing Co., 1978.

Herzog, Arthur. *The War-Peace Establishment*. Harper & Row, 1965.

Hodgson, Godfrey. *America in Our Time: From World War II to Nixon*. Doubleday, 1976.

Hofstetter, C. Richard. "Political Disengagement and the Death of Martin Luther King." *Public Opinion Quarterly* (Summer 1969): 174-79.

Horowitz, David. "Revolutionary Karma vs. Revolutionary Politics." *Ramparts*, March 1971.

Huston, James A. "Selective Service in World War II." *Current History*, June 1968.

Jacobs, Clyde E., and John F. Gallagher. *The Selective Service Act: A Case Study of the Governmental Process*. Dodd, Mead, 1967.

Johnson, Haynes, and George C. Wilson. *Army in Anguish*. Pocket Bks., 1972.

Johnson, Keith R. "Who Should Serve?" *The Atlantic Monthly*, February 1966.

Johnson, Lyndon Baines. *The Vantage Point*. Holt, Rinehart & Winston, 1971.

Jones, Landon Y. *Great Expectations: America and the Baby Boom Generation*. Coward, McCann & Geoghegan, 1980.

Kearns, Doris. *Lyndon Johnson and the American Dream*. Signet, 1976.

Keniston, Kenneth. *The Uncommitted: Alienated Youth in American Society*. Dell, 1965.

———. *Young Radicals: Notes on Committed Youth*. Harcourt, Brace & World, 1968.

Kerr, Clark. *The Uses of the University*. Harvard Univ. Pr., 1972.

Kissinger, Henry A. *White House Years*. Little, Brown, 1979.

Knight, Arthur. "Celluloid Monument." *Saturday Review*, August 3, 1957.

Knightley, Phillip. *The First Casualty*. Harcourt Brace Jovanovich, 1975.

Kolodziej, Edward A. *The Uncommon Defense and Congress, 1945-1963*. Ohio State Univ. Pr., 1966.

Kopkind, Andrew. "Goodbye to All That." *The New Republic*, November 19, 1966, 7-8.

———. "The Greening of America: Beyond the Valley of the Heads." *Ramparts*, March 1971.

Ladner, Joyce. "What 'Black Power' Means to Negroes in Mississippi." *Trans-Action*, November 1987, 7-15.

LaFeber, Walter. *America, Russia, and the Cold War, 1945-1963*. Wiley, 1967.

Lane, Robert E., and Michael Lerner. "Why Hard Hats Hate Hairs." *Psychology Today*, November 1970, 45-48.

Leuchtenburg, William E. *A Troubled Feast: American Society Since 1945*. Little, Brown, 1973.

Lewis, Anthony, and the *New York Times*. *Portrait of a Decade: The Second American Revolution*. Random, 1964.

Lewy, Guenter. *America in Vietnam*. Oxford Univ. Pr., 1978.

Lifton, Robert Jay. *Home From the War*. Simon & Schuster, 1973.

Lippmann, Walter. *The Cold War: A Study in U.S. Foreign Policy*. Harper, 1947.

Lipset, Seymour Martin. *Rebellion in the University*. Little, Brown, 1971.

Little, Roger W., ed. *Selective Service and American Society*. Russell Sage Foundation, 1969.

Loory, Stuart H. *Defeated: Inside America's Military Machine*. Random, 1973.

Lukas, J. Anthony. "The Council on Foreign Relations—Is It a Club? Seminar? Presidium? 'Invisible Government'?" *New York Times Magazine*, November 21, 1971.

McNamara, Robert. *The Essence of Security: Reflections in Office*. Harper & Row, 1968.

MacPherson, Myra. *Long Time Passing: Vietnam and the Haunted Generation.* Doubleday, 1984.

Manning, Robert, and Michael Janeway, eds. *Who We Are.* Atlantic-Little, Brown, 1969.

Matusow, Allen J. *The Unravelling of America: A History of Liberalism in the 1960s.* Harper & Row, 1984.

Mecklin, John. *Mission in Torment.* Doubleday, 1965.

Meconis, Charles A. *With Clumsy Grace: The American Catholic Left, 1961-75.* Seabury Pr., 1979.

Meehan, Thomas. "The Yale Faculty Makes the Scene." *New York Times Magazine,* February 7, 1971.

Menashe, Louis, and Ronald Radosh, eds. *Teach-Ins, USA: Reports, Opinions, Documents.* Praeger, 1967.

Meyer, Philip. "Aftermath of Martyrdom: Negro Militancy and Martin Luther King." *Public Opinion Quarterly* (Summer 1969): 160-73.

Michener, James. *Kent State: What Happened and Why.* Random, 1971.

Miller, Jim, ed. *The Rolling Stone Illustrated History of Rock and Roll.* Random, 1976.

Miller, Merle. *Lyndon: An Oral Biography.* Ballantine Bks., 1981.

Morgan, Thomas B. "Reporters of the Lost War." *Esquire,* July 1984, 49-60.

Moorefield, Story. "The Remarkable GI Bill." *American Education* 10, no. 7 (August-September 1974): 25.

Muse, Benjamin. *The American Negro Revolution.* Indiana Univ. Pr., 1968.

The National Economy and the Vietnam War. Committee for Economic Development. April 1968.

Nichols, Lee. *Breakthrough on the Color Front.* Random, 1954.

Nixon, Richard M. *RN: The Memoirs of Richard Nixon.* Grosset & Dunlap, 1978.

Oates, Stephen B. *Let the Trumpet Sound: The Life of Martin Luther King, Jr.* NAL, 1982.

O'Sullivan, John, and Alan M. Meckler, eds. *The Draft and Its Enemies: A Documentary History.* Univ. of Illinois Pr., 1974.

Parmenter, Tom. "Breakdown of Law and Order." *Trans-Action,* September 1967, 13-21.

Peeters, Paul. *Massive Retaliation: The Policy and Its Critics.* Henry Regnery Co., 1959.

Perlo, Victor. *The Unstable Economy: Booms and Recessions in the United States Since 1945.* International Publishers, 1973.

Peterson, Richard E., and John A. Bilorusky. *May 1970: The Campus Aftermath of Cambodia and Kent State.* Carnegie Commission on Higher Education, 1971.

Ploski, Harry A., and Ernest Kaiser, eds. *The Negro Almanac.* The Bellwether Co., 1971.

Polenberg, Richard. *One Nation Divisible.* Viking Pr., 1970.

Powers, Thomas. *The War at Home: Vietnam and the American People, 1964-1968.* Grossman Publishers, 1973.

"PR for POWs." *New Republic,* June 19, 1971.

Rainwater, Lee. "Open Letter on White Justice and the Riots." *Trans-Action,* September 1967, 22-32.

———, and William L. Yancey. "Black Families and the White House (The Political Implications of the Moynihan Report Controversy)." *Trans-Action,* July-August 1967, 6-53.

Reich, Charles. *The Greening of America.* Bantam, 1970.

Ridgway, James. *The Closed Corporation.* Random, 1968.

Riesman, David. "Some Reservations About Black Power." *Trans-Action,* November 1967, 20-22.

———, and Christopher Jencks. *The Academic Revolution.* Doubleday, 1968.

Robinson, John P. "Public Reaction to Political Protest: Chicago 1968." *Public Opinion Quarterly* 34(Spring 1970): 1-9.

Rogin, Michael Paul. *The Intellectuals and McCarthy: The Radical Specter.* MIT Pr., 1967.

Rollins, Peter C. "Television's Vietnam: The Visual Language of Television News." *Journal of American Culture* 4(1981): 114-35.

Rovere, Richard. "Notes on the Establishment in America." *The American Scholar* (Fall 1961).

———. *Senator Joe McCarthy.* Harcourt, Brace and Co., 1959.

Sale, Kirkpatrick. *SDS.* Vintage Bks., 1973.

Salisbury, Harrison E. *The Shook-Up Generation.* Harper & Row, 1958.

———. *Without Fear or Favor.* New York Times Bks., 1980.

Sanders, Jacquin. *The Draft and the Vietnam War.* Walker & Co., 1966.

Schell, Jonathan. *The Time of Illusion.* Vintage Bks., 1976.

Schlesinger, Arthur. *A Thousand Days: John F. Kennedy in the White House.* Houghton Mifflin, 1965.

Schlissel, Lillian, ed. *Conscience in America: A Documentary History of Conscientious Objection in America.* Dutton, 1968.

Schrag, Peter. "Covering the Academic Fires." *Change* 2, no. 4 (July-August 1970): 10-12.

Schwartz, Daniel. "Watershed Between the Decades." *The Nation,* November 26, 1973.

Scott, Joan Wallach. "The Teach-In: A National Movement or the End of an Affair?" *Studies on the Left* 5, no. 3 (Summer 1965): 82-87.

Seale, Bobby. *Seize the Time.* Random, 1968.

Searle, John R. *The Campus War.* New World Publishing Co., 1971.

Sears, David O., and John B. McConahay. *The Politics of Violence: The New Urban Blacks and the Watts Riot.* Houghton Mifflin, 1973.

Seligman, Daniel. "Youth Rebellion." *Fortune,* January 1968, 68.

Shannon, William V. "The Vietnam Election." *Commonweal,* December 2, 1966, 249-50.

Shaw, Arnold. *The Rockin' '50s.* Hawthorn Bks., 1974.

Smelser, Neil J., and Gabriel Almond, eds. *Public Higher Education in California.* Univ. of California Pr., 1974.

Smith, Gaddis. *Dean Acheson.* Cooper Square Publishers, 1972.

Smith, Mark E., III, and Claude J. Johns, eds. *American Defense Policy.* 2d edition. Johns Hopkins Univ. Pr., 1968.

Stadtman, Verne A. *The University of California 1868-1968.* McGraw-Hill, 1970.

Stavisky, Sam. "Who Will Be Drafted This Time?" *Saturday Evening Post,* January 20, 1951.

Stevens, Robert Warren. *Vain Hopes, Grim Realities: The Economic Consequences of the Vietnam War.* New Viewpoints, 1976.

Stone, I.F. *The Haunted Fifties.* Random, 1963.

Stratford, Mary. "How It Was Then." *The Baltimore Afro-American,* Souvenir edition, August 27, 1983.

The Student Voice. The Student Non-Violent Coordinating Committee, October 1963.

Swomley, John M., Jr. *The Military Establishment.* Beacon Pr., 1964.

Tarr, Curtis W. *By the Numbers: The Reform of the Selective Service System, 1970-1972.* National Defense Univ., 1981.

Taylor, Maxwell D. *Swords and Plowshares.* Norton, 1972.

———. *The Uncertain Trumpet.* Harper and Brothers, 1959.

Taylor, Stuart. "Violence at Kent State May 1 to 4, 1970." *The Student Perspective.* College Notes and Texts, Inc., 1971.

Thorne, David, and George Butler. *The New Soldier by John Kerry and Vietnam Veterans Against the War.* Collier Bks., 1971.

Time-Life Bks., eds. *This Fabulous Century.* Vols. 6 & 7. Time-Life Bks., 1970.

Truman, Harry S. *Memoirs.* Vol. 2, *Years of Trial and Hope, 1946-1952.* Doubleday, 1956.

Tryon, Warren S. "The Draft in World War I." *Current History,* June 1968.

Verba, Sidney et al. "Public Opinion and the War in Vietnam." *American Political Science Review,* June 1967, 317-33.

Vietnam Veterans Against the War. *The Winter Soldier Investigation: An Inquiry into American War Crimes.* Beacon Pr., 1972.

Viorst, Milton. *Fire in the Streets: America in the 1960s.* Simon & Schuster, 1979.

Walton, George. *The Tarnished Shield: A Report on Today's Army.* Dodd, Mead, 1973.

Weiss, Peter. "Bomb Crater in the American Dream." *The Nation,* October 5, 1970.

WGBH-TV. *Vietnam: A Television History.* Part 11, *Homefront USA.* Transcript. 1983.

"What About the POWs?" *Look,* May 5, 1970.

White, Theodore H. *The Making of the President 1960.* Atheneum, 1961.

———. *The Making of the President 1964.* Atheneum, 1965.

———. *The Making of the President 1968.* Atheneum, 1969.

Whiteside, Thomas. "Corridor of Mirrors: The Television Editorial Process, Chicago." *Columbia Journalism Review* (Winter 1969).

Widick, B.J. "The Suffering Majority." *The Nation,* May 25, 1970, 616-19.

Wilder, Thornton. "The Silent Generation." *Harper's,* April 1953.

Wilhelmsen, Frederick D., ed. *Seeds of Anarchy: A Study of Campus Revolution.* Argus Academic Pr., 1969.

Wills, Garry. *The Kennedy Imprisonment: A Meditation on Power.* Little, Brown, 1982.

———. *Nixon Agonistes.* Houghton Mifflin, 1970.

Wilson, Logan, ed. *Emerging Patterns in American Higher Education.* American Council on Education, 1965.

Witcover, Jules. "The Press and Chicago: The Truth Hurt." *Columbia Journalism Review* (Fall 1968): 5-9.

———. "Where Washington Reporting Failed." *Columbia Journalism Review* (Winter 1970-71).

Wittner, Lawrence S. *Rebels Against War: The American Peace Movement 1941-1960.* Columbia Univ. Pr., 1969.

Wolin, Sheldon S., and John H. Schaar. *The Berkeley Rebellion and Beyond: Essays on Politics and Education in the Technological Society.* Vintage Bks., 1970.

"Woodstock Festival." *New Yorker,* August 30, 1969, 17-21.

Woodward, C. Vann. "What Happened to the Civil Rights Movement?" *Harper's,* January 1967, 29-37.

Yankelovich, Daniel A. *The New Morality: A Study of American Youth.* McGraw-Hill, 1974.

Yarmolinsky, Adam. *The Military Establishment.* Harper & Row, 1971.

Yergin, Daniel. *Shattered Peace.* Houghton Mifflin, 1977.

Zangrando, Robert L. "The Direction of the March." *Negro History Bulletin* 27, no. 3 (December 1963).

II. Government and Government-Sponsored Published Reports

BDM Corporation. *A Study of the Strategic Lessons Learned in Vietnam.* Vols. 1-8. National Technical Information Service, 1980.

Byrne, James J. *Employment and Unemployment Among Vietnam Era Veterans: An Analysis of the 1979 National Survey of Veterans.* Research Monograph 14-A, U.S. Veterans' Administration, August 1981.

Congressional Quarterly Service. *Congress and the Nation 1945-1964.* GPO, 1965.

Eisenhower, Dwight D. *Public Papers of the Presidents of the United States: Dwight D. Eisenhower.* GPO, 1958-1961.

Executive Office of the President. *Economic Report of the President.* GPO, 1960, 1965, 1967, 1973.

Grant, W. Vance, and Leo J. Eiden. *Digest of Education Statistics.* National Center for Education Statistics, U.S. Department of Education, 1982.

Hershey, Lewis B. *Outline of Historical Background of Selective Service (From Biblical Days to June 30, 1965).* Selective Service System, 1965.

National Advisory Commission on Civil Disorders. *Report of National Advisory Commission on Civil Disorders.* Bantam, 1968.

National Advisory Commission on Selective Service. *In Pursuit of Equity: Who Serves When Not All Serve?* GPO, 1967.

National Commission on the Causes and Prevention of Violence. *Report of Daniel Walker. Rights in Conflict.* Bantam, 1968.

President's Commission on Campus Unrest. *Report of President's Commission on Campus Unrest.* GPO, 1970.

Selective Service System. *Annual Report of the Director.* GPO, 1965-1969.

Truman, Harry S. *Public Papers of the Presidents of the United States: Harry S Truman.* GPO, 1964.

U.S. Congress. House. Committee on Armed Services. *Review of the Administration and Operation of the Selective Service System.* June 1966.

U.S. Congress. Senate. Committee on Armed Services. *Amending and Extending the Draft Law and Related Authorities.* 90th Congress, 1st sess., 1967.

_____. *Worldwide Military Commitments.* 90th Congress, 1st sess., 1967.

_____. *Authorization for Military Procurement, Research and Development, Fiscal Year 1969, and Reserve Strength.* 90th Congress, 2d sess., 1968.

U.S. Department of Commerce, Bureau of the Census. *Historical Statistics of the U.S. Colonial Times to 1970.* GPO, 1975.

_____. *Current Population Reports Series P-20, No. 155. Negro Population: March 1965.* 1966.

_____. *The Social and Economic Status of the Black Population in the United States: An Historical View, 1970-1978.* GPO, 1979.

_____. *Statistical Abstract of the United States.* GPO, 1946-47, 1959, 1962, 1966-67, 1970, 1974.

U.S. Department of Defense. *Report on Study of the Draft.* GPO, 1966.

_____. Office of the Secretary, Historical Office. *The Department of Defense: Documents on Establishment and Organization, 1944-1978.* GPO, 1978.

U.S. Department of Labor, Bureau of Labor Statistics. *The Negroes in the U.S.: Their Economic and Social Situation.* GPO, 1966.

U.S. Veterans' Administration. *Legacies of Vietnam: Comparative Adjustment of Veterans and their Peers.* GPO, 1981.

III. The authors consulted the following newspapers and periodicals:

Business Week, 1965-1972; *Life,* 1945-1973; *Monthly Labor Review,* 1965-1972; *New York Times,* 1945-1973; *Newsweek,* 1945-1973; *San Francisco Examiner,* 1964-1965; *Time,* 1945-1973; *U.S. News and World Report,* 1963-1972; *Wall Street Journal,* 1968; *Washington Post,* 1960-1973.

IV. Archives

The authors consulted documents held at the following institutions:

Lyndon Baines Johnson Library, Austin, Texas; John F. Kennedy Library, Boston, Massachusetts; Kent State University, Office of the Registrar, Kent, Ohio; Martin Luther King, Jr., Library and Archives, Atlanta, Georgia; Simpson Historical Research Center, Maxwell Air Force Base, Alabama; U.S. Army Center of Military History, Washington, D.C.; U.S. Army Military History Institute, Carlisle Barracks, Pennsylvania; U.S. Army Training and Doctrine Command, Fort Monroe, Virginia; U.S. Marine Corps History and Museums Division, Headquarters, USMC, Washington, D.C.; U.S. Naval Historical Center, Washington, D.C.

V. Interviews

Rev. Daniel Berrigan, S.J., antiwar activist; John Chancellor, NBC News; Roger Hilsman, former Assistant Secretary of State; Jerry Lewis, Dept. of Sociology, Kent State University; Richard Lieberman, former student, Kent State University; Gregory A. Rogers, office of the Dean of Student Affairs, Kent State University.

Credits

Cover Photo
Bernard Boston

Part I
p. 5, Joe Scherschel—LIFE Magazine, © 1961, Time Inc. pp. 8-9, Standard Oil of New Jersey Collection, Photographic Archives, University of Louisville. p. 9, inset, Photographic Archives, University of Louisville. p. 11, Drawing by David Levine. Reprinted with permission from *The New York Review of Books,* © 1970, Nyrev Inc. p. 13, Bettmann Archive. pp. 14-15, Henri Cartier-Bresson—Magnum. p. 15, inset, George Lacks—LIFE Magazine, © 1947, Time Inc. pp. 16-17, Robert Phillips—Black Star. pp. 18-19, John Dominis—LIFE Magazine, © 1951, Time Inc. p. 23, top, UPI/Bettmann Archive, courtesy National Archives; bottom, Hank Walker—LIFE Magazine, © 1960, Time Inc. p. 24, Loomis Dean—LIFE Magazine, © 1951, Time Inc. p. 26, left inset, "I Love Lucy," CBS Television Show; right inset, CBS. pp. 26-27, UPI/Bettmann Archive. p. 27, inset, Grey Villet—LIFE Magazine, © 1960, Time Inc. p. 29, Jack Fields. p. 31, I. Wilmer Counts, courtesy *The Arkansas Democrat.* p. 32, © 1955, Warner Bros. Inc. All rights reserved. p. 33, Jay Leviton—Atlanta, courtesy Black Star. pp. 34-35, Bruce Davidson—Magnum. p. 37, Cecil Stoughton—JFK Library. pp. 38-39, Charles Moore—Black Star. p. 41, Paul Schutzer—LIFE Magazine, © 1969, Time Inc.; inset, Francis Miller—LIFE Magazine, © 1963, Time Inc. pp. 42-43, Fred Ward—Black Star. p. 43, top, Paul Schutzer—LIFE Magazine, © 1963, Time Inc.; bottom, Steve Schapiro—Black Star. p. 44, Noel Clark—LIFE Magazine, © 1963, Time Inc. p. 45, Charles Harbutt—Archive Pictures Inc. pp. 46-47, Yale Joel—LIFE Magazine, © 1965, Time Inc.

Suburban Frontier
p. 48, inset, Bernard Hoffman—LIFE Magazine, © 1950, Time Inc. pp. 48-49, Joe Scherschel—LIFE Magazine, © 1958, Time Inc. pp. 50-51, Cornell Capa—Magnum. p. 51, inset, Wayne Miller—Magnum. pp. 52-53, Jon Brenneis—LIFE Magazine, © 1954, Time Inc. p. 53, inset, Yale Joel—LIFE Magazine, © 1954, Time Inc. pp. 54-55, Yale Joel—LIFE Magazine, © 1958, Time Inc. p. 55, inset, Ralph Crane—LIFE Magazine, © 1960, Time Inc.

Part II
p. 57, Benedict J. Fernandez. pp. 58-59, Charles Moore—Black Star. pp. 60-61, © James H. Karales, 1965. p. 62, Danny Lyon—Magnum. p. 63, George Tames—NYT PICTURES. p. 65, Joe Flowers—Black Star. p. 67, inset, AP/Wide World; bottom, Elaine Mayes. p. 68, left inset, Wayne Miller—Magnum; right inset, Ted Streshinsky. pp. 68-69, Paul Fusco—Magnum. p. 73, Benedict J. Fernandez. p. 74, top, Peter Simon; bottom, Andrew Sacks. pp. 74-75, Benedict J. Fernandez. p. 77, Joel E. Boxer, courtesy Life Picture Service. p. 79, Dennis Brack—Black Star. p. 83, top, AP/Wide World; bottom, © James H. Karales, 1963. pp. 84, 85, Ken Heyman. p. 87, Benedict J. Fernandez. pp. 88-89, Bruce Davidson—Magnum. p. 89, inset, Ken Heyman.

War Comes Home
pp. 90-95, Costa Manos—Magnum. p. 96, Tal McBride—Philip Bermingham Photography, with permission from Vietnam Veterans Memorial Fund, Inc. p. 97, Costa Manos—Magnum.

Part III
p. 99, Perry Riddle. p. 101, Benedict J. Fernandez. p. 102, Danny Lyon—Magnum. p. 103, left, Herb Greene; right, Jim Marshall. pp. 105, 106-7, Steve Schapiro—Black Star. p. 107, inset, Maury Englander—Bethel. pp. 108-9, Fred W. McDarrah. pp. 110-11, Declan Haun—LIFE Magazine, © 1967, Time Inc. p. 112, Lee Balterman—LIFE Magazine, © 1967, Time Inc. p. 115, Benedict J. Fernandez. pp. 116-17, Jill Freedman—Archive Pictures Inc. pp. 120-21, Charles Harbutt—Archive Pictures Inc. p. 121, inset, UPI/Bettmann Archive. p. 123, Jack Kightlinger—LBJ Library. p. 124, inset, © 1967, Ramparts Magazine Inc. Permission granted by Bruce W. Stilson. pp. 124-25, Charles Gatewood. p. 125, right, *Berkeley Barb,* courtesy Doe Library at University of California/Berkeley. p. 129, Fred W. McDarrah. p. 131, Mark Godfrey—Archive Pictures Inc. p. 133, top, Paul Sequeira; bottom, News Group Chicago, Inc., 1968. Reprinted with permission of the *Chicago Sun-Times.* p. 134, top, Paul Sequeira; bottom, News Group Chicago, Inc., 1968. Reprinted with permission of the *Chicago Sun-Times.* pp. 134-35, News Group Chicago, Inc., 1968. Reprinted with permission of the *Chicago Sun-Times.* pp. 136-37, Hiroji Kubota—Magnum.

Woodstock
p. 138, inset, John Dominis—LIFE Magazine, © 1969, Time Inc. pp. 138-39, Bonnie Freer. p. 140, inset, Benno Friedman. pp. 140-41, Jim Marshall. p. 141, inset, Benno Friedman. pp. 142-43, Burke Uzzle—Woodfin Camp. p. 143, left inset, Bill Eppridge—LIFE Magazine, © 1969, Time Inc.; right inset, Burke Uzzle—Woodfin Camp. p. 144, inset, Burke Uzzle—Woodfin Camp. pp. 144-45, Ken Heyman.

Part IV
p. 147, Stern—Black Star. p. 149, Mary Ellen Mark—Archive Pictures Inc. p. 152, inset, Dan Mattson, courtesy Southeast Asia Resource Center. pp. 152-53, Bill Eppridge—LIFE Magazine, © 1971, Time Inc. p. 154, Ted Lau—TIME Magazine. pp. 156-57, George W. Gardner. pp. 160-61, Baron Wolman. p. 161, inset, UPI/Bettmann Archive. p. 162, Paul Fusco—Magnum. p. 163, Don Snyder. p. 164, inset, Jeffrey Blankfort—Jeroboam. pp. 164-65, Elihu Blotnick. p. 165, insets, Jeffrey Blankfort—Jeroboam. pp. 166-67, Burke Uzzle—Woodfin Camp. p. 171, *Akron Beacon Journal.* p. 173, John Filo, courtesy VALLEY NEWS DISPATCH. p. 174, UPI/Bettmann Archive. p. 175, Dennis Brack—Black Star. p. 176, East Street Gallery—Black Star. pp. 180-81, Bernard Edelman. p. 181, top, bottom, Barbara Pfeffer. p. 182, Bernard Edelman. pp. 184-85, James Conroy.

p. 32—Rock 'n' Roll Rebellion
"Rip It Up": Words and music by Robert Blackwell and John Marascalco. Copyright © 1956, Venice Music c/o ATV Music Corp. Used by permission. All rights reserved.
"Good Golly Miss Molly": Words and music by John Marascalco and Robert Blackwell. Copyright © 1957, Parker Music Co. Used by permission.

p. 102—A Chorus of Protest
"Blowin' in the Wind": Words and music by Bob Dylan. Copyright © 1962, Warner Bros., Inc. All rights reserved. Used by permission.
"Turn! Turn! Turn!": Words from the Book of Ecclesiastes. Adaptation and music by Pete Seeger. TRO - © Copyright 1962, Melody Trails, Inc., New York, NY. Used by permission.
"My Generation": Words and music by Peter Townshend. © Copyright 1965, Fabulous Music Ltd., London, England. TRO-Devon Music, Inc., New York, controls all publication rights for the U.S.A. and Canada. Used by permission.
"I Feel Like I'm Fixin' to Die Rag": Words and music by Joe McDonald. © 1965, Alkatraz Corner Music 1977. Used by permission. All rights reserved.
"Volunteers": Performed by the Jefferson Airplane on the "Volunteers" album. Composed by Paul Kantner and Marty Balin. © 1969, Icebag Corp.-BMI. All rights reserved. Reprinted by permission of the publisher.
"Fortunate Son": Words and music by J.C. Fogerty. Copyright © 1969, Jondora Music-BMI. Used by permission.
"Ohio": Written by Neil Young. Copyright © 1970, Cotillion Music, Inc. & Broken Arrow Music. Used by permission. All rights reserved.
"Revolution": Words and music by John Lennon and Paul McCartney. Copyright © 1968, Northern Songs Ltd. All rights for the United States and Mexico controlled by Maclen Music, Inc., c/o ATV Music Corp. Used by permission. All rights reserved.

Index

Names, Acronyms, Terms

AID—United States Agency for International Development. Administered economic aid to countries around the world, including South Vietnam.

AWOL—absent without leave.

CENTO—Central Treaty Organization. Formed in 1955 to bring military and economic aid to the Middle East. Engineered by the U.S. but under the formal leadership of Great Britain, the pact joined together Turkey, Iran, Iraq, and Pakistan "to create a solid band of resistance against the Soviet Union."

China Lobby—group of influential, conservative American politicians, journalists, and businessmen who supported the regime of Chiang Kai-shek and the Chinese Nationalists against Mao and the Communists.

CIA—Central Intelligence Agency.

CO—conscientious objector.

CORE—Congress of Racial Equality. Interracial civil rights organization founded in the North in 1942. By the midsixties it had rejected nonviolence, purged white members, and denounced U.S. involvement in Vietnam.

DMZ—demilitarized zone. Established by the Geneva accords of 1954, provisionally dividing North Vietnam from South Vietnam along the seventeenth parallel.

FCC—Federal Communications Commission.

GI Bill—popular name for the Serviceman's Readjustment Act, signed in 1944 and repeatedly updated, which provided benefits for eligible, discharged veterans.

IDA—Institute for Defense Analysis. An independent, nonprofit consortium that conducted research for the Department of Defense. Its work on Vietnam included the original proposal for an electronic barrier at the DMZ. Founded in 1956, the IDA was affiliated with twelve universities, including Columbia.

JCS—Joint Chiefs of Staff. Consisted of chairman, U.S. Army chief of staff, chief of naval operations, U.S. Air Force chief of staff, and marine commandant (member ex officio). Advises the president, the National Security Council, and the secretary of defense.

Kerner Commission—National Advisory Commission on Civil Disorders, headed by Governor Otto Kerner of Illinois, which, in 1968, reported on and analyzed racial riots.

MACV—Military Assistance Command, Vietnam. U.S. command over all U.S. military activities in Vietnam, originated in 1962.

Marshall Plan—post-World War II American program of aid initiated in 1947 to spur economic recovery in Europe.

MIA—missing in action.

The Mobe (after 1968 "The New Mobe")—The National Mobilization Committee To End the War in Vietnam. Umbrella organization created during the fall of 1966 to coordinate antiwar activities.

NAACP—National Association for the Advancement of Colored People.

NCO—noncommissioned officer.

NSC—National Security Council. Established in 1947 to "advise the president with respect to the integration of domestic, foreign, and military policies relating to the national security," it was composed of the president; the secretaries of state, defense, army, navy, and air force; and the chairman of the National Security Resources Board.

POW—prisoner of war.

PTSD—Post-Traumatic Stress Disorder. Psychological syndrome of delayed reaction to unusually stressful events. Recognized by the early 1980s as a malady affecting many "heavy combat" veterans of the Vietnam War.

ROTC—Reserve Officers Training Corps.

SANE—National Committee for a Sane Nuclear Policy.

SAS—Students' Afro-American Society (Columbia University).

SCLC—Southern Christian Leadership Conference. Organized in 1957 and headed by Dr. Martin Luther King, SCLC organized nonviolent campaigns for full citizen rights and integration for blacks.

SDS—Students for a Democratic Society. Founded in 1961, this self-proclaimed vanguard of the "New Left" included on its agenda civil rights, university reform, and an end to poverty before concentrating its energy later in the decade on opposition to American involvement in Vietnam.

SEATO—Southeast Asia Treaty Organization. Organized in 1954 between Thailand, Pakistan, and the Philippines and the U.S., Britain, France, Australia, and New Zealand to form an alliance against Communist subversion, especially in Indochina.

SNCC—Student Non-Violent Coordinating Committee. Civil rights group formed in 1957 to win political power for Southern blacks through nonviolent protest. Became an increasingly strident advocate of "Black Power" in the midsixties.

SSS—Selective Service System.

Truman Doctrine—President Truman's declaration of the American policy "to support free peoples who are resisting attempted subjugation by armed minorities or outside pressures." The doctrine was first pronounced as a justification for American aid to Greece and to Turkey in 1947.

VA—Veterans' Administration.

VVAW—Vietnam Veterans Against the War.

Walker Commission—investigated the confrontation of demonstrators and police during the Democratic Convention in Chicago, 1968. Headed by Daniel Walker, it was officially the Chicago Study Team of the National Commission on the Causes and Prevention of Violence.